Life

Beginnings of Life
Animal Life
Plant Life
Evolution of Life
Behavior and Ecology of Life

Ricki Lewis

State University of New York at Albany

Contributing Authors

Animal Biology, Behavior and Ecology

Judith Goodenough
University of Massachusetts at Amherst

Plant Biology

Randall C. Moore
Wright State University

Wm. C. Brown Publishers

Book Team

Editor *Kevin Kane*
Developmental Editor *Margaret J. Manders*
Production Editor *Sherry Padden*
Visuals/Design Consultant *Marilyn Phelps*
Designer *Mark Elliot Christianson*
Art Editor *Janice M. Roerig*
Photo Editor *Carol Smith*
Permissions Editor *Vicki Krug*
Visuals Processor *Joseph P. O'Connell*

 Wm. C. Brown Publishers

President *G. Franklin Lewis*
Vice President, Publisher *George Wm. Bergquist*
Vice President, Operations and Production *Beverly Kolz*
National Sales Manager *Virginia S. Moffat*
Group Sales Manager *Vince DiBlasi*
Vice President, Editor in Chief *Edward G. Jaffe*
Marketing Manager *Craig S. Marty*
Managing Editor, Production *Colleen A. Yonda*
Manager of Visuals and Design *Faye M. Schilling*
Production Editoral Manager *Julie A. Kennedy*
Production Editoral Manager *Ann Fuerste*
Publishing Services Manager *Karen J. Slaght*

WCB Group

President and Chief Executive Officer *Mark C. Falb*
Chairman of the Board *Wm. C. Brown*

Life
Front cover photo by © Robert Hernandez/Allstock

Part 1: Beginnings of Life
Front cover illustration by Mark Elliot Christianson based on photographs
by © Lloyd M. Beidler/Science Photo Library/Photo researcher, Inc.

Part 2: Animal Life
Front cover photo by © Erwin & Peggy Bauer

Part 3: Plant Life
Front cover photo by © Michael Fogden/Oxford Scientific Films

Part 4: Evolution of Life
Front cover photo by © Henry Ausloos/Animals Animals

Part 5: Behavior and Ecology of Life
Front cover photo by © Larry Lefever/Grant Heilman Photography

Photo Research by Toni Michaels

The credits section for this book begins on page C-1, and is considered
an extension of the copyright page.

Library of Congress Catalog Card Number: **Life**: 91-70426

ISBN **Life** Casebound, recycled interior stock: 0-697-05392-X
ISBN **Life** Paper binding, recycled interior stock: 0-697-14187-X
ISBN **Part 1: Beginnings of Life** Paper binding, recycled interior stock: 0-697-14193-4
ISBN **Part 2: Animal Life** Paper binding, recycled interior stock: 0-697-14195-0
ISBN **Part 3: Plant Life** Paper binding, recycled interior stock: 0-697-14197-7
ISBN **Part 4: Evolution of Life** Paper binding, recycled interior stock: 0-697-14199-3
ISBN **Part 5: Behavior and Ecology of Life** Paper binding, recycled interior stock: 0-697-14201-9
ISBN **Life** Boxed set, recycled interior stock: 0-697-14189-6

Printed in the United States of America by Wm. C. Brown Publishers,
2460 Kerper Boulevard, Dubuque, IA 52001

10 9 8 7 6 5 4 3 2 1

Publisher's Note to the Instructor

Recycled Paper

Life—in all its numerous binding options (listed here)—is printed on **recycled paper stock.** All of its ancillaries, as well as all advertising pieces for *Life*, will also be printed on recycled paper, subject to market availability.

Our goal in offering the text and its ancillary package on **recycled paper** is to take an important first step toward minimizing the environmental impact of our products. If you have any questions about recycled paper use, *Life*, its package, any of its binding options, or any of our other biology texts, feel free to call us at 1-800-331-2111. Thank you.

Kevin Kane
Senior Editor
Biology

Binding Option	Description	ISBN
Life, casebound	The full-length text (chapters 1-40), with hardcover binding.	0-697-05392-X
Life, paperbound	The full-length text, paperback covered and available at a significantly reduced price, when compared with the casebound version.	0-697-14187-X
Part 1 *Beginnings of Life*, paperbound	Part 1 features the first 4 units or 15 chapters of the text, covering the scientific method, the unity and diversity of life, basic chemistry, cell biology, reproduction and development, and genetics. This paperback option is available at a significantly reduced price when compared with both the full-length casebound and paperbound versions.	0-697-14193-4
Part 2 *Animal Life*	Part 2 features chapters 16-27 on the anatomy and physiology of animals—invertebrate, vertebrate, and human. This paperback is also available at a significantly reduced price when compared with the full-length versions of the text.	0-697-14195-0
Part 3 *Plant Life*	Part 3 features chapters 28-32 on plant form and function, with popular applications chapters on "Plants Through History" (28) and Plant Biotechnology (32). Paperback bound, it is available for a fraction of the full-length casebound or paperbound prices.	0-697-14197-7
Part 4 *Evolution of Life*	Part 4 features chapters 33-35 on evolution. Paperback bound, it is also available for a fraction of the full-length casebound or paperbound prices.	0-697-14199-3
Part 5 *Behavior and Ecology of Life*	Part 5 features chapters 36-40 on behavior and ecology. Paperback bound, it also sells for a fraction of the full-length book price.	0-697-14201-9
Life, the Boxed Set	The entire text, offered in an attractive, boxed set of all five paperback "splits." It is available at the same price as the full-length casebound text.	0-697-14189-6

Brief Contents

Contents

UNIT 7

Evolution 617

UNIT 8

Behavior and Ecology 665

The *Life*
Learning System

Key Concepts

At the ends of major sections within each chapter, summaries briefly highlight key concepts in the section, helping students focus their study efforts on the basics.

Dramatic Visuals Program

Colorful, informative photographs and illustrations enhance the learning program of the text as well as spark interest and discussion of important topics.

CHAPTER

3

The Chemistry and Origin of Life

Chapter Outline

The Characteristics of Life
Organization
Metabolism
Irritability and Adaptation
Reading 3.1 The Definition of Death
Reproduction
What Is the Simplest Form of Life?
Chemistry Basics
The Atom
Atoms Meeting Atoms
Life's Chemical Components
Characteristics of Water
Water in the Human Body
Organic Compounds of Life
Inorganic Compounds in
Life—Minerals
The Origin of Life on Earth
Spontaneous Generation
Life from Space
Common Ancestry
Chemical Evolution
Reading 3.2 Recipes for Starting
Life—Simulating Early Earth
Conditions

Learning Objectives

By the chapter's end, you should be able to answer these questions:

1. What characteristics distinguish living things from nonliving things?

2. What are the simplest forms of life?

3. What chemical components constitute living things?

4. What chemical compounds are important to human health?

5. How might living matter have evolved from nonliving chemicals?

38

Chapter Outlines

Each chapter begins with an outline. These will allow students to tell at a glance how the chapter is organized and what major topics have been included in the chapter. The outlines include the first and second level heads for the chapter.

Learning Objectives

Each chapter begins with a list of concepts stressed in the chapter. This listing introduces the student to the chapter by organizing its content into a few meaningful sentences. The concepts provide a framework for the content of each chapter.

---

68   *Cell Biology*

KEY CONCEPTS

The structural unit of an organism is the cell. Organisms are unicellular or multicellular. Complex cells contain specialized structures called organelles. All cells have structures in common to carry out basic life processes, but different numbers of organelles give cells distinct characteristics.

Viruses—Simpler Than Cells

The simplest form of life is a unicellular organism with no organelles, such as a bacterium. However, in chapter 3 we encountered several types of "infectious agents" that appear to be living while they are infecting cells but otherwise seem to be nonliving chemicals. Before describing how we examine cells and their contents, it is interesting to take a comparative look at the viruses, both to point out their noncellular organization and because they exert very noticeable effects on human health, causing such minor ills as colds and influenza and such deadly ones as AIDS. Reading 4.1 describes effects of the herpes simplex virus.

A virus consists of a nucleic acid (DNA or RNA) surrounded by protein. Figure 4.2 illustrates the human immunodeficiency virus (HIV), which causes AIDS. A virus must be within a cell to reproduce, and hence it is called an obligate parasite. Many viruses, such as HIV, cannot survive outside of a living cell. Some other viruses are afforded protection from the physical environment by their protein coverings. A virus reproduces by injecting its DNA or RNA into the host cell, where it situates itself within the host's DNA. In fact, viral DNA sequences can probably be found within your own chromosomes. (An RNA virus, such as HIV, is called a retrovirus and must first make a replica of its RNA in DNA form.)

Once viral DNA integrates into the host's DNA, it can either remain there and be replicated along with the host's DNA whenever the cell divides, but not cause harm, or the viral DNA can actively take over the cell, leading eventually to the cell's death. To do this, some of the virus's genes direct the host cell to replicate viral DNA rather than the host DNA. As viral DNA accumulates in the cell, some of it is used to manufacture proteins. (Recall from chapter 3 that the function of DNA is to provide information from which the cell constructs proteins.) Within hours or days, the

infected cell fills with viral DNA and protein. Some of the proteins wrap around the DNA to form new viral particles. Finally, a viral enzyme is produced that cuts through the host cell's outer membrane. The cell bursts, releasing new viruses.

Viruses are known to infect all kinds of organisms, including animals, plants, and bacteria. A particular type of virus, however, infects only certain species, which constitute its *host range.* (Refer back to figure 3.6 for an illustration of a tomato infected by the tomato bunchy top virus.)

Figure 4.3 illustrates what happens to a moth infected by a type of virus called a baculovirus.

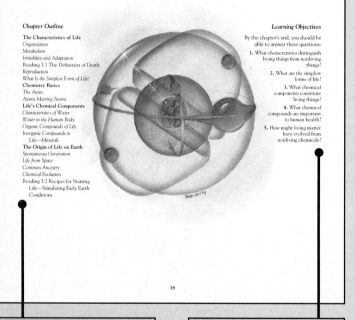

Figure 4.2
A virus is a nucleic acid coated with protein. The human immunodeficiency virus (HIV), which causes AIDS, consists of RNA surrounded by several layers of proteins. Once inside a human cell (usually a T cell, part of the immune system), the virus uses an enzyme to convert its RNA to DNA, which then inserts into the host DNA. HIV damages the human body's protection against disease by killing T cells and by using these cells to make more of itself.
From "AIDS viron" (January 1987 cover painting), copyright © 1987, by Scientific American, Inc., George V. Kelvin, all rights reserved.

Readings

Throughout *Life*, selected readings both elaborate and entertain. Some describe experiments, some provide health information, and others are closer looks at specific topics. All readings are written by the author.

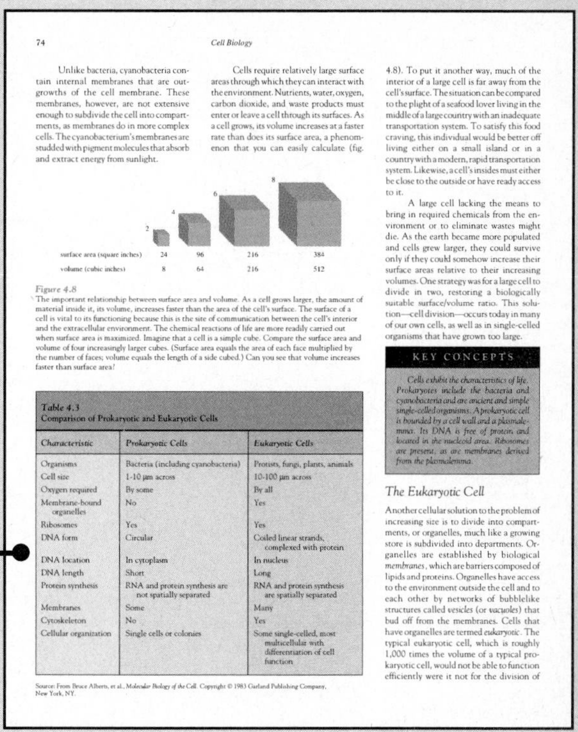

Tables

Numerous strategically-placed tables list and summarize important information, making it readily accessible for efficient study.

Boldfaced Words

New terms appear in boldface print as they are introduced within the text and are immediately defined in context. If any of these terms are reintroduced in later chapters, they are italicized. Key terms are defined in the text glossary with appropriate page reference.

To Think About

Located at the end of each chapter, these questions are springboards for class discussions and term paper topics.

Chapter Summaries

At the end of each chapter is a summary. This should help students more easily identify important concepts and better facilitate their learning of chapter concepts

Questions

The end-of-chapter questions often continue the storytelling style of the chapter, using anecdotes and experiments from the chapter to illustrate and apply concepts.

Suggested Readings

A list of readings at the end of each chapter suggests references that can be used for further study of topics covered in the chapter. The items listed in this section were carefully chosen for readability and accessibility.

Sample page — Cellular Architecture, 97

Reading 5.2 Liposomes—New Drug Delivers

In 1961, English investigator Alec Bangham poured water into a flask containing a film of phospholipid molecules as part of his research on blood clotting. He was surprised to see that the lipid turned milky. Looking at the material under a microscope, Bangham saw that the phospholipid film had broken into thousands of tiny bubbles, each surrounding some of the water. The bubbles ranged in diameter from 250 Angstroms (Å) to several micrometers. Bangham called the liposomes, meaning "bodies of lipid."

[remaining text of reading — see sample]

Figure 1
Liposomes are microscopic bubbles composed of lipid bilayers. They form spontaneously when certain concentrations of fatty molecules are mixed with water. The diameters of these liposomes are about 0.00015 millimeters.

Sample page — Cell Biology, 74

Figure 4.8
The important relationship between surface area and volume. As a cell grows larger, the amount of material inside it, its volume, increases faster than the area of the cell's surface.

| surface area (square inches) | 24 | 96 | 216 | 384 |
| volume (cubic inches) | 8 | 64 | 216 | 512 |

Table 4.3
Comparison of Prokaryotic and Eukaryotic Cells

Characteristic	Prokaryotic Cells	Eukaryotic Cells
Organisms	Bacteria (including cyanobacteria)	Protists, fungi, plants, animals
Cell size	1–10 μm across	10–100 μm across
Oxygen required	By some	By all
Membrane-bound organelles	No	Yes
Ribosomes	Yes	Yes
DNA form	Circular	Coiled linear strands, complexed with protein
DNA location	In cytoplasm	In nucleus
DNA length	Short	Long
Protein synthesis	RNA and protein synthesis are not spatially separated	RNA and protein synthesis are spatially separated
Membranes	Some	Many
Cytoskeleton	No	Yes
Cellular organization	Single cells or colonies	Some single-celled, most multicellular with differentiation of cell function

Source: From Bruce Alberts, et al., *Molecular Biology of the Cell*. Copyright © 1983 Garland Publishing Company, New York, NY.

KEY CONCEPTS

Sample page — Thinking Scientifically, 11

SUMMARY

QUESTIONS

Sample page — Overview of Biology, 12

TO THINK ABOUT

SUGGESTED READINGS

Preface

Life was written with the nonbiology major in mind, but contains enough information to be suitable for a majors' course too.

Diversity in Action

While human examples and applications are emphasized, *Life*'s diversity is treated early in a separate chapter, later in an appendix on taxonomy, and is logically integrated into all chapters. The animal biology chapters, for example, explore a deep-sea shrimp's vision, an insect's exoskeleton, a cow's digestion, and much more. The behavior and ecology chapters are filled with glimpses into the lives of a variety of organisms, from aardwolves to fire ants to naked mole rats. The reader of *Life* will learn many new things, but also encounter familiar territory. The science of biology will not seem foreign—it will be fun and make sense.

Discovery and Evolution

Two conceptual threads weave their way through *Life*. The book opens with the first theme, discovery. The story of how the sweetener aspartame was discovered takes the student through the scientific method and experimental design, yet points out how the initial detection of the food additive was very much a surprise.

In chapter 2, "The Diversity of Life," taxonomy is alive and vibrant in the treetops of a Peruvian wildlife preserve, where biologists catalog the abundance of insect life; and in such an unlikely place as an urban fish market. A pair of children playing with spectacles led to the development of the compound microscope, as described in chapter 4. In chapter 6, "Biological Energy," the student can be the discoverer by using the reactions of photosynthesis to develop a photograph on a leaf. The inborn errors of metabolism, PKU (chapter 15, "Genetic Disease: Diagnosis and Treatment") was discovered thanks to a mother's alertness of her infant's odd-smelling diapers. And a simple treatment for newborn jaundice (chapter 24, "The Digestive System") was discovered by an observant English nurse changing "nappies" in the sunlight. Chapter 15 also tells the story of how a seemingly drunken sailor and his 5,000 living descendants helped provide the first genetic marker.

Not all discovery is accidental. The look at "Molecular Genetics" in chapter 13 is liberally sprinkled with descriptions of the most elegant experiments ever performed. The scientific method is reviewed in chapter 36, "The Behavior of Individuals," as students at the University of Miami track singing birds, and in chapter 38 "Populations," through ecologists conducting wildlife surveys. The creation of an artificial mini-biosphere, described in chapter 39 "Ecosystems," is an exciting view of scientific investigation—whether it works or not.

The second conceptual thread, evolution, accustoms the reader to continually wonder, "How did all of this happen?" How did a duo of protein and nucleic acid join forces long ago to form the first cell? How could random mutations in those early cells build the metabolic pathways of today? How did eukaryotic cells come by their highly successful "bags within a bag" organization? How do species arise, change, become extinct? How have our ideas about evolution themselves evolved?

Humor, History, and Human Values

An occasional foray into humor can help students learn. Consider the example of epistasis in chapter 11, borrowed from the soap opera "General Hospital," or the opening to chapter 34 "The Forces of Evolutionary Change," a love story between a moose and a dairy cow.

Historical references add interest and chronicle the evolution of ideas. The confusing multiple phenotypes of the blood disorder porphyria, for example, may have led the "mad king" George III to provoke the American Revolution. The study of genetics begins with early agricultural efforts nearly 10,000 years ago. How different were Edward Jenner's problems with how best to test his smallpox vaccine (chapter 28, "Plants Through History") from today's scientists' attempts to test AIDS vaccines? The state of the American temperate forest today reflects pioneer activity over the past centuries. Recent history brings the ecology chapters alive, from Mt. St. Helens to the Yellowstone fires to the nuclear explosion at Chernobyl.

Examining human values teaches the student to develop informed opinions and judgments about biologically relevant issues—a skill that will last long after the steps of glycolysis or the parts of the cell are forgotten. Should a pregnant woman who smokes or drinks alcohol be responsible for the health effects on her fetus? Should an employer be told the results of an employee's genetic marker test for Alzheimer's disease? Should we take extraordinary measures to save extremely premature babies if they will be handicapped after (or by) the treatment? Should we even attempt to clean animals drenched in oil from tanker spills? Should we limit reproduction? These disturbing queries are most often found in the "To Think About" sections at the chapters' ends, both so that they will not distract from learning major facts and concepts and so that the student is left thinking.

Integrating Technology

Technology has given new, exciting meaning to some difficult subjects. Discussing the development of extraembryonic structures segues into a peek at chorionic villus sampling. Liposomes are but an extension of cell membrane structure and function. Teaching DNA replication is no longer a hurdle, now that we have the polymerase chain reaction to demonstrate elegantly the power of the process. Filling in the details of food webs no longer requires being on the scene of a meal, thanks to stable isotope tracing (chapter 39, "Ecosystems").

The chapters on plant anatomy and physiology are bracketed by two unique applications chapters—chapter 28, "Plants Through History," chronicles our harvesting of the major crop plants, and chapter 32, "Plant Biotechnology," looks at how molecular and cellular techniques are likely to continue that harvest, via the genetic alteration of plant life.

Finally, Appendix A, "Microscopy", provides a closer look at the technology that really breathed life into biology, from the first crude lenses to today's powerful confocal microscopes. Yet the very technology that has taught us so much and made our lives so comfortable can get out of control, upsetting the delicate balance of life. Chapter 40 "Environmental Concerns," describes these problems, but emphasizes natural resiliency, leaving the reader, ultimately, with a sense of hope and purpose:

> *"This book has shown you the wonder that is life, from its constituent chemicals, to its cells, tissues, and organs, and all the way up to the biosphere. Do nothing to harm life—and do whatever you can to preserve its precious diversity. For in diversity lies resiliency, and the future of life on earth."*

Pedagogy

A great deal of creative energy has gone into the pedagogical aids, and some are quite different from those in the run-of-the-mill textbook. (For a visual walkthrough of these aids, examine the *Life* Learning System preview in this book's frontmatter.) The end-of-chapter "Questions" often continue the storytelling style of the chapter, using anecdotes and experiments from the literature to illustrate and apply concepts. The "To Think About" questions are springboards for class discussions and term paper topics. "Suggested Readings" go far beyond *Scientific American* and other textbooks, including sources such as *Science News, FDA Consumer* and the *New York Times*—sources that students are more likely to read, understand, and appreciate.

"Learning Objectives," which open the chapters, "Key Concepts" following major sections, and end-of-chapter summaries reinforce main points.

"Readings" throughout the chapters both elaborate and entertain. Some describe experiments: "Enticing Cells to Divide in the Laboratory," "Recipes for Starting Life—Simulating Early Earth Conditions," "Tracking Development in Different Organisms;" some provide health information, "Cardiovascular Spare Parts," "Jon and Linda—The Plight of an Infertile Couple," "Our Overdrugged Elderly," "Steroids and Athletes—An Unhealthy Combination," "The War on Cancer;" others are closer looks, "A Closer Look at an Organelle—The Lysosome," "Tumor Necrosis Factor," "Odd Human Traits," or "The Herpes Simplex Virus." Some are practical, "Nutrition and the Athlete," "Food Inhalation and the Heimlich Maneuver" and many highlight diversity "Falling Felines," "Rumbles, Roars, Screeches, and Squeals—Animal Communication," or "Sexual Seasons."

Ancillaries

Instructor's Manual/Test Item File

Prepared by Heather McKean and James Hanegan of Eastern Washington University, the instructor's manual offers helpful suggestions for course outlines and developing daily lectures. Each chapter provides key concepts, key terms, chapter outlines, learning objectives, answers to the text's end-of-chapter questions, and suggested audiovisual materials. There are also 25 to 50 objective questions in a *Test Item File* in the back of the manual. (ISBN 0-697-10181-9)

Laboratory Manual

Written by Alice Jacklet, a colleague of mine at SUNY-Albany, the *Laboratory Manual* strongly emphasizes and guides students through *the process of scientific inquiry*. Beautifully illustrated in full-color, it features 20 self-contained exercises that can easily be reorganized to suit individual course needs. (ISBN 0-697-05637-6)

Laboratory Resource Guide

This helpful prep guide offers instructions for assembling lab materials and preparing reagents, as well as suggestions for using the Lab Manual in different kinds of lab settings. (ISBN 0-697-10178-9)

Customized Laboratory Manual

Inexpensive, one-color separates of each lab in the Laboratory Manual are available for individual use, for combination with labs of local origination, or for combination with labs from other Wm. C. Brown manuals. All materials will be custom, spiral-bound for your convenience. Contact your local Wm. C. Brown sales representative for more details.

Readings in Biology

A compilation of original journal and magazine articles by Ricki Lewis is also available to students at a nominal price. The readings, which correlate closely with the sequence of topics in the text, present additional high-interest information on cell biology, genetics, reproduction, and animal biology. (ISBN-0-697-12059-7)

Student Study Guide

Also written by Heather McKean and James Hanegan, the study guide offers students a variety of exercises and keys for testing their comprehension of basic as well as difficult concepts. (ISBN 0-697-05636-8)

TestPak

This computerized classroom management system/service includes a data base of objective test questions, copyable student self-quizzes, and a grade-recording program. Disks are available for IBM, Apple, and MacIntosh PC computers and require no programming experience. If a computer is not available, instructors can choose questions from the *Test Item File* and phone or FAX in their request for a printed exam, which will be returned within 48 hours.

Transparencies and Slides

More than 200 overhead *transparencies* or a comparable *slide set* is available for free to all adopters, on request. The acetates and slides feature key illustrations from the text that, in most cases, have images and labels that have been significantly enlarged for more effective classroom display. (Transparencies: 0-697-10179-7; Slides: ISBN 0-697-10167-3)

Customized Transparency Service

For those adopters interested in receiving acetates of text figures not included in the standard transparency package, a select number of acetates will be custom-made upon request. Contact your local Wm. C. Brown sales representative for more details.

Extended Lecture Outline Software

This instructor software features extensive outlines of each text chapter with a brief synopsis of each subtopic to assist in lecture preparation. Written in ASCII files for maximum utility, it is available in IBM, Apple, or Mac formats. It is free to all adopters, upon request.

You Can Make a Difference
by Judith Getis

This short, inexpensive supplement offers students practical guidelines for recycling, conserving energy, disposing of hazardous wastes, and other pollution controls. It can be shrink wrapped with the text, at minimal additional cost. (ISBN 0-697-13923-9)

How to Study Science
by Fred Drewes, Suffolk County Community College

This excellent new workbook offers students helpful suggestions for meeting the considerable challenges of a science course. It offers tips on how to take notes; how to get the most out of laboratories; as well as on how to overcome science anxiety. The book's unique design helps to stir critical thinking skills, while facilitating careful note-taking on the part of the student. (ISBN 0-697-14474-7)

The Life Science Lexicon
by William N. Marchuk, Red Deer College

This portable, inexpensive reference helps introductory-level students quickly master the vocabulary of the life sciences. Not a dictionary, it carefully explains the rules of word construction and derivation, while giving complete definitions of all important terms. (ISBN 0-697-12133-X)

Biology Study Cards
by Kent Van De Graaff, R. Ward Rhees, and Christopher H. Creek, Brigham Young University

This boxed set of 300, two-sided study cards provides a quick, yet thorough visual synopsis of all key biological terms and concepts in the general biology curriculum. Each card features a masterful illustration, pronunciation guide, definition and description in context. (ISBN 0-697-03069-5)

Special Software and Multi-Media Ancillaries

Life on Earth Videotapes

This critically acclaimed, twin-cassette package by David Attenborough, features thirteen programs, each about 25 minutes in duration, on Life's Diversity. Each cassette also features "Chapter Search," an on-screen numerical code for quick-scan access to each of the cassettes' thirteen programs and subtopics. The *Life on Earth* videotapes are available for free to all adopters of the text, upon request. (ISBN 0-697-14631-6)

Program Summary

1. THE INFINITE VARIETY
   Nature's secrets found in ancient places.
2. BUILDING BODIES
   First signs of life in the seas.
3. THE FIRST FORESTS
   The world of plants, primitive and grand.
4. THE SWARMING HORDES
   The ingenious adaptability of insects.
5. CONQUEST OF THE WATERS
   Complexities of the great groups of fish.
6. INVASION OF THE LAND
   The emergence of amphibian creatures.
7. VICTORS OF THE DRY LAND
   Reptiles and the dinosaur dynasty.
8. LORDS OF THE AIR
   Feathers, wings and birds in flight.
9. THE RISE OF THE MAMMALS
   Where dinosaurs failed, mammals succeeded.
10. THEME AND VARIATIONS
    The extremes of mammal evolution.
11. THE HUNTS AND THE HUNTED
    Patterns of behavior in the animal kingdom.
12. LIFE IN THE TREES
    Spotlighting monkeys and their relatives.
13. THE COMPULSIVE COMMUNICATORS
    The development and achievements of humans.

Bio Sci II Videodisk

This critically acclaimed laser disk, produced by Videodiscovery for Wm. C. Brown, features more than 12,000 still and moving images, with a complete, bar-coded directory. Contact your Wm. C. Brown sales representative for more details. (ISBN 0-697-12121-6)

Mac-Hypercard and IBM Linkway Biostacks

These easy-to-use MacIntosh and IBM disks allow instructors to access the Bio Sci II laserdisk through a series of programmed lecture sequences. Contact your Wm. C. Brown representative for more details. (Mac Hypercard: 0-697-13273-1; IBM Linkway Biostacks, 3.5: 0-697-13275-7; IBM Linkway Biostacks, 5.2: 0-697-13274-9)

The Gundy-Weber Knowledge Map of the Human Body
by G. Craig Gundy, Weber State University

This thirteen disk, Mac-Hypercard program is for use by instructors and students alike. It features masterfully prepared computer graphics, animations, labeling exercises, self-tests and practice questions to help students examine the systems of the human body. Contact your local Wm. C. Brown representative or call 1-800-351-7671.

The Knowledge Map Diagrams

1. Introduction, Tissues, Integument System (0-697-13255-2)
2. Viruses, Bacteria, Eukaryotic Cells (0-697-13257-9)
3. Skeletal System (0-697-13258-7)
4. Muscle System (0-697-13259-5)
5. Nervous System (0-697-13260-9)
6. Special Senses (0-697-13261-7)
7. Endocrine System (0-697-13262-5)
8. Blood and the Lymphatic System (0-697-13263-3)
9. Cardiovascular System (0-697-13264-1)
10. Respiratory System (0-697-13265-X)
11. Digestive System (0-697-13266-8)
12. Urinary System (0-697-13267-6)
13. Reproductive System (0-697-13268-4)

Demo - (0-697-13256-0)
Complete Package - (0-697-13269-2)

GenPak: A Computer Assisted Guide to Genetics
by Tully Turney, Hampden-Sydney College

This Mac-Hypercard program features numerous, interactive/tutorial (problem-solving) exercises in Mendelian, molecular, and population genetics at the introductory level. (ISBN 0-697-13760-0)

Acknowledgments

Most of the credit for this book goes to the stories of life themselves. But thanks must also go to the scores of magazine editors who have shown me how to explain concepts clearly and concisely, yet retain a distinctive style; to the manuscript reviewers who corrected my errors and contributed so many valuable insights; to Gail Marsella, Randy Moore, Tom Gregg, Tom Wissing, and Judy Goodenough for assistance with selected chapters; to a fantastic bookteam; to my editor, Kevin Kane, and my developmental editor, Marge Manders, at Wm. C. Brown, who managed to keep me going at those times when the automatic pilot faltered; to my parents, who encouraged a little girl who brought home all sorts of creatures and to my parents-in-law who never lost faith; to my three daughters, whom I gestated along with this book; and most of all to my husband, Larry, who faithfully photocopied zillions of pages, listened to countless reviews, and never tired of hearing, yet one more time, "I've only got one more sentence left!" This really is the last sentence.

UNIT

7

Evolution

CHAPTER

33

Darwin's View of Evolution

Learning Objectives

By the chapter's end, you should be able
to answer these questions:

1. What can be learned about the evolution of species when cataloging the types of organisms that populate islands over known periods of time?

2. What natural phenomena does the science of evolution consider?

3. How do geology and geography influence evolution?

4. How did Charles Darwin's observations of the distribution of organisms throughout the world contribute to his theory of evolution?

5. What is natural selection, and how does it explain and underlie evolutionary change?

About 8 million years ago, the island of Mauritius rose in volcanic fury from the depths of the Indian Ocean. By the sixteenth century, the island's surface was covered with low-lying plains and dense, tall forests teeming with colorful birds, scurrying insects, and basking reptiles. The organisms that made the island their home were well adapted to the climate, terrain, and other organisms of Mauritius. Some of the organisms interacted in interesting ways.

Consider the flightless, 30-pound (14-kilogram) relative of the pigeon, the dodo bird, which stood 3 feet (1 meter) tall and nibbled the hard fruits of the abundant Calvaria tree. Were it not for the destruction of the outer hard layer of the Calvaria fruits by the dodo's digestive tract, the seeds of the majestic trees could not germinate. This mutual dependence of two types of organisms is termed **coevolution.**

Food was plentiful on Mauritius, and the populations of its resident species flourished. Life progressed in this splendor and diversity on the little island until the 1500s, when Spanish and Portuguese sailors arrived. It was the beginning of the end for many longtime island inhabitants. The men feasted on dodo meat, and their pet monkeys and pigs ate dodo eggs. The Calvaria trees gradually died out as their route for seed dispersal and germination vanished with the dodo. Today only a few ancient Calvarias remain. Rats and mice swam ashore from the ships to attack native insects and reptiles. Exotic animals accompanying the human invasion also evicted island species from their homes. Indian myna birds took over nesting holes of the native echo parakeet, while Brazilian purple guava and oriental privet plants crowded seedlings of native trees that had been undisturbed for centuries. Soon, the forest that had previously been home mostly to birds, insects, and reptiles had become a mammalian haven, populated largely by newcomers.

By the mid-1600s, only 11 of the original 33 species of native birds remained. The dodo was exterminated by 1681, earning a dubious distinction as the first recorded extinction due to direct human intervention (fig. 33.1). The dodo is known today solely from bones. For years the bird was thought to be mythical. Others of Mauritius's reptile, plant, and insect species may face similar bleak futures.

About 3 million years after Mauritius erupted from the Indian Ocean, the first of a chain of other volcanic islands was born, rising in the central Pacific, 2,000 miles (3,218 kilometers) from the closest continents. After the new land cooled, the invasion of life began. Seeds floated in on mats of vegetation or drifted in on the wind or on migrating birds. Insects and a lone type of mammal, a bat, flew in too. From this original gathering of plants and animals evolved, over the millennia, a diverse collection of new varieties. The original 15 species of land birds diversified into more than 80 species; the 20 founding land molluscs were ancestral to more than 1,000 species living there today; one or two colonizing fruit fly varieties led to hundreds of modern species (fig. 33.2).

Islands continued to erupt from the volcanic earth, and the main island of Hawaii was born a mere half million years ago. Its five volcanoes, two exceeding

Figure 33.1
The dodo—a modern extinction caused by humans. The great, flightless dodo and the Calvaria tree coevolved, the bird dependent upon the tree for food, and the tree dependent on the bird for seed germination.

Figure 33.2
The hundreds of species of fruit flies that inhabit the Hawaiian Islands descended from only one or two colonizing species. This fly hails from the island of Oahu.

13,780 feet (4,200 meters) above sea level, provide a wide range of different habitats, which are frequently altered by fresh lava flows. Local populations confined to isolated habitats accumulate their own distinct sets of adaptations, so that the island is home to hundreds of species seen nowhere else on the planet.

The Hawaiian Islands, like Mauritius, have seen many species vanish. Some species just cannot compete with others for food and shelter. The arrival of humans to the Hawaiian Islands in A.D. 400 transformed the lush lowland forests into fields of crops, destroying the homes of many resident species. The large, flightless birds were eaten, and the vibrantly colored birds were killed and their feathers used to adorn the clothing of Polynesian settlers. Europeans who arrived a dozen centuries later destroyed the land further, hastening the extinctions of even more species.

About 40 million years ago, a group of small volcanoes arose from the sea just off the coast of Ecuador. Over the years the resulting volcanic islands cooled sufficiently so that organisms living on the mainland of South America were able to colonize them, flying or riding natural rafts of floating vegetation to a new habitat. Gradually, these first islands were covered over by the sea, as newer islands arose from volcanic eruptions farther away from the mainland. Perhaps the first group of islands and the second group coexisted for a time, and some of the organisms on the islands closer to the mainland moved to the newer island, which was farther from the mainland.

Today's Galápagos archipelago is a group of volcanic islands 600 miles (965 kilometers) west of Ecuador. The particular species that chanced to inhabit these islands were but a subset of all those present on the mainland. They survived only if they, and their descendants, were adapted to the particular environmental challenges posed by the island habitat. The modern Galápagos Islands are home to an unusual assortment of organisms. The name Galápagos comes from the Spanish for "tortoise," one of the island's most noticeable residents (fig. 33.3).

Figure 33.3
Galápagos tortoises. When he visited the Galápagos Islands, Charles Darwin found that the natives could tell which island a particular tortoise came from by the length of its neck and other obvious adaptations. This tortoise has evolved a long neck, which enables it to reach its vegetable food.

Islands Reveal Evolution in Action

These panoramas of island life are constructed from geological and historical evidence, with the details filled in from present-day ideas about evolution. Islands provide a microcosm for viewing evolution on an accelerated scale, something that life on the mainland does not provide as readily. **Evolution** is the process by which the genetic composition of populations of organisms changes over time. In sexually reproducing organisms, when genetic changes accumulate that prevent members of one population from successfully breeding with members of another population, two **species** have diverged from the ancestral group.

If we are lucky enough to know when an island formed and have evidence indicating which species were the first to colonize it, and we know which species live there today, the events that took place in between can be reconstructed. It is likely that over time, certain individuals were better able to survive and leave offspring than other individuals, because they had inherited variations of traits that were helpful, or **adaptive,** in that particular environment. The island populations accumulated adaptive traits to the point that they eventually became so unlike their distant relatives that originally settled the island that they theoretically could no longer mate with them. Thus did new species arise. The isolation of the island environment prevented members of island populations from breeding with individuals on other landmasses, keeping their collections of traits separate. One way that new species are born is from the isolation afforded by islands.

Macroevolution and Microevolution

Evolution is a continuing process that explains the history of life on earth, as well as the diversity of life forms on the planet today. Evolution includes large-scale events, such as the appearance of new species **(speciation)** and the disappearance of species **(extinction).** These large changes are termed **macroevolution.** Evolution also includes more subtle, incremental single-trait changes that accumulate to the point that two groups of organisms can no longer interbreed. These changes are termed **microevolution.**

Whereas macroevolutionary events tend to span very long periods of time, microevolutionary changes can happen so rapidly that they can be seen experimentally. In one experiment, two populations of a species of fruit fly were bred, each from an original pair of flies. One population was reared at 61°F (16°C) and the other at 80°F (27°C). After 12 years, the flies raised at the colder temperature were on the average 10% larger than the flies raised at the higher temperature.

Microevolutionary change can also be seen yearly as influenza viruses change their surface proteins, reflecting underlying genetic mutation. This is why we must constantly develop new flu vaccines, and it is also why it has been difficult to devise a vaccine against the virus that causes AIDS, which also evolves rapidly.

Evolutionary biologists debate whether macroevolutionary changes reflect the buildup of step-by-step microevolutionary changes or if the more sweeping events involve some other, as yet unknown, genetic mechanism. Although clearly both macroevolutionary and microevolutionary processes are at work, the precise relationship between them is not well understood.

Early in the nineteenth century, biologists realized that inherited traits (rather than acquired traits) are important in evolution. Although later the discovery of genes explained the mechanics of evolutionary change, the idea of evolution as a gradual change in life forms actually grew out of many observations made by several individuals (Reading 33.1). These concepts were crystallized into a coherent theory by Charles Darwin in the nineteenth century. Darwin's theory was radical for its time, but it was so compelling, and so beautifully argued and illustrated, that it achieved scientific acceptance rather easily. Darwin's famous theory of evolution has its roots in the evolution of the earth.

KEY CONCEPTS

The isolation afforded by islands offers views of evolution in action. Evolution is genetic change in a population. Large-scale events such as speciation and extinction illustrate macroevolution. Single-trait changes demonstrate microevolution. The precise relationship between microevolutionary and macroevolutionary events is not known.

The Influence of Geology—Clues to Evolution in Rock Layers

In a sense, it can be said that the science of evolution got its start in ditch digging. The field of geology arose in the latter half of the nineteenth century, as people puzzled over the layers (strata) in the earth that were revealed when ditches were dug or mountains climbed. It had been recognized since the 1600s that lower rock layers were older than those above them, a phenomenon called the **principle of superposition.** Several interesting theories attempted to explain how rock layers came to be (fig. 33.4).

Neptunism, named after the Roman god of the sea, held that a single great flood organized the earth's surface, with the waters receding to reveal the mountains, valleys, plains, and rock strata present to this day. According to Neptunism, the earth has not changed since this initial catastrophic event. A variation of Neptunism, called **mosaic catastrophism,** held that a series of great floods molded the earth's features and were responsible for extinctions of some life forms and creations of others. Mosaic catastrophism explained why preserved remains of sea-dwelling organisms were sometimes found in different rock strata. The single flood of Neptunism could not account for this observation.

At odds with Neptunism and mosaic catastrophism was **uniformitarianism,** the continual remolding of the earth's surface. This idea was proposed by a physician and farmer named James Hutton, who liked to take long walks in the Scottish countryside.

Reading 33.1 Some Thoughts on Evolution Through History

THROUGHOUT RECORDED HISTORY AND UNDOUBTEDLY BEFORE THAT AS WELL, HUNDREDS OF THINKERS HAVE PONDERED HOW THE GREAT VARIETY OF LIVING THINGS CAME TO BE, AND HOW THEY ARE RELATED TO ONE ANOTHER, IF AT ALL. Here are a few hypotheses to explain the evolution of life.

One of the earliest thinkers to place human beginnings into a scheme with the origin of other organisms was a fourth-century B.C. Greek physician, Empedocles. He proposed that the appearance of animals was the most recent part of the evolution of the universe. First, parts of animal bodies appeared, and then the parts mixed together randomly to form animals. The first combinations were poorly adapted monsters that did not survive or reproduce and hence did not perpetuate. Eventually, the animals with which we are familiar today formed, and these survived.

Like Empedocles, Aristotle, who lived a century later, considered the appearance of animals to follow the evolution of nonliving matter. He thought that inorganic matter evolved into organic matter, which led to soft living matter, which gave rise to perfect life forms. But he thought each species arose independently and did not change.

Aristotle envisioned a "Great Chain of Being," a detailed ordering of many life forms arranged into a single line of descent. The Chain of Being was uneven—it did not represent all types of organisms in the same degree of detail. Different human races were considered to be distinct types of organisms, and their "order," from less advanced to more advanced, often reflected the ethnic background of the orderer. Yet many species and entire groups of organisms were missing from the Great Chain of Being. Like many plans before it, the Chain of Being traced the evolution of the supposedly imperfect to the perfect. This differs markedly from the modern view of evolutionary change as fostered by adaptations to a particular environment, rather than attainment of a subjective perfection.

The term "evolution" in reference to the appearance of life forms over time was coined by Swiss naturalist Charles Bonnet in the eighteenth century. He envisioned earth's natural history as a series of major catastrophes. After each event, the organisms of the past period became fossils, and new types of organisms appeared, moved up a notch on a scale of increasing biological complexity. The most recent event, according to Bonnet, catapulted apes to human status.

The first thinker to extract a theory from these sometimes arbitrary orderings of organisms was French taxonomist Jean Baptiste Lamarck (1744–1829). He originated some of the ideas found in Darwin's work, such as the evolution of species from preexisting ones and the ability of animals to adapt to a changing environment. He is most remembered, however, for his theory of the inheritance of acquired characteristics, in which evolutionary change results from the appearance of new body parts or functions in response to want or need. According to this view, characteristics acquired during an individual's lifetime are passed to its offspring. An often-quoted example of the inheritance of acquired characteristics is the long neck of the giraffe. The animal "needed" a long neck to reach its treetop food, so the neck grew, a little each generation. Once acquired, a trait was passed on to the next generation. Lamarck is also noted for his law of use and disuse. A used organ would be maintained from generation to generation; an unused organ would gradually disappear.

Darwin was not exactly sure how natural variations arose. The field of evolution had to wait until the early twentieth century, when knowledge of genetics supplied the missing information.

Hutton possessed a great scientific gift—the ability to connect observations to explain phenomena. What set Hutton's mind to contemplating the history of the earth were similarities of rocks in different parts of a particular locale. Why did pebbles brought in by the tide resemble rocks in the hills looking out over the ocean? Why did the rock layers in mountains contain evidence of organisms that clearly had lived in the sea? Hutton noted the weathering of exposed rock on the land and the gradual deposition of sediments in bodies of water. He proposed that the earth's surface features were not formed in just one event, or even several, but were continually being built up and broken down. According to Hutton, the seas receded to reveal new, uplifted sediments, as ancient mountains were eroded down, slowly contributing future sediments to the seas.

These geological changes must have taken a very long time—certainly longer than the 6,000 to 10,000 years of earth's existence according to the Bible. The long time of earth history was inferred because the forces of geological change—erosion and deposition of sediments—occur very slowly, yet vast geological change was clearly evident in many places.

Hutton published his ideas in a book, *Theory of the Earth*, in 1785, earning him long after his death the title "father of geology." His contemplation of the vast stretches of time necessary to account for rock formations, plus the existence of fossils, led Hutton to propose a theory of evolution startlingly like the one that would be described by Charles Darwin in the next century. However, Hutton died before this book could be completed, and the manu-

script was discovered in 1947, long after Charles Darwin was recognized as the father of evolution.

Although Hutton did not live long enough to pursue his ideas on the evolution of life, a contemporary was having thoughts along the same lines. William Smith was a grade-school-educated surveyor who dug canals in the English countryside in the late 1700s. Like others before him, Smith was fascinated by the precise rock layers revealed by his excavating, so much so that his friends nicknamed him Strata Smith. Smith noticed that each stratum seemed to have its own characteristic assortment of **fossils** (evidence of past life). Even if the layer meandered, or was sharply disrupted for a distance, when it straightened out or reappeared it always contained fossils of the same types of organisms.

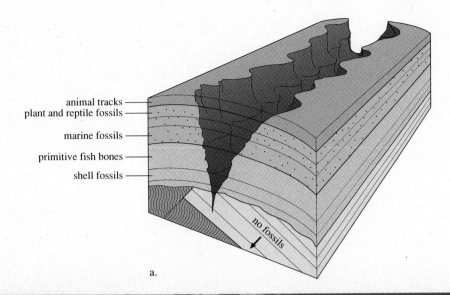

animal tracks
plant and reptile fossils
marine fossils
primitive fish bones
shell fossils

no fossils

a.

b.

Figure 33.4

Rock layers reveal earth history and sometimes life history. Layers of sedimentary rock form from sand, mud, and gravel deposited in ancient seas. The rock layers on the bottom are older than those on top. Rock strata sometimes contain evidence of organisms that lived when the layer was formed. The position of such fossils within rock layers provides clues about when the organism they represent lived. Sediments are visible along the Grand Canyon. Hiking here is like taking a journey through time. Although the rim now rises over 6,500 feet (2,000 meters) above sea level, when the rock formed it was beneath an ancient ocean.

Because lower strata were older than strata closer to the surface, the positions of certain fossils within rock layers indicated the relative times of existence of the organisms they represent. Fossils could now be put into a relative time frame.

Early in the nineteenth century, another geologist, Charles Lyell, continued Hutton's approach of envisioning long-ago earth features suggested by present-day rock formations. Lyell suggested that sandstone was once sand, shale rock was once mud, and islands were once active volcanoes. He described these ideas in his three-volume *Principles of Geology*, a set of which were to accompany a young man named Charles Darwin on a fascinating voyage. So impressed was Darwin with Lyell's presentation of uniformitarianism that, years later, he would write: "Therefore a man should examine for himself the great piles of superimposed strata, and watch the rivulets bringing down mud, and the waves wearing away the sea-cliffs, in order to comprehend something about the duration of past time, the monuments of which we see all around us."

KEY CONCEPTS

The organization of remains of ancient life in rock layers reveals information about when the organisms lived in time and with respect to each other.

The Voyage of the HMS *Beagle*

It was against the backdrop of the birth of geology and the principle of uniformitarianism that Charles Darwin was born in 1809, the son of a physician and grandson of noted physician and poet Erasmus Darwin. Young Charles did not do particularly well in school, preferring to wander about the countryside examining rock outcroppings, collecting shells, and observing birds and insects. Under family pressure he began to study medicine but abandoned it because he could not stand to watch children undergoing surgery without anesthesia. Next he tried studying for the clergy, but could not maintain interest, leading his father to comment, "You're good for nothing but shooting guns, and rat catching, and you'll be a disgrace to yourself and all of your family."

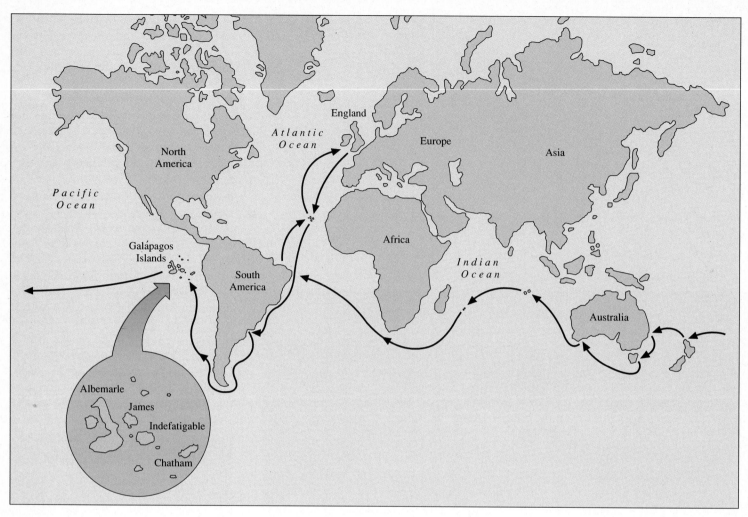

Figure 33.5
The 5-year journey of the HMS *Beagle*. During his voyage, Charles Darwin recorded his observations of geological formations and the distribution of living things. His voluminous notes would serve as the basis for his theory of evolution, synthesized years later.

While Darwin reluctantly explored the subject areas his family thought right for him, he also followed his own interests. He became an avid and valued participant on several geological field trips and met professors in the new science of geology. Darwin's investigations of rock layer formations meshed well with his boyhood love of nature, and so when he was offered a position as captain's companion aboard the HMS *Beagle*, he accepted, despite his father's objections. He would later become the ship's naturalist. Before the ship set sail for its 5-year voyage 2 days after Christmas in 1831, botany professor John Henslow, who had arranged Darwin's new job, gave the young man the first volume of Charles Lyell's *Principles of Geology*. Darwin picked

up the second two volumes later in South America. The trilogy was to influence Darwin's thinking profoundly (fig. 33.5).

Darwin read Lyell's geology text as he battled continual seasickness, and he became utterly convinced that uniformitarianism—the gradual changing of the earth's features over long periods of time—was correct. Lyell's ideas fit nicely with what Darwin had observed on his excursions prior to boarding the HMS *Beagle*. Yet Darwin came from a religious family, and he did not set sail with any particular goal of developing a comprehensive theory of evolution. He was actually in search of proof of the biblical version of creation, which he was raised to believe. However, the combination of this unusually perceptive "trained observer," as Darwin has

been called, and a voyage to some of the most unusual and undisturbed places on the planet, set the stage for the collection of bountiful evidence upon which the theory of evolution would be built.

Darwin's Observations

Charles Darwin recorded his observations as the ship journeyed down the coast of South America. He paid close attention to forces that uplifted new land, such as earthquakes and volcanoes, and the constant erosion that wore it down. Over and over, he saw what Lyell had written about. Darwin marveled at the intermingling of sea and land in the earth's layers; of fossils of forest plants interspersed with sea sediments; of shell fossils in a mountain cave. The gradual changes evi-

a.

b.

Figure 33.6

Convergent evolution provides common solutions to common challenges. Darwin was puzzled by organisms that lived in similar habitats in different parts of the world but differed in some ways. *a.* For example, the North American wolf and the Tasmanian wolf look remarkably alike, but the North American variety is a placental mammal (which nourishes the unborn through a maternal organ, the placenta) whereas the Tasmanian wolf is a marsupial (which nourishes immature young in a maternal pouch). *b.* Eyes have evolved independently 40 times to meet the need for a light-sensing organ. The eyes of humans and octopuses are coincidentally very similar. Otherwise the two species have little in common. *c.* These three animals look similar. Each has a back fin, flippers, a bilobed tail, and a streamlined body, all of which are adaptations to an aquatic existence. Yet the top animal is an ancient reptile (an ichthyosaur); the middle one is a modern fish; and the bottom animal is a dolphin, a mammal.

c.

L. O'Keefe

denced in the layers of earth were echoed in the fossils found within them. Darwin suggested that fossils, like sediments, were arranged in a chronological sequence, with those most like present forms occupying the highest, or most recent, layers. Like a geologist, he tried to extrapolate past occurrences from contemporary observations and wondered how a particular type of organism got to be where he saw it.

Darwin was particularly aware of differences between organisms, both on a global scale and in localized environments. He noted that different species seen at different latitudes paralleled the different species seen at different elevations on a mountain. Why was this so? If there was a one-time period of special creation, as the Bible held, then why was one sort of animal or plant created for a mountaintop or frigid plain and another for a warmer habitat? Even more puzzling was the fact that similar habitats in different parts of the world were populated by similar-looking types of organisms that could nonetheless have important differences between them.

For example, Africa, Australia, and South America all have large, flightless birds, but the ostrich, emu, and rhea are clearly not the same type of animal. The North American wolf and Tasmanian wolf look almost identical, and live in similar environments, yet their methods of nurturing their unborn young are vastly different (fig. 33.6). Today we know that organisms of different species can evolve similar adaptations to similar environments, a phenomenon called **convergent evolution.**

Darwin kept detailed notes on the living things he saw and also on geological formations. However, there is some debate as to whether he realized the influence of geography on the distribution of organisms as he observed it or whether he did so after the journey. He wrote after the voyage that wherever he found a barrier—a desert, river, or mountain—different sorts of organisms populated the two sides. Islands were the ultimate barriers and often lacked the types of organisms that could not get to them. Why would a Creator have put only a few types of organisms on islands, Darwin wondered?

In the fourth year of the voyage, the HMS *Beagle* spent a month in the Galápagos Islands. Although Darwin spent half of the time shipbound due to illness and visited only 4 of the 11 islands, the notes and samples that he brought back would form the backbone of his theory of evolution.

KEY CONCEPTS

As a young man, Charles Darwin journeyed around the world for 5 years aboard the HMS Beagle, and his observations formed the basis of his theory of evolution. Darwin noticed the constant upheaval in geologic processes, the distribution of fossils in rock strata, differences and similarities between organisms, and the correlation of organisms' characteristics to their environments.

After the Voyage

Darwin returned to England in 1836 and published the first account of the *Beagle's* voyage, *A Naturalist's Voyage on the Beagle*, 3 years later. In that time he spoke with several other naturalists and geologists whose observations and interpretations helped mold Darwin's thoughts on the evolutionary process.

In March 1837, Darwin spoke with an ornithologist (an expert on birds), who was very excited by the finches brought back from different islands of the Galápagos. By examining beak structure, the ornithologist could tell that some of the birds ate small seeds, some ate large seeds, others ate leaves or fruits, and some ate insects (fig. 33.7). In all, Darwin had brought back or described 14 distinct types of finch, each

probing bill; insect eater; feeds in trees   **warbler finch**

probing bill; insect eater; uses twigs or cactus spine to probe insects from cactus   **woodpecker finch**

grasping bill; insect eater   **large tree finch**

crushing bill; cactus seed eater   **large ground finch**

Figure 33.7
The differences in beak structure of the 14 species of finch seen on the Galápagos Islands reflect the birds' different food sources.

different from the finches seen on the mainland. A special creation of slightly different finches on each island did not make much sense. Darwin thought it more likely that the different varieties of finch on the Galápagos were descended from a single ancestral type of bird that dwelled on the mainland. Some birds flew over to the islands and, finding a relatively unoccu-

pied new habitat, flourished. Gradually, the finch population branched into several directions, with some groups now eating insects, some eating fruits and leaves, and others consuming different-sized seeds. Darwin called this gradual change from an ancestral type "descent with modification." The different neck lengths of the islands' giant tortoises might also reflect descent with modification. Darwin wondered how and why these variations might have arisen.

In September 1838, Darwin read a book that enabled him to make some sense of the diversity of finches on the Galápagos Islands and of other examples. Economist and theologian Thomas Malthus's "Essay on the Principle of Population," written 40 years earlier, stated that the size of a human population is limited by food availability, disease, and war. Wouldn't populations of other organisms, in the wild, face similar limitations of resources? If so, then individuals who were better able to obtain those resources would survive to reproduce, contributing some individuals like themselves to the next generation (fig. 33.8). This would explain the observation that more individuals were produced in a generation than survived. Over time, the challenges posed by the environment would "select" these better-equipped variants, and gradually the population would change. Darwin compared the selection of adaptive traits by the environment to the **artificial selection** by breeders of certain traits in domesticated pigeons. He called this differential survival and reproduction of better-adapted variants **natural selection.**

Natural selection beautifully explained the diversity of finches on the Galápagos. Originally, some finches flew over from the mainland to populate one island. When that first island population grew too large for all individuals to obtain enough small seeds, those who could eat other things, perhaps because of a quirk in beak structure, began to eat other foods. Finding the new food plentiful, these once-unusual birds gradually made up more of the population. Because each of the islands had slightly different habitats, different varieties of finches were selected on each one. The divergence of several new types from a single ancestral type is termed **adaptive radiation.**

Figure 33.8
Maple saplings compete for natural resources. Near a forest floor, young trees of various sizes attempt to obtain sufficient space, sun, and water to grow and survive. Few of them will succeed.

Darwin's theory of natural selection as the process behind evolutionary change was unveiled in a 35-page sketch published in 1842, and 2 years after that as a 230-page analysis. (Other forces behind evolution are discussed in the next chapter.) In 1856, his treatise expanded but not yet published, Darwin was disturbed to receive a 4,000-word manuscript from British naturalist Alfred Russell Wallace with the rather long-winded title, *On the Tendency of Varieties to Depart Indefinitely From the Original Type*. It was as if Wallace had peered into Darwin's mind. Actually Wallace, like Darwin, had seen the principles of evolution demonstrated among the diverse life forms of South America.

Darwin and Wallace presented their ideas at a scientific meeting later that year. In 1859, Darwin finally published 490 pages of the even longer-titled *On the Origin of Species by Means of Natural Selection, or Preservation of Favoured Races in the Struggle for Life*. It became an overnight success. The direction of biological thought had been changed forever.

KEY CONCEPTS

Darwin noted "descent with modification" in different varieties of finches from the Galápagos. He deduced that natural populations would be affected by the availability of resources and environmental conditions, such that only the better adapted of each generation would survive to reproduce. Darwin termed the differential survival and reproduction of better-adapted variants natural selection. Divergence of several species from one is called adaptive radiation.

Natural Selection—The Mechanism Behind Darwinian Evolution

On his 5-year voyage on the HMS *Beagle*, Darwin saw evidence of the change in life forms through time—evolution. Perhaps his most important observation was not the specifics of beak structure in finches or neck length in giant tortoises but simply that a great deal of variation exists among members of a species. (You can confirm this just by glancing around a classroom and noting the differences among students.) Darwin envisioned natural variation as the raw material of evolution. Depending upon environmental conditions and competition for resources, certain variants would be more fit than others and therefore more likely to have offspring healthy enough to have offspring of their own. The traits that make these individuals healthier in the particular environment are passed on. An individual who is successful in mating is considered to be "fit," and reproductive success is what is meant by the term **survival of the fittest.**

The traits that contribute to reproductive success need not directly affect reproduction. Any trait that ensures an individual's survival can make reproduction more likely. Wrote Darwin, "When we see leaf-eating insects green, and bark-feeders mottled-grey; the alpine ptarmigan white in winter, the red-grouse the colour of heather, we must believe that these tints are of service to these birds and insects in preserving them from danger."

Traits that directly boost reproductive success increase in a population due to a type of natural selection called **sexual selection** (fig. 33.9). Such traits include elaborate feathers in male birds, horns in species ranging from beetles to giant elk, and the courtship songs sung by various insects and birds that attract a mate.

Natural selection does not produce perfection, but it reflects transient adaptation to a prevailing environmental condition. Selective forces act upon preexisting characteristics; they do not create new, perfectly adapted variants. The furry fox that survives a frigid winter to bear pups in the spring is not "perfect" and would certainly not seem so in an unusually mild winter or sweltering summer. Similarly, bighorn sheep whose dwindling numbers grace the crags of the northern Rockies today were far more plentiful at the height of the ice age, when they flourished in the cooler climate.

Natural selection can mold the same population in different directions under different environmental circumstances. Consider the finches on the tiny Galápagos Island of Daphne Major. In a very dry season in the early 1980s, birds with large beaks were more likely to survive because most of the seeds that they eat are large and dry. In 1983, 8 months of extremely heavy rainfall allowed many small seeds to accumulate. Over the next 2 years, finches with small beaks, who could easily eat the tiny seeds, came to predominate.

Although Darwin was quite convinced that the interaction between naturally occurring variants and environmental conditions provides the force behind evolution, he did not know the source of those important variants. He recognized that the natural variations that play a part in the accumulation of new traits and the origin of species are those that are passed on to future generations, but he did not know how they arose or were transmitted.

A predecessor of Darwin, French taxonomist Jean-Baptiste Lamarck, thought that inherited variations were acquired during an individual's lifetime through want or need and then passed on to the next generation. According to this viewpoint, the fox with the heavy coat would have

a.

b.

c.

d.

Figure 33.9

Sexual selection. The individual who is most successful in attracting a mate is the most fit, according to Darwin. *a.* The male bowerbird builds intricate towers of sticks and grass to attract a mate. *b.* The male bird of paradise displays bright plumes and capes in his quest for sexual success. Diverse organisms use horns to battle rivals for access to the hornless sex, from the battling Hercules beetles (*c*) to the extinct Irish elk, with its 80-pound antlers (*d*).

Table 33.1
Darwin's Main Ideas

1. Living things are varied. Within a species, no two individuals (except identical siblings) are exactly alike.

2. More individuals are born than survive to reproduce.

3. Individuals compete with one another for the resources that enable them to survive.

4. Within populations, the characteristics of some individuals make them more able to survive and reproduce in the face of certain environmental conditions than others.

5. As a result of this environmentally selected "survival of the fittest," only those individuals with adaptive traits live long enough to pass these traits on. Over time, this natural selection can change the characteristics of populations, even molding new species.

---

consciously grown it to help him survive the frigid winter, rather than the Darwinian interpretation of the animal's inheriting genes conferring a heavy coat that just happened to be adaptive in the fox's environment. Darwin thought that new characteristics were acquired by an individual's somatic cells, and then transmitted to the sex cells, so that they could be passed to subsequent generations. Table 33.1 presents Darwin's main ideas.

It is ironic that as Darwin spent his later years pondering the source of inherited variation, a contemporary thinker, a breeder of peas in an Austrian monastery, Gregor Mendel, was formulating the answer. But it would be another half a century until the science of genetics would arise to explain the science of evolution.

KEY CONCEPTS

Natural selection acts on preexisting variants. Fitness refers to reproductive success. In a given environment, some individuals will be more fit than others, as a result of particular inherited variations, some of which directly affect sexual behavior and some of which affect fitness indirectly. Lamarck thought that evolution was driven by traits acquired during an individual's lifetime to suit a particular need and were then passed on.

SUMMARY

The biological science of *evolution* examines changing characteristics of populations of organisms that can lead to adaptation and to the formation and demise of species. Islands provide vivid examples of evolutionary change because their geographical isolation separates individuals with particular combinations of traits from ancestral organisms and selects those traits that are adaptive in the particular environment. Evolution consists of both the large-scale, species-level changes of *macroevolution* and the trait-by-trait changes of *microevolution*.

The field of geology laid the groundwork for evolutionary thought. Some people explained the distribution of rock strata with the idea of *Neptunism* (a single flood) or *mosaic catastrophism* (a series of floods), but it was *uniformitarianism* (the continual remolding of the earth's surface) that was most consistent with the planet's appearance. Uniformitarianism suggests that geological change took a very long time. The sequence of rock strata suggests a time frame, with the lowest layers older than layers closer to the earth's surface. It follows that fossils found within rock strata are also organized according to their time of deposition, which demonstrates the *principle of superposition*. Charles Darwin was greatly influenced by geology.

Darwin was an ordinary student given an extraordinary opportunity to observe the distribution of organisms in many diverse habitats as naturalist aboard the HMS *Beagle* on its 5-year journey. In the years following the voyage, Darwin thought over his observations, conferred with biologists and geologists, and was greatly influenced by Thomas Malthus's "Essay on the Principle of Population." From these sources, Darwin eventually synthesized his theory of the origin of species by means of *natural selection*. His theory states that those individuals who are best adapted to their environments are more likely to produce fertile offspring and will pass on their adaptive traits to the next generation. Eventually, enough changes would accumulate so that its members could no longer mate with members of the ancestral population, and a new species would result. The different beak shapes among the several species of finches found on the Galápagos Islands illustrate natural selection. Natural selection does not produce perfection but rather successful adaptation to the environment.

QUESTIONS

1. What characteristic of islands is responsible for the impact they have had on the evolution of species?

2. What is the difference between microevolutionary and macroevolutionary change?

3. How did James Hutton, William Smith, Charles Lyell, and Thomas Malthus influence the thinking of Charles Darwin?

4. What is natural selection? How can natural selection explain evolutionary change?

5. What sorts of traits lead to "fitness" in a Darwinian sense?

6. The term "highly evolved" is often interpreted to mean "perfect." Why is this definition inaccurate if applied to Darwinian evolution?

TO THINK ABOUT

1. Many islands have populations of large, flightless birds found nowhere else in the world. How might they have gotten to the islands?

2. Which theory best explains Darwinian evolution—Neptunism, mosaic catastrophism, or uniformitarianism? Give a reason for your answer.

3. An early and major objection to Darwin's concept of natural selection as the mechanism behind evolution was that it refutes the pleasant idea that we humans are advanced and special when compared to other species. How does Darwinian evolution do this?

4. You have a pet cocker spaniel and believe that if you snip off the end of his tail, then breed him, his puppies will be born with snipped-off tails. Is this idea consistent with Darwinian evolution? What principle is it an example of, and who suggested it?

5. Herbert Spencer was an eighteenth-century English sociologist who believed in applying Darwin's concepts to human society. He popularized the phrase "survival of the fittest" and suggested that the unemployed, the sick, and other "burdens on society" be allowed to die rather than be objects of public assistance and charity. What do you think of this idea and of the validity of his interpretation of the concept of natural selection?

SUGGESTED READINGS

Darwin, Charles. 1958 (1859). *On the origin of species by means of natural selection*. New York: Mentor Books. Darwin's writing is very detailed, but offers fascinating examples and interpretations of the natural world.

Diamond, Jared. October 1990. Bob Dylan and moa's ghosts. *Natural History*. Can extinct, large birds explain the unique distribution of species in New Zealand?

Eldredge, Niles. 1982. *The monkey business*. New York: Washington Square Press. Is evolution really a fact?

Gould, Stephen Jay. *Wonderful life* (1989). *The flamingo's smile* (1986). *Hen's teeth and horse's toes* (1983). *The panda's thumb* (1980). *Ever since Darwin* (1977). New York: W.W. Norton. Humorous and fact-packed evolutionary essays. Gould also writes a monthly column on evolution for *Natural History* magazine.

Monastersky, R. June 13, 1987. Natural selection: Bird seeds of change. *Science News*, vol. 131. Natural selection of beak size among finches on Daphne Major in the Galápagos follows fluctuations in yearly rainfall.

Stone, Irving. 1980. *The origin*. Garden City, N.Y.: Doubleday. A fictionalized but highly informative account of the adventures of a brilliant thinker, Charles Darwin.

34

The Forces of Evolutionary Change

Chapter Outline

Learning Objectives

By the chapter's end, you should be able to answer these questions:

1. What is a population?

2. What is a gene pool?

3. Under what conditions does evolutionary change not occur?

4. How can algebra be used to describe whether or not microevolution is occurring?

5. How can migration, nonrandom mating, mutation, and natural selection alter gene frequencies?

6. How do some genetic diseases remain in populations, even though they decrease reproductive success?

7. How do species arise?

8. How do species become extinct?

BECK/PERRITY

Bullwinkle J. Moose first appeared on dairy farms in upstate New York in 1980. A refugee from the dense moose populations in nearby New England and Canada, Bullwinkle was one of only 20 moose in all of New York state. Most were males, who were more likely to survive the rigors of migration than females. Bullwinkle developed an attraction to the next best thing to the cows of his own species—domesticated dairy cows (fig. 34.1). The moose's vision was poor, and from a distance the heifers did not look much different from moose cows. Their low-pitched moos were similar to the moans that female moose utter to lure mates. The scent of the dairy cows was enough like that of moose cows that Bullwinkle dug his hooves into the ground and urinated around a small area, marking a territory as a prelude to mating. He then approached a plump heifer.

Once Bullwinkle mounted the heifer, though, the courtship ceased. For in the end, a moose is a moose and a cow is a cow—members of two different species. The moose's genitalia did not fit the cow's, and the activity ended without completion. Bullwinkle continued to frequent upstate New York farms in search of dairy cows until 1987, when he finally found a mate of his own kind, near Tupper Lake.

Not all species are as different appearing as the moose and the dairy cow. For example, two species of fruit fly, *Drosophila persimilis* and *Drosophila pseudoobscura*, look identical, down to the tiniest bristle. The flies will not mate with each other, however, perhaps because of a lack of communication. If the antennae of a female of one species are snipped off, she will indeed mate with a male of the other species.

How does a group of organisms become able to mate successfully only among themselves? In other words, how do species form? Charles Darwin noted that evolution of species was the consequence of different traits being selected by particular environments. Eventually, such accumulated adaptations in a group of organisms changes them to the point that they cannot mate with others not of the group. On a small scale, then, evolution reflects the changing representations of particular traits among groups of individuals. On a large scale, evolution is the formation and the extinction of species.

Figure 34.1

Members of two species cannot successfully mate with one another. In some areas of New England and upstate New York, male moose are rare and will occasionally approach a dairy cow with romance in mind.

Evolution After Darwin—The Genetics of Populations

The "raw material" of evolution is inherited natural variation. The role of genes in evolution is different from genetic functions considered so far—as biochemical instructions that form the biological basis of traits passed through families. Genes influence evolution at the population level. A **population** is a broad term for any group of interbreeding organisms. Human populations include the students in a class or a school or people in a town, a nation, or the entire world.

All the genes in a population constitute its **gene pool**. The proportion of different alleles of each gene determines the characteristics of that population. A Swedish population, for example, would have a preponderance of "blond" hair color alleles; a population of black Africans would have very few, if any, such alleles but would have many alleles conferring darker hair shades.

Microevolution occurs when the frequency of an allele in a population changes. A gene's frequency can be altered when new alleles are introduced into a population by mutation; when individuals migrate between populations; when an environmental condition is more easily tolerated by those who have a particular phenotype (natural selection); and when genes are eliminated because individuals with certain genotypes do not reproduce. Hence, many conditions must be met for evolution *not* to occur.

When Gene Frequencies Stay Constant—Hardy-Weinberg Equilibrium

Genotypes and phenotypes can be predicted when a gene is passed from parents to offspring by using probability or Punnett squares (chapter 11). Changes in gene frequencies in populations from generation to generation can also be calculated, and from these values phenotypes and genotypes can be deduced.

In 1980, a mathematician, H.H. Hardy, and a physician interested in genetics, W. Weinberg, independently proposed that phenotype and genotype frequencies could be determined by applying a simple algebraic expression, the binomial expansion $p^2 + 2pq + q^2 = 1.0$, where p^2 represents homozygous dominant individuals, q^2 represents homozygous recessive individuals, and $2pq$ represents heterozygotes (fig. 34.2). The Hardy-Weinberg equation is analogous to a monohybrid cross ($Aa \times Aa$), which results in a single way to generate each homozygote (AA or aa) and two ways to get a heterozygote (Aa or aA). An example of how phenotype and genotype frequencies are calculated is presented in Reading 34.1.

The Hardy-Weinberg equation can reveal single-gene frequency changes that underlie evolution. If the proportion of genotypes remains the same from generation to generation, as indicated by the

Algebraic Expression	What It Means
$p + q = 1$	All dominant alleles plus all recessive alleles add up to all of the alleles for a particular gene in a population.
$p^2 + 2pq + q^2 = 1$	For a particular gene, all homozygous dominant individuals (p^2) plus all heterozygotes ($2pq$) plus all homozygous recessives (q^2) add up to all of the individuals in the population.

Figure 34.2
Using algebra to follow gene frequencies.

equation, then evolution is not occurring for that gene. This situation is called **Hardy-Weinberg equilibrium.** It is an idealized state, only possible if the population is large, if it mates randomly, and there is no mutation, migration, or natural selection.

KEY CONCEPTS

The genes in a population comprise its gene pool. Microevolution reflects changes in gene frequencies in populations. These changes can be traced using the Hardy-Weinberg equation. Microevolution is not occurring if gene frequencies stay constant from generation to generation, a condition called Hardy-Weinberg equilibrium, which is only met if mating is random and the population large, with no migration, mutation, or natural selection.

When Gene Frequencies Change

Migration and Nonrandom Mating

It is easy to see how rarely, if ever, Hardy-Weinberg equilibrium exists by considering the most familiar population—our own. The population of New York City, for example, has been built by waves of immigration. The original Dutch settlers of the 1600s lacked many of the genes present in today's metropolis, contributed by the English, Irish, Slavic peoples, blacks, hispanics, Italians, Asians, and many others.

Although New York City is often described as a "melting pot," many people, there and elsewhere, choose mates who have particular characteristics, and therefore mating is not random. Mates are chosen for any number of reasons, such as physical appearance, ethnic background, or intelligence. Even the fact that women often tend to seek mates who are taller than they are removes the randomness from mating.

Nonrandom mating is also quite common in populations of other species. It is especially pronounced in agriculture, where semen from one prize bull may be used to artificially inseminate thousands of cows. Occasionally such an extreme situation arises in a human population, when a particular male fathers many, many children. In the Cape population of South Africa, for example, a Chinese immigrant known as Arnold had a very rare dominant genetic disease that causes the teeth to fall out before age 20. Arnold was extremely fertile and had seven wives. Of his 356 living descendants, 70 have the dental disorder. The frequency of this allele in the Cape population is exceptionally high, compared to elsewhere in the world, thanks to Arnold.

Genetic Drift

Gene frequencies can change when a small group is separated from a larger population, a phenomenon called **genetic drift.** By chance, the small group may not represent the whole. Could the average academic ability of 200 students in a biology class, for

Reading 34.1 Using Algebra to Track Gene Frequencies

ALGEBRA CAN BE USED TO DESCRIBE THE ALLELE, GENOTYPE, AND PHENOTYPE FREQUENCIES IN A POPULATION. When these values change—as they nearly always do—evolution is occurring.

Consider a population of 100 foxes, in whom coat thickness is determined by a single gene. Allele C confers a thick coat, and allele c a thin coat. The frequency of dominant alleles is symbolized by the letter p and recessive alleles by q. The sum of p and q is one, so that if the frequency of one allele is known, the other is calculated by subtracting from one.

Among the foxes, the frequency of C alleles is 0.70, and therefore the frequency of c alleles is 0.30. The number of thin-coated foxes is calculated first, because this phenotype has only one corresponding genotype, cc. The proportion of thin-coated foxes is q^2, or the chance of having two c alleles, which equals (0.30) x (0.30), or 0.09, or 9%. Nine percent of 100 foxes equals 9 thin-coated animals.

The number of foxes with thick coats can be determined by subtracting 9 from 100, but applying the appropriate parts of the Hardy-Weinberg equation gives a more precise answer by indicating genotype—that is, the number of thick-coated foxes that are homozygous dominant (CC) and the number that are heterozygous (Cc). The number of CC foxes equals p^2, or (0.70) x (0.70), or 49% of 100, which is 49 foxes. The number of heterozygotes is $2pq$, or (2) x (0.70) x (0.30), or 42% of the total, or 42 foxes. Adding p^2 and $2pq$ gives the expected 91 foxes with thick coats. Note that although only 9 foxes out of 100 have thin coats, 42 foxes carry the allele for a thin coat.

If none of the foxes dies or leaves the group, if no new foxes of reproductive age enter, if the fur genes do not mutate, if natural selection does not favor one phenotype over another, and if each fox contributes equally to the next generation—then allele frequencies and the proportions of each genotype will remain unchanged in the next generation. Evolution is not occurring. But it is highly unlikely that all of these conditions will be met. Many different scenarios could alter the genetic makeup of this population, with respect to coat thickness. Here are a few:

Twenty foxes wander away and become separated from the main group. If, by chance, 8 of the animals have thin coats, the allele frequency of c in the new, small population will be quite higher than it was in the ancestral population. (migration and genetic drift)

A very harsh winter kills 5 of the 9 thin-coated foxes. The allele frequency of c is decreased in the new population of 91 foxes. (natural selection)

If thick-coated foxes preferentially seek thick-coated foxes as mates, the frequency of the c allele will decline somewhat, but thin-coated individuals will still be born approximately 25% of the time when heterozygotes mate. (nonrandom mating)

If in each generation three C alleles mutate to c, the allele frequencies will change accordingly. (mutation)

Can you think of other scenarios that would alter allele frequencies in this population?

example, be determined by considering only those students who earned a grade of F on the final exam—or an A?

An example of genetic drift in human populations is the **founder effect**, which occurs when small groups of people leave their homes to found new settlements. The new colony may have different genotype frequencies than the original population. The fact that Native Americans in North America do not have type B blood illustrates the founder effect. Type B blood is seen in the Asian population from whom the Indians are descended. Perhaps the founding band of Asian settlers who crossed the Bering Strait to America many thousands of years ago did not include a person with type B or AB blood, or if it did, he or she may not have had children survive to pass on the trait.

The founder effect can also increase the proportion of an allele in a population. Consider the 2,500,000 people of the Afrikaner population of South Africa, who are descended from a small group of Dutch immigrants. Today, 30,000 Afrikaners have porphyria variegata, a dominantly inherited enzyme defect whose only symptom is a severe reaction to barbiturate anesthetics. (The disorder was not recognized until these drugs entered medical practice.) All of the affected people are descended from one couple who came from Holland in the 1680s. Today's gene frequency in South Africa is far higher than that in Holland because this couple contributed significantly to the early Afrikaner population.

Genetic drift can occur when members of a small community choose to mate only among themselves, resulting in inbreeding. This happened in the Dunker community of Germantown, Pennsylvania. The frequencies of some genotypes are different among the Dunkers than among their neighbors who are not part of their society and different from people living today in the part of Germany that the Dunkers left between 1719 and 1729 to settle in the New World (table 34.1 and fig. 34.3).

Genetic drift also results from a **population bottleneck**, a situation in which many members of a population die, and the numbers are then restored by mating among a few individuals. The new population has a much more restricted gene pool than the larger, ancestral population. The current world population of cheetahs provides evidence of severe population bottlenecks (fig. 34.4). Until 10,000 years ago, these cats were prevalent in many areas. Today, only two isolated populations live in South and East Africa, numbering only a few thousand animals. Examination of protein sequences from 55 cheetahs found them to be quite uniform in genetic makeup—evidence of a population bottleneck. The cheetahs of the South African population are so alike genetically that even unrelated animals can accept skin grafts from each other. Researchers attribute the genetic uniformity of cheetahs to two bottlenecks—one occurring at the end of the most recent ice age, when habitats were altered, and mass slaughter by nineteenth-century cattle poachers.

Mutation

A major source of genetic variation is mutation, the changing of one allele into another. (Genetic variability also arises from crossing over and independent assortment during meiosis, but these events recombine existing traits rather than introducing new ones.) Spontaneous mutation occurs when a DNA base is in a transient, unusual form at the precise instant that the DNA is replicated, inserting a mismatched DNA base into the new DNA strand (fig. 34.5). If the base change occurs in a part of a gene corresponding to a portion of a protein necessary for its function, then an altered trait may result. If the mutation is in a gamete, then the change can be passed to future generations and therefore ultimately affect an allele's frequency in the population.

The spontaneous mutation rate varies for different genes and in different organisms. Based on prevalence of certain disease-causing genes, it is estimated that each human gene has about a 1 in 100,000 chance of mutating. If there are about 50,000 human genes, then 1 in every 2 gametes (50,000 genes multiplied by a mutation rate per gene of 1/100,000) theoretically carries a new mutation. But because most mutations are recessive and will be masked by a normal allele in the next generation, the mutation situation is not as ominous as it may appear. Dominant mutations, however, are expressed immediately. An achondroplastic dwarf born to normal parents is an example of a spontaneous, dominant mutation.

The frequency of a mutant allele is maintained in a population in heterozygotes and by reintroduction by further mutation. It is removed when homozygous individuals arise who cannot reproduce successfully due to their double dose of the mutant allele. Because of heterozygosity and mutation, all populations have some alleles that would be harmful if homozygous. The collection of deleterious alleles in a population is called the **genetic load**.

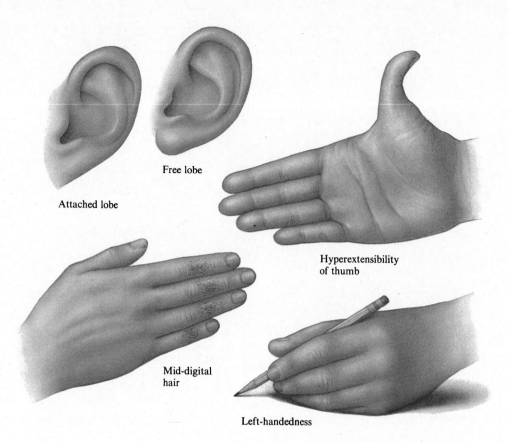

Figure 34.3
Three interesting traits more common among the Dunkers and that occur at unique frequencies are attached earlobes, the ability to bend the thumb backwards, hair on the middle of the fingers, and left-handedness.

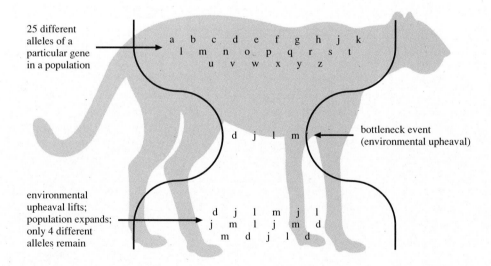

Figure 34.4
A population bottleneck occurs when the size of a genetically diverse population drastically falls, is maintained for a time at this level, and then expands again. The rebuilt population loses some genetic diversity if different alleles are lost in the bottleneck event. The two dwindling cheetah populations in South and East Africa vividly illustrate the result of a population bottleneck. The cheetahs are more genetically alike than are mice bred specifically for genetic uniformity. Cheetahs are difficult to breed in zoos because sperm quality is poor and many newborns die—both due to the lack of genetic diversity.

Table 34.1
Genetic Drift and the Dunkers

Blood Type	Population		
	U.S.	Dunker	European
ABO system			
A	40%	60%	45%
B+AB	15%	5%	15%
Rh-	15%	11%	15%
MN system			
M	30%	44.5%	30%
MN	50%	42%	50%
N	20%	13.5%	20%

Each person probably has four or five such deleterious recessive alleles. It may take a very long time, however, for mutant alleles to reveal themselves, because two individuals who have children together must carry the same mutant allele for each child to have a 25% chance of being affected by the particular condition. Many such recessive mutations were induced by the radiation released from the atomic bombs dropped over Japan in 1945. Geneticists estimate that it will take 30 generations for those mutations to start showing up in homozygous form. By 1990, genetic problems were not any more prevalent among Japanese offspring of parents exposed to the bomb than among people of the same age elsewhere. (This may not be true for non-genetic problems.)

When mating occurs among blood relatives, the chance of conceiving a homozygous recessive individual occurs as soon as two people mate who carry the same mutant allele, inherited from a shared ancestor. This is why in some states it is illegal for first cousins to wed. They have one-eighth of their genes in common, and it becomes likely that a pair of harmful recessive alleles could match up.

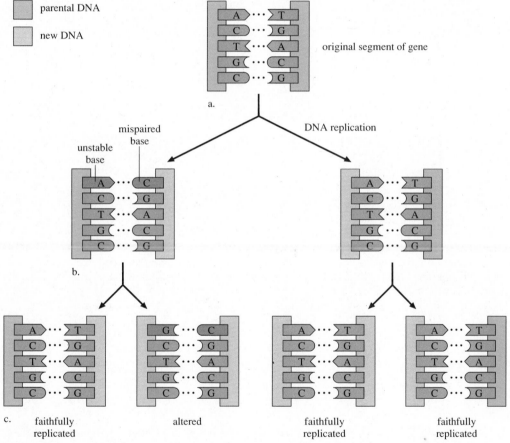

c.   faithfully   altered   faithfully   faithfully
    replicated   replicated   replicated

KEY CONCEPTS

Hardy-Weinberg equilibrium rarely, if ever, exists in nature. In genetic drift, such as the founder effect and population bottlenecks, gene frequencies change when small populations form from larger ones. Spontaneous mutations in germ cells alter allele frequencies. Harmful alleles constitute a population's genetic load. They are maintained in heterozygotes, introduced by mutations, but eliminated by natural selection.

Figure 34.5
Mutation can alter traits. *a.* In DNA, nearly all of the time, base A pairs with base T (and vice versa) and C pairs with G (and vice versa). However, DNA bases are very slightly unstable chemically, and for fleeting moments they exist in altered forms. *b.* If a DNA replication fork encounters a base in its unstable form, a mismatched base pair can result. *c.* After another round of replication, one of the daughter cells has a different base pair than the one in the corresponding position in the original DNA segment. Such a substituted base pair can alter the structure of a gene. If the gene's function is affected, the individual's phenotype may be changed. Because natural selection acts upon phenotypes (a gene's expression), mutation can contribute to evolutionary change.

Natural Selection

Gene frequencies that are altered in response to environmental change are vividly illustrated by the 100 or so insect species that have undergone color changes enabling them to blend into their backgrounds as their environments become polluted. This adaptive response is termed **industrial melanism**. Figure 3.4 illustrates the selection of dark pigmentation in the peppered moth *Biston betularia* in rural England.

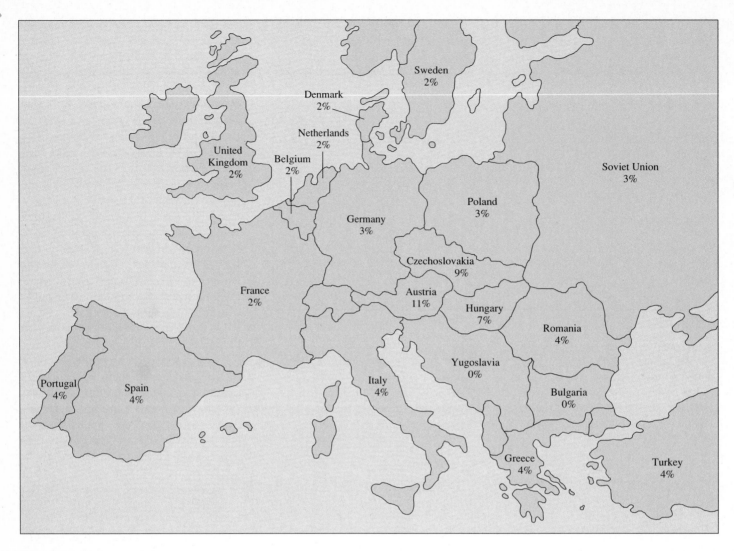

Figure 34.6

Tay-Sachs disease and balanced polymorphism. Just as being a carrier for sickle cell disease protects against malaria, being a carrier for the neurodegenerative Tay-Sachs disease may protect against tuberculosis. Tay-Sachs is quite common in Jewish people whose families came to the United States from Eastern Europe. In these populations, up to 11% of the Jewish people are carriers. Tuberculosis ran rampant in the Eastern European Jewish settlements during World War II, but often healthy relatives in families with Tay-Sachs resisted the infection. The protec-tion against tuberculosis offered by Tay-Sachs disease heterozygosity remained among the Jewish population in Eastern Europe because they could not leave the crowded ghettos. The allele for Tay-Sachs increased in frequency as tuberculosis selectively felled those who did not carry the allele and as the people had children with each other. The map displays the percentage of Tay-Sachs carriers among the Jewish populations in different countries, based on carrier frequencies of American Jews whose ancestors came from these countries.

Before the Industrial Revolution, dark moths were rare because they were easy prey for birds, who spotted them against the background of tree bark turned white from the growth of lichens (see chapter 2, Reading 2.1, "Fungus + Algae = Lichen"). After industrialization, air pollution killed the lichens, darkening the tree bark, and the dark moths were now more easily hid-den than the white moths and better able to survive and reproduce. Changes in the coloration of moth populations began in the 1700s and became more pronounced in the 1950s. By 1956, 95% of the moth population was dark—just about the re-verse of the situation before the environ-mental change.

The predominant color of moth populations also varies with the degree of industrialization in a particular geographic region. Dark moths were most common in Liverpool, a sooty, factory town, and were rarely seen in pristine, rural northern Wales. Today, only a small portion of northern England has populations of mostly dark moths, a trend attributed to 20 years of efforts to control smoke pollution.

Natural selection is also evident in the declining virulence of certain human infectious diseases over many years. The spread of tuberculosis in the Plains Indians of the Qu'Appelle Valley Reservation in Saskatchewan, Canada, illustrates the forces of evolution at work. When tubercu-losis first appeared on the reservation in the mid-1880s, it struck people swiftly and lethally, infecting many organs and killing 10% of the population. By 1921, tuberculosis in the Indians tended to affect only the lungs, and 7% of the population died annually from it. By 1950, mortality was down to 0.2%.

Outbreaks ran similar courses in other human populations, appearing in crowded settlements where the bacteria were easily spread from person to person in exhaled droplets. In the 1700s, tuberculosis raged through the cities of Europe and was brought to the United States with immigrants in the early 1800s, where it likewise swept through the cities. As in the Plains Indians population, tuberculosis incidence and virulence fell dramatically in the cities of the industrialized world in the first half of the twentieth century—before widespread use of antibiotics.

What tamed tuberculosis? It may have been natural selection, operating on both the bacterial and human populations. Some people inherited resistance to the infection, enabling them to produce protected children. Plus, the most virulent bacteria killed their hosts so quickly that there was no time to pass on the germs. As the deadliest bacteria were selected out of the population, and as people with inherited resistance contributed disproportionately to the next generation, the effect of tuberculosis on human health gradually became more benign, evolving from an acute, systemic infection to an increasingly rare chronic lung infection.

Types of Natural Selection

Industrial melanism and the decline in severity of tuberculosis illustrate **directional selection**, in which a previously "normal" characteristic of a population alters in response to a changing environment as the number of better-adapted individuals increases. Natural selection can have other effects. In **disruptive selection**, two extreme expressions of a trait are the most fit. A population of marine snails, for example, lives among tan rocks encrusted with white barnacles. The snails are either white and camouflaged while near the barnacles or tan and hidden while on the bare rock. Only animals that are not white or tan, or that lie against the opposite-colored background, will be seen, and eaten, by predatory shore birds.

In **stabilizing selection**, extreme phenotypes are less adaptive, and an intermediate phenotype has greater survival and reproductive success. Consider human birthweight. Newborns who are under 5 pounds (2.27 kilograms) or over 10 pounds (4.54 kilograms) are less likely to survive than babies weighing between 5 and 10 pounds.

Balanced Polymorphism—The Sickle Cell Story

A form of stabilizing selection called **balanced polymorphism** allows a genetic disease to remain in a population even though the illness clearly diminishes the fitness of affected individuals. The disease persists because carriers have some advantage over those who have two copies of the normal allele.

Balanced polymorphism maintains sickle cell disease, an autosomal recessive disorder that causes anemia, joint pain, a swollen spleen, and frequent, severe infections (chapter 14). Carriers of sickle cell disease are resistant to malaria, an agonizing cycle of chills and fever that is caused by a protistan parasite, *Plasmodium falciparum*, which spends the first stage of its life cycle in the salivary glands of the mosquito *Anopheles gambiae* (fig. 28.15). When an infected mosquito bites a human, the malaria parasite enters the red blood cells and is taken to the liver. The infected red blood cells eventually burst, releasing the parasite all over the body.

In 1949, British geneticist Anthony Allison found that the frequency of sickle cell carriers in tropical Africa was quite high in regions where malaria was present all year long. Blood tests from children hospitalized with malaria found that nearly all were homozygous for the normal allele. The few sickle cell carriers among them had the mildest cases of malaria. Was the presence of malaria somehow selecting for the sickle cell allele by felling those people who did not inherit it? The fact that sickle cell disease is far less common in the United States, where malaria is not present, supports a protective effect of sickle cell heterozygosity.

The rise of sickle cell disease parallels the cultivation of crops that provide breeding grounds for the *Anopheles* mosquito. About 1,000 B.C., Malayo-Polynesian sailors from southeast Asia traveled in canoes to East Africa, bringing new crops of banana, yam, taro, and coconut. When the jungle was

cleared to grow these crops, the open space enticed the mosquitos to flourish. The insects, in turn, provided a habitat for part of the life cycle of the malaria parasite.

The sickle cell gene is believed to have been brought to Africa by people migrating from southern Arabia and India, or it may have arisen by mutation directly in East Africa. However it happened, those people who inherited one copy of the sickle cell allele were better able to fight off the fever and chills of malaria. Something about their red blood cells is inhospitable to the parasite. The healthier carriers had more children, passing on the protective allele to half of them. Gradually, the frequency of the sickle cell allele in East Africa rose, from 0.1% to a spectacular 45% in 35 generations. The price was paid for this genetic protection whenever two carriers produced a child who suffered from sickle cell disease.

A cycle set in. Settlements with large numbers of sickle cell carriers escaped debilitating malaria and were therefore strong enough to clear even more land to grow food—and support the disease-bearing mosquitos. Even today, sickle cell disease is more prevalent in agricultural societies than among people who hunt and gather their food. Figure 34.6 shows another example of balanced polymorphism.

> ### KEY CONCEPTS
>
> *In directional selection, better-adapted individuals are selected in a changing environment. In disruptive selection, two extreme expressions of a trait have a survival advantage. In stabilizing selection, the intermediate between two extreme phenotypes is more likely to survive. Balanced polymorphism is a form of stabilizing selection in which a harmful allele is maintained in a population because the heterozygote has some advantage.*

How Species Arise

Charles Darwin saw the evolution of species as a gradual series of adaptations molded by a changing environment selecting certain naturally occurring variants (Reading 34.2). He called this process of one species slowly becoming another "descent with modification." When genetic differences

Figure 34.7
Geographical isolation leads to allopatric
speciation. The bluish gray pupfish inhabits a
warm spring called Devil's Hole at the base of
a mountain near Death Valley, Nevada. The
summer pupfish population numbers about
600 individuals and the winter residents only
200. What makes these minnow-sized fish of
evolutionary note is that their home has been
isolated from other bodies of water for 50,000
years. In that time, the genetic makeup of the
fish has shifted so greatly that they can no
longer mate successfully with pupfish from
populations beyond the spring. An entire new
species has evolved in a mere flicker of
geological time.

Figure 34.8
Hybrids between two species are usually infertile. The liger is the result of mating between a tiger
and a lion, but this animal is not fertile. Only four such animals are known in the United States.
The first liger we know of was bred by accident, in 1950, at a circus that had undoubtedly kept
tigers and lions together. In the wild, these great cats will not normally mate.

prevent members of one population from
producing fertile offspring with members of
another, a new species is born.

Speciation depends upon natural selection and the physical distribution of
organisms, or **biogeography**. These factors
contribute to speciation in two stages. First,
a population becomes geographically separated, perhaps by an earthquake, flood, or
volcanic eruption, so that members of the
two newly formed groups cannot interact.
Over time, the populations may evolve
different allele frequencies because the
forces of natural selection, nonrandom
mating, migration, and mutation act independently in each group. In addition,
the original geographic isolation may have,
by chance, created two subgroups with
different allele frequencies. Two populations that are geographically isolated from
one another are said to be **allopatric**, and
formation of new species initiated by geographic isolation is called **allopatric speciation** (fig. 34.7).

For a new species to form, geographic
isolation must be followed by reproductive
isolation. That is, members of the two
separated populations should not be able to

reproduce successfully with each other if
the geographic barrier is lifted. Two closely
related groups of organisms that occupy the
same region but cannot reproduce successfully with each other are called **sympatric species.** Sympatric speciation may
arise following geographical isolation or by
itself.

Reproductive isolating mechanisms
prevent production of fertile offspring. The
point in development when two species fail
to produce viable offspring can occur before
or after mating.

Premating Reproductive Isolation

Premating reproductive isolation is not
always as obvious as the mismatched genitals
of the male moose and the dairy cow. In
ecological isolation, members of two
populations prefer to mate in different
habitats. In **temporal isolation**, they have
different mating seasons. In **behavioral
isolation**, the organisms perform different
repertoires of courtship cues as the male
and female approach one another.

These mechanisms are like a man and
a woman seeking mates, perhaps going to
different parties (ecological) on different

nights (temporal) and speaking different
languages (behavioral). Two species of toad
descended from a single ancestral type provide a vivid example of premating reproductive isolation. *Bufo americanus* breeds in the
early spring in small, shallow puddles or dry
creeks, whereas *Bufo fowleri* breeds in the late
spring in large pools and streams. Each type
of toad also has a unique mating call.

Postmating Reproductive Isolation

Sometimes organisms mate, but fertile
offspring do not result. The incompatibility can occur as early as fertilization, if the
genetic material of the two species is
packaged into chromosomes differently. A
dog's gamete, with 39 chromosomes, could
not form a healthy zygote with a cat's
gamete, which has 19 chromosomes. Rarely,
hybrid offspring result when individuals of
different species mate, but they tend to be
infertile and so have no evolutionary impact. A mule, for example, is a hybrid
between a horse and a donkey. Sometimes
two animals that would not mate in the
wild do so in captivity. This happens with
tigers and lions, but their hybrid offspring,
seen only in zoos, are not fertile (fig. 34.8).

Reading 34.2 *The Pace of Evolution—Like a Tortoise or a Hare?*

CHARLES DARWIN BELIEVED THAT EVOLUTION TOOK A VERY LONG TIME, WITH ONE LIFE FORM TRANSFORMING INTO ANOTHER THROUGH A SERIES OF INTERMEDIATE STAGES. He noted, however, that such gradualistic evolution was not well supported by the fossil record because of a lack of intermediate, or transitional, forms. Darwin and others attribute the seeming incompleteness of the fossil record to several factors:

Lack of preservation of animals that did not have hard body parts;
Some species did not exist long enough to leave behind much evidence;
Many species were not widespread;
Geological upheavals that destroyed evidence.

Another explanation for some of the many gaps in the fossil record is that evolution may not always be gradual.

In 1944, paleontologist George Gaylord Simpson suggested that some of the gaps in the fossil record may actually be what they seem to be—true gaps, representing the sudden appearance of a species. Simpson estimated that perhaps 10% of all speciation falls into this "quantum evolution" category. In 1944, Simpson's concept of evolution by "leaps and starts" was not accepted by strict Darwinian gradualists.

In 1972, the idea of fast speciation interspersed with long periods when species changed little or not at all (stasis) was again raised by two young paleontologists, Stephen Jay Gould of Harvard University and Niles Eldredge of the American

Figure 1
Land-dwelling tree frogs of genus *Eleutherodactylus* skip the tadpole stage and hatch directly from an egg as a small frog. This mature body form so early in life widens the range of habitats that the animal can occupy, thus giving it a selective advantage over frogs that spend the earlier parts of their lives as tadpoles.

Museum of Natural History. This time, the concept was termed **punctuated equilibrium** to reflect the long periods of stasis interrupted by times of fast evolutionary change. The fossil record, they claim, lacks transitional forms simply because in some cases of speciation, they do not exist.

Instances of very rapid evolution support the operation of punctuated

equilibrium. Consider the several species of cichlid fish that live only in Lake Nabugaboo, Uganda, a body of water separated from Lake Victoria by a sand spit. These species have evolved over just the past 4,000 years. Even more recently, banana-eating moths have evolved in Hawaii since Polynesian settlers introduced bananas a few centuries ago. The appearance of new infectious diseases in our lifetime, such as toxic shock syndrome and Lyme disease, may reflect rapid evolution in the microorganisms that cause these illnesses.

How might changes drastic enough to lead to speciation occur rapidly? The answer may lie in the genes, for a single gene can have a profound effect on the appearance or functioning of an organism. A gene that alters the timing of early developmental events may cause obvious changes in the adult. An inherited delay in pigmentation in the embryo, for example, could greatly change the adult's appearance, which could in turn have great selective consequences in a plant or animal whose survival depends upon protective coloration. Frogs of genus *Eleutherodactylus* (fig. 1) skip the tadpole stage, hatching from an egg as a small frog. This characteristic could have evolved by an alteration in a single gene—a drastic and sudden change that would have increased survival. A single genetic "switch" altering timing of cell division could have produced the prolonged brain growth that is characteristic of our own species.

Reproductive isolation due to chromosome incompatibility can occur among individuals of the same species, if something creates subgroups with different organizations of genetic material. This happened, with the help of geographic isolation, in the plant *Clarkia rubicunda*, common along the coast of central California. A severe drought in the region of the Golden Gate Bridge in San Francisco nearly decimated the local population of *C. rubicunda*. By chance, the only survivors had several chromosomal abnormalities. These plants cross-fertilized among themselves, estab-

lishing a new population where the chromosomal aberrations were the norm. When the drought ended, *C. rubicunda* came in from surrounding regions, but they could not produce offspring with the Golden Gate group. The gametes of the two groups could no longer unite, although both types of plants were descended from the same ancestors. A new species, *C. franciscana*, had arisen.

Instantaneous reproductive isolation also results from **polyploidy**, when the number of chromosome sets increases (fig. 34.9). Polyploidy can occur when meiosis

fails, producing, for example, diploid sex cells in a diploid individual. If diploid sex cells in a plant self-fertilize, a **tetraploid** individual results, having four sets of chromosomes.

When chromosome sets derive from the same species, the organism is called an **autopolyploid**. Autopolyploids of the rose, for example, have 14, 21, 28, 35, 42, or 56 chromosomes—presumably descended from an ancestral species having 7 chromosomes. Polyploids can also form when gametes from two different species fuse, creating a hybrid from which an **allopolyploid** may develop.

a.

b.

Figure 34.9
Polyploidy in plants. A triploid plant is unlikely to give rise to a new species because the three copies of each chromosome cannot segregate during meiosis into daughter cells having a consistent number of chromosomes. As a result, a triploid seed grows into a plant that has few seeds—not very valuable for evolution but a favorite of gardeners who prefer seedless varieties of plants, such as the triploid "seedless" watermelon (*b*). A watermelon is normally diploid.

For example, an "old world" species of cotton has 26 large chromosomes, whereas a species found in Central America and South America has 26 small chromosomes. The type of cotton that is commonly cultivated for cloth is an allopolyploid of the old world and American types. It has 52 chromosomes.

Polyploidy may occur in the wild as a response to unusually low temperatures. Agriculturalists often induce polyploidy, however, because such plants generally have larger leaves, flowers, and fruits. This is done using the drug colchicine, which is an extract of the autumn crocus plant. Colchicine dismantles the spindle apparatus, which normally aligns and then separates the chromosomes in dividing cells. Lacking a spindle, the replicated chromosomes cannot be distributed into two daughter cells, and a polyploid results. Many new varieties of crops are induced polyploids, including alfalfa, apples, bananas, barley, potatoes, and peanuts.

So great is the genetic difference between a polyploid and the plant from which it arises that geographic isolation is not even necessary for speciation. The fact that nearly half of all flowering plant species are natural polyploids indicates that this form of reproductive isolation has been fairly important in plant evolution.

Polyploidy is rarely seen in animals, because the disruption in sex chromosome constitution usually leads to sterility. One exception is the grey tree frog *Hyla versicolor*, which is a tetraploid probably derived from the identical-appearing *Hyla chrysoscelis*, a diploid. Once in a great while a human infant is born who is triploid, but massive birth defects usually end life within days. Certain cells in the healthy human body, however, are normally polyploid. Some liver cells, for example, are octoploid, with eight sets of chromosomes.

KEY CONCEPTS

New species arise when genetic changes prevent the members of one population from mating with the members of another. This may occur rapidly or over a long period of time. Speciation depends upon natural selection and biogeography. Allopatric speciation occurs when two populations are physically separated and develop different gene frequencies because of differences in natural selection, nonrandom mating, mutation, and migration. In sympatric speciation, which may follow allopatric speciation, two closely related groups in the same area cannot reproduce with each other.

Premating reproductive isolation can be ecological, temporal, or behavioral. Postmating reproductive isolation occurs when the genetic material is different, or packaged into chromosomes differently, in two groups of organisms. Mating between members of two animal species may produce an offspring, but it is not fertile. Polyploidy creates new species because the number of chromosome sets increases. An autopolyploid has chromosomes from one ancestral species; an allopolyploid has chromosomes from two different species.

How Species Become Extinct

Not all species emerge in healthy numbers from population bottlenecks or evolve into new species following geographical isolation. Just as speciation does not produce "perfect" organisms, but well-adapted ones, extinction is not a badge of biological failure. Extinction reflects the inability of organisms to adapt to an environmental challenge.

What Causes Mass Extinctions?

Earth history has been marked by at least a dozen periods of mass extinctions (table 34.2). (Geological time periods are discussed in chapter 35.) **Paleontologists**, who study evidence of past life, can find clues in the earth's sediments to the catastrophic events that heralded the disappearances of many species over relatively short expanses of time. Although explanations of the causes of mass extinctions are highly controversial among scientists, two general hypotheses have emerged in recent years.

The **impact theory** suggests that a meteor or comet crashed to earth. If it hit land, then dust, soot, and other debris sent skyward would block the sun, setting into motion a deadly chain reaction. Without sunlight, plants would not be able to photosynthesize, and they would die. The animals that ate plants, and the animals that

Table 34.2
Mass Extinctions

Time	Species Affected	Suggested Cause
3 bya* (Precambrian)	Anaerobic bacteria	Oxygen in atmosphere
545 mya+ (end of Cambrian)	Trilobites, other marine invertebrates	Meteor impact
440 mya (Ordovician)	Marine invertebrates	Gondwana formed
370 mya (end of Devonian)	Most fish and invertebrates	Meteor impact; Gondwana moved; asteroid shower
240 mya (Permian)	96% of all species	Pangeae formed
200 mya (end of Triassic)	75% marine invertebrates	Meteor impact
140 mya (end of Jurassic)	Marine species	Not known
90 mya (mid-Cretaceous)	Dinosaurs	Flowering plants
60 mya (Cretaceous/Tertiary boundary)	Dinosaurs, marine species	One or more meteor impacts
11,000 years ago	Large mammals	Drought, hunting

*billion years ago
+million years ago

Mass Extinctions Through Geological Time

Extinctions probably occurred even before life as it is known today evolved, with the periodic wiping out of primordial cell-like structures as more efficient ones formed. After each mass extinction, the survivors repopulated the earth. It is interesting to ponder our own fate had different subsets of species vanished or survived.

An early mass extinction reflected the drastic change in the atmosphere—oxygenation—that happened as cyanobacteria evolved. The oxygen they released was toxic to the reigning anaerobic species, many of which died out as the more efficient energy users flourished.

About 440 million years ago, life in the seas was severely disrupted as a huge continent, called Gondwana, formed and covered the South Pole, causing an ice age. The glaciers drew water from the oceans, robbing many species of their habitats. Then 370 million years ago, geological upheaval struck again. Sulfur-containing minerals found in disturbed rock layers in the Canadian Rockies indicate a mixing of ancient ocean layers. Iridium is also here, as is evidence of glaciation. At this time, many fish species and nearly 75% of all marine invertebrates perished.

The Permian period of 240 million years ago saw the greatest mass extinction of them all, when 96% of species died in several waves of death spanning 8 million years. The cause of the Permian extinction is thought to be the fusion of landmasses into a single gigantic continent, Pangaea. The present-day location of the continents suggests that they may once have been connected, with the continental shelf of South America fitting like a puzzle piece along that of western Africa. Remains of the same species of now-extinct organisms are found along the coasts of both South America and West Africa, supporting the hypothesis that the great landmasses were once contiguous.

Just 40 million years after the Permian extinction, earth's inhabitants faced yet another changing environment. Once again, 75% of marine invertebrate species vanished. A crater in Quebec, Canada, roughly half the size of Connecticut, may be evidence of a meteor impact that had devastating repercussions.

ate those animals, would die too. An extraterrestrial object landing in the ocean would be equally devastating by mixing water layers. Oxygen-poor deeper waters would be shot upward in the turbulence, and upper-dwelling organisms adapted to the oxygen carried in their watery surroundings would die of oxygen starvation.

Evidence for the impact theory includes centimeter-thin layers of earth that are rich in iridium, an element rare here but common in meteors (fig. 34.10). Quartz crystals found in iridium deposits are cracked at angles that suggest an explosion. Where layers of rock unusually devoid of fossils are found near an iridium layer, the impact theory of mass extinction is suggested.

Alternatively, the restlessness of the planet's rocks may explain some mass extinctions. The geological theory of **plate tectonics** views the earth's surface as several rigid plates that can move, like layers of ice on a lake. These plates continually drift away from oceanic ridges, where new molten rock bubbles forth. Older regions of tectonic plates sink back into the earth's interior at huge trenches.

When continents drifted, coalesced, or broke apart, the environmental changes thrust upon organisms must have been profound. Suddenly organisms that had survived well in their particular habitats found themselves among unfamiliar species, whose members possibly competed for limited resources. Weather conditions changed, with ice ages and droughts killing off many species. The shifting of continents often altered shorelines, diminishing shallow sea areas packed with life.

Either a meteor crash or moving continents could explain the chaotic conditions associated with mass extinctions—or perhaps these changes occurred alone. Whatever the initial cause, at various times in earth history, sea levels have dropped, bodies of fresh water flooded their banks, temperatures fluctuated, volcanoes blew their tops, vegetation patterns changed, and tracts of land bridging continents ebbed and flowed. In India, for example, a lava flow the size of France is a reminder of a huge volcanic eruption that may have coincided with the extinction of dinosaurs. Might a long-ago volcano have spewed enough debris into the atmosphere to block the sun, lowering temperatures and triggering mass starvation? A volcano would also have released sulfur emissions, causing global acid rain and threatening life in the waters.

a.

b.

Figure 34.10

Evidence for an impact. *a.* A pencil-thin rock layer found everywhere on earth may hold clues to a global meteorite impact about 60 million years ago. The band of rock is rich in iridium, an element rare on earth but prevalent in meteors. On this seaside cliff in Zumaya, Spain, paleontologists and geologists probe the exposed iridium layer. *b.* Further evidence in support of the impact theory is that quartz grains from the iridium-rich region are cracked in a way only possible in a nuclear explosion or meteor impact. Opponents of the impact theory, however, maintain that the cracks could have arisen in a volcanic explosion.

Another impact is hypothesized for the mass extinctions that peaked about 65 million years ago, when 75% of all plant and animal species, including the great dinosaurs, disappeared. In the seas, plankton, microscopic food for many larger marine dwellers, died as well. These extinctions did not all happen at once. Ocean chemistry changes span 2 million years around this time, suggesting a series of impacts rather than a single cataclysmic event.

The most recent round of mass extinctions may have been at least partially caused by our own species. The last ice age occurred during the Pleistocene epoch, from about 1.6 million to 10,000 years ago. In the last 2,000 years of this time period, 35 classes of mammals became extinct in North America. Unlike previous mass extinctions, when many types of organisms perished, the species that disappeared 11,000 years ago were mostly large, plant-eating mammals.

Were the Pleistocene herbivores hunted to extinction? According to the **Pleistocene overkill hypothesis,** at this time humans from Asia crossed a land bridge over the Bering Strait to a corridor east of the Canadian Rockies, traveling down through North America. Along the way, they encountered 50 to 100 million large herbivores, which they hunted to extinction. Flint spears found in remains of mammoths, mastodonts, horses, tapirs, and camels support the overkill hypothesis. The arrival of humans could have been devastating on this continent because it was rather sudden. In contrast, humans and their immediate ancestors had lived in Europe, Asia, and Africa far longer, and herbivore species there may have had the time to adapt to human predation.

Figure 34.11
A Pleistocene scene. The selective extinction of large herbivores (such as the saber-toothed tiger, mastodonts and mammoths, and giant sloths, peccaries, beavers, bears, deer, antelope, and lions) at a time when humans were hunting their way from Alaska to Mexico suggests that the two events may be related. This last round of extinction may have been caused by our own species.

Figure 34.12
A zoo of extinct organisms. This curator of England's Tring Zoological Museum cradles the only organism in this assemblage that is not extinct—an aye-aye from Madagascar. But it may be next.

The disappearance of large mammals may have led to extinctions of smaller animals. The **keystone herbivore hypothesis** suggests that the demise of the large herbivores led to overgrowth of vegetation that these animals ate, and this vegetation change threatened the existence of smaller herbivores (fig. 34.11).

The earth has not seen the last mass extinctions. Largely because of human intervention in the environment, species are vanishing with disturbing rapidity. Among the list of the recently extinct include the 10-foot (3-meter) moa bird, the zebralike quagga, the passenger pigeon, and the dodo bird (fig. 34.12). Within the next 25 years, a million more species may be lost.

Although humans have hastened the extinctions of some species, we have also made efforts to save endangered species (fig. 34.13). Consider the flightless Guam rail bird. In 1968, 80,000 of them lived on the island of Guam. Today, only 50 birds remain, occupying an area of dense brush that runs along an air strip used by B52 bombers at Anderson Air Force Base. The birds' habitat was scheduled to be destroyed because the heavy vegetation could provide cover for terrorists. But preservation overcame politics, and not only has the Guam rail's last refuge been spared, but birds are being relocated in an attempt to increase their numbers.

The whooping crane, the tallest bird in North America, has also benefited from human intervention. In 1941, only 21 birds were known to exist. In 1975, conservationists in northern Alberta placed whooping crane eggs in the nests of closely related species such as the sandhill crane. Soon, the unrelated birds nurtured the whooping crane eggs. By 1985, 140 whooping cranes made up the population. With efforts such as these, perhaps we can make a positive difference in the biological destiny of our planet.

KEY CONCEPTS

Extinction results when species cannot adapt to a changing environment. The earth's dozen or more mass extinctions may have been triggered by meteor impacts or continent movements, which disrupted climatic conditions. Disturbance to the sea would have mixed the oxygen distribution, and disturbance to the land would have raised huge dust clouds. Specific mass extinctions have been linked to oxygenation of the atmosphere, formation of large continents, meteor impacts, and human predation.

Reading 34.3 *Dogs and Cats—Products of Artificial Selection*

THE PAMPERED POODLE AND GRACEFUL GREYHOUND MAY WIN IN THE SHOW RING, BUT IN TERMS OF GENETICS AND EVOLUTION, THEY ARE POOR SPECIMENS. Human notions of attractiveness can lead to bizarre breeds that may not have evolved naturally. Beneath carefully bred quirks lurk small gene pools and extensive inbreeding—all of which spell disaster to the health of many highly prized and highly priced show animals.

The sad eyes of the basset hound make him a favorite in advertisements, but his runny eyes can be quite painful (fig. 1). His short legs make him prone to arthritis, his long abdomen encourages back injuries, and his characteristic floppy ears often hide ear infections. The eyeballs of the Peking-ese protrude so much that a mild bump can pop them right out of their sockets. The tiny jaws and massive teeth of pugdogs and bulldogs lead to dental and breathing problems, plus sinusitis, bad colds, and their notorious "dog breath." Folds of skin on their abdomens easily become infected.

Larger breeds, such as the Saint Bernard, are plagued by bone problems and short life spans.

We artificially select natural oddities in cats too, our choices of feline traveling companions throughout history has left a legacy of human civilization in the form of cat populations. One of every 10 New England cats has six or seven toes on each paw, thanks to a multitoed ancestor in colonial Boston (fig. 2). Elsewhere, these cats are quite rare. The sizes of the blotched tabby populations in New England, Canada, Australia, and New Zealand reflect the time of colonization by cat-loving Britons. The Vikings brought the orange tabby to the islands off the coast of Scotland, rural Iceland, and the Isle of Man, where these feline favorites flourish today.

A more modern entrant among cat fanciers is the American curl cat, whose origin is traced to a stray female who wandered into the home of a cat-loving family in Lakewood, California, in 1981.

She had unusual, curled-up ears, and several of her litters made it obvious that the trait is inherited (fig. 3). The cause—a dominant gene that leads to formation of extra cartilage lining the outer ear. Cat breeders attempting to fashion this natural peculiarity into an official show animal are hoping that the gene does not have other, less loveable effects. Cats with floppy ears, for example, are known to have large feet, stubbed tails, and lazy natures.

Figure 2
Multitoed cats are common in New England but rare elsewhere.

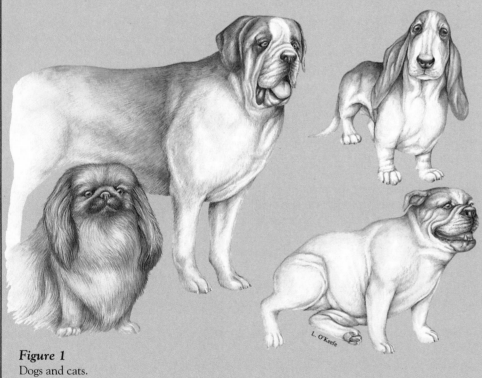

Figure 1
Dogs and cats.

Figure 3
American curl cat

Figure 34.13

The Przewalski's horse, from Russia and China, was nearly extinct when breeders intervened. Twelve of the animals were bred to the related Mongolian domesticated horse to produce 409 "reconstructed" Przewalski's horses that today live in zoos. The animal in the wild is extinct.

SUMMARY

Evolution begins with changes in allele frequencies within the *gene pools* of populations. If allele frequencies are not changing from generation to generation, *Hardy-Weinberg equilibrium* exists and evolution is not occurring. If allele frequencies are known, the binomial expansion $p^2 + 2pq + q^2$ can be used to calculate the proportion of genotypes and phenotypes in a population. The equation reveals allele frequency changes when migration, nonrandom mating, mutation, or natural selection is operating.

In *genetic drift,* allele frequencies change in small populations split off from larger ancestral populations because of chance sampling of alleles. In human populations, a form of genetic drift is the *founder effect,* where a few individuals start a new colony. Genetic drift is also encountered in *population bottlenecks,* when a group of organisms is nearly killed off and the few survivors replenish the population with a restricted gene pool. Mutation can alter gene frequencies by introducing new alleles. Harmful recessive alleles are selected against in homozygotes, and are maintained by heterozygotes and reintroduced by mutation. The deleterious alleles in a population constitute its *genetic load.*

Natural selection is a major driving force behind evolution. In *directional selection,* a trait shifts in one direction. In *disruptive selection,* extreme expressions are selected at the expense of intermediate forms. In *stabilizing selection,* an intermediate phenotype has an advantage. In *balanced polymorphism,* alleles that damage fitness in the homozygote are selected because the heterozygote has an advantage over those lacking the allele.

Speciation is usually caused by a combination of changing allele frequencies and geographical isolation of two populations, which results in two groups whose members can no longer reproduce successfully with each other. *Premating reproductive isolation* prevents two individuals from mating due to ecological, temporal, or behavioral differences. *Postmating reproductive isolation* results from incompatible chromosomes. Hybrid offspring of two species are infertile. *Polyploidy* causes rapid speciation in plants by introducing extra sets of chromosomes and immediate reproductive isolation.

Extinction results from the inability of a species to adapt to a changing environment. The earth has had several periods of mass extinctions, which may be related to meteor impacts and geological upheavals such as continental shifts. Either of these forces can lead to drastic environmental changes, such as mixing ocean layers or blocking the sun, that ultimately make survival impossible for many species.

QUESTIONS

1. The fraggles are a population of mythical, mouselike creatures that live in underground tunnels and chambers beneath a large vegetable garden, which supplies their food. Of the 100 fraggles in this population, 84 have green fur and 16 have gray fur. Green fur is controlled by a dominant allele F and gray fur by a recessive allele f. Assuming Hardy-Weinberg equilibrium is operating, answer the following questions:
   a. What is the frequency of the gray allele f?
   b. What is the frequency of the green allele F?
   c. How many fraggles are heterozygotes (Ff)?
   d. How many fraggles are homozygous recessive (ff)?
   e. How many fraggles are homozygous dominant (FF)?

2. One spring, a dust storm blankets the usually green garden of the fraggles in gray. Under these conditions, the green fraggles become very visible to the Gorgs, monstrous beasts who tend the gardens and try to kill the fraggles underfoot to protect their crops. The gray fraggles, however, blend into the dusty background and find that they can easily steal radishes from the garden. How might this event affect microevolution in this population of fraggles?

3. How did natural selection in this century render tuberculosis a less dangerous disease than it had been in the past century?

4. Women who are extremely thin cease to have menstrual periods. It is thought that this happens because they have too little body fat to support a pregnancy. Women who are extremely obese have fewer children than women of normal weight, because they are also more likely to suffer from heart disease or diabetes, which makes pregnancy difficult. Assuming that extreme thinness and obesity are at least partially genetically determined, what type of natural selection is at work here?

5. Reading 10.1 shows a chimeric animal that is derived from an embryo built of sheep cells and goat cells. How does the reproductive ability, and therefore the potential impact of evolution, of this goat/sheep differ from that of a liger or mule?

6. What evidence would suggest an extraterrestrial rather than an earth-based cause of a mass extinction?

TO THINK ABOUT

1. Conflicting hypotheses are often proposed to account for evolutionary events, such as the pace of evolution and the cause of mass extinctions. Those who do not believe that evolution has taken place sometimes cite these differences of opinion as evidence that even scientists doubt that evolution occurs. Scientists, however, maintain that conflicting hypotheses, or theories that could have been possible simultaneously, do not argue against evolution at all but demonstrate the process of scientific thinking. What is your opinion on the matter? Why are hypotheses particularly important in understanding evolutionary processes compared to other fields of biology?

2. What are three characteristics of human populations in the United States that violate the conditions of Hardy-Weinberg equilibrium?

3. According to the definition of speciation, do you think that the Great Dane and miniature poodle should be considered separate species?

4. In gene therapy, a defective gene is replaced with a functioning one. In what part of an organism would this have to be performed to have the potential to influence evolution? Why?

5. Which evolutionary principles are illustrated by the following scenarios taken from science fiction films?
   a. An environmental catastrophe forces one group of humans underground and a smaller group to remain above. One group evolves into grotesque "mutants" and the other into a sleek, handsome race.
   b. We cause our own numbers to dwindle dangerously close to extinction following a nuclear holocaust. Only a handful of individuals survive to reestablish the population.
   c. An approaching comet renders the earth uninhabitable. Certain humans are chosen to leave the doomed earth to settle another planet.

SUGGESTED READINGS

Cohn, Jeffery P. October 1990. Endangered wolf population increases. _BioScience_. Can humans help to restore wolf populations?

Diamond, Jared M., and Jerome I. Rotter. September 10, 1987. Observing the founder effect in human evolution. What maintains the frequencies of human genetic diseases? _Nature_, vol. 329. Genetic quirks in populations can sometimes be traced to the individuals in whom they arose. Some fascinating examples.

Gore, Rick. June 1989. Extinctions. _National Geographic_. A panorama of earth's dozen largest mass extinctions, including the spectacular evidence.

Kettlewell, B. 1973. _The evolution of melanism_. Oxford: Clarendon. Natural selection is vividly displayed by protective coloration in moths.

Phillips, Kathryn. June 1990. Where have all the frogs and toads gone? _BioScience_, vol. 40 no. 6. Are some of these animals headed for extinction?

Stanley, Steven M. 1981. _The new evolutionary timetable_. New York: Basic Books. Is the pace of evolution like a tortoise or a hare?

Stebbins, G. Ledyard, and Francisco J. Ayala. August 28, 1981. Is a new evolutionary synthesis necessary? _Science_, vol. 213. A classic paper placing rapid evolution in the framework of traditional Darwinian theory.

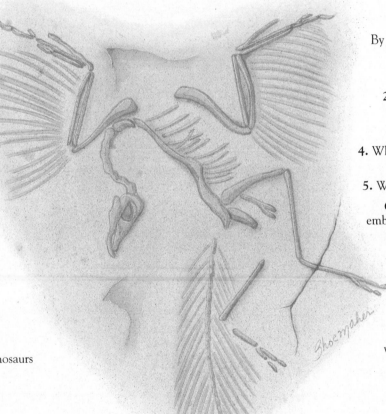

Learning Objectives

By the chapter's end, you should be able to answer these questions:

1. What is a fossil?

2. Why are fossils important to the study of evolution?

3. How do fossils form?

4. What methods are used to determine the age of a fossil?

5. Why is the fossil record incomplete?

6. How can comparative anatomy, embryology, and biochemistry provide clues to evolutionary relationships between species?

7. What were some of the major events in life history that we know about?

8. What sorts of animals living within the past 40 million years were probably our direct ancestors?

Large vultures lived about 12,000 years ago in caves in the walls of the Grand Canyon, so high that only other birds could reach them. The vultures were ancestors of the California condors, which today live only in zoos. The condors of 12,000 years ago had a plentiful food supply of diverse, large mammals. Adult birds would soar about searching for carcasses, bringing back remains of horses, bison, mammoths, camels, and mountain goats for the fledgling birds back in the cave, who were too young to scavenge on their own (fig. 35.1).

To reconstruct the lives of the ancient condors, caves in the Grand Canyon wall were excavated. The great birds left traces of their existence in preserved feather fragments and bones. Some of the vultures were quite young, as evidenced by preserved egg shell fragments and the size of holes in some of the smaller bones. The caves were too high for the large mammals of the time to reach, yet piles of their bones lay about. These mammals must have been brought to the caves by the vultures, as modern condors did, until the last wild bird perished in 1987. By noting the layer of rock within which the remains were found, and by chemically analyzing dried protein in a preserved beak, an approximate date of 120 centuries ago was assigned to the find.

Preserved remains of once-living organisms provide a major tool for deciphering the biological past. Similarities between modern species also offer compelling evidence for evolution. **Paleontologists** use these clues to reconstruct evolutionary relationships between species, which are called lineages, or **phylogenies.** For example, the close evolutionary relationship between humans and chimpanzees is suggested by the ways in which the bones and muscles are arranged and function, by similar chromosome organization, and by nearly identical amino acid sequences of many proteins.

In the biological science of evolution, the pictures painted by these different types of evidence replace the experimental portion of the scientific method, because the best possible experiment—going back in time to actually witness what happened—is impossible. Nonetheless, the evidence for evolution is abundant and rich.

a.

b.

Figure 35.1
a. The California condor is a species recently gone extinct in the wild. *b.* Condors once dwelled in caves high in the walls of the Grand Canyon.

Fossils

How Fossils Form

A **fossil** is evidence of prehistoric life. Many fossils are hard parts of organisms that have been replaced by minerals. An inch-long horn coral dies on an ancient sea bottom in what is now Indiana and is covered, over the eons, with layers of sand and mud. Gradually, the mud hardens into rock. Meanwhile, the horn coral decomposes, leaving an impression of its shell. Millions of years later, a person walking along land that was once that sea bottom sees the impression. Perhaps the mold was filled in with more mud, which also hardened into rock. The explorer may then find a cast of the horn coral, a rocky replica of the ancient animal.

The living matter of trees can be replaced with minerals, producing petrified wood that reveals cellular structures when sliced thin and viewed under a microscope. Evidence of our recent relatives often consists of teeth, which are even harder than bone and the likeliest anatomical parts to be preserved. Bones are fossilized when minerals replace cells.

The most striking fossils form when sudden catastrophes rapidly bury organisms in an oxygen-poor environment. Without oxygen, tissue damage is minimal, and the area is too hostile for scavengers to feed on the dead. Under these unusual conditions, even soft-bodied life forms can leave exquisitely detailed portraits of their anatomies. A block-long section of the Canadian Rockies called the Burgess shale, for example, houses an incredibly varied collection of 530-million-year-old soft invertebrates, preserved, the evidence suggests, in a sudden mudslide. Similarly, a family of rhinoceroslike styracosaurs living along the Milk River in Montana about 75 million years ago was preserved in time by a sudden flood. Today the rock strata in the hills are littered with styracosaur skull and limb fragments, the original bone tissue replaced with mineral.

Muds and floods are not the only agents of fossilization. A gold prospector found a perfectly preserved baby mammoth in the ice of the Arctic circle in Siberia. "Dima" was about 9 months old when she perished 40,000 years ago and stood 3 feet (1 meter) tall and weighed about 140 pounds (64 kilograms) (fig. 35.2). In Los Angeles,

mammals were preserved in the La Brea tar pits. Insects and frogs were trapped in sticky tree resin, which then hardened around them, forming translucent tombs known as amber.

Microscopes can aid in identifying fossils whose sources are not as obvious as horn corals, dinosaur bones, and insects in amber. Fossilized grasses, for example, are recognized with the help of a scanning electron microscope. Colonies of microscopic organisms are sometimes preserved. Fossilized coatings of cyanobacteria that lined ancient sea floors 2.5 billion years ago are found in western Australia. In the United States, similar fossils date from 500 million years ago. Fossils need not even be remains themselves. Dinosaur footprints and worm borings reveal how the animals that made them traveled. The pigments in fossilized dinosaur dung offer clues to what the great reptiles ate.

Fossils offer only fleeting glimpses into life's history. Much evidence was destroyed by the formidable forces of nature—erosion, tides, volcanoes, continental shifts, earthquakes, storms, and even meteor impacts. Plus, some species may have lived for such short periods of time, or dwelled in such restricted areas, that their fossils, if they left

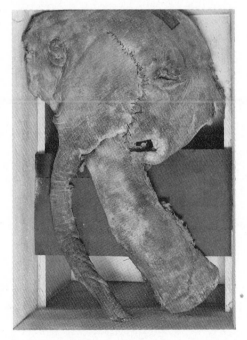

a.

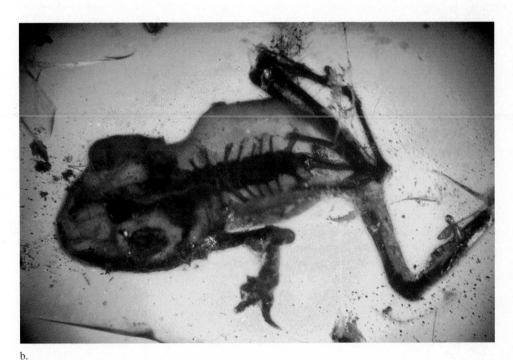

b.

Figure 35.2
Fossils. *a.* This frozen mammoth was found in Alaska and is preserved in a refrigerator at the American Museum of Natural History. *b.* About 40 million years ago, this *Eleutherodactylus* frog was trapped in tree resin. The frog has two broken limbs and other signs of struggle and injury. Perhaps a bird captured the animal, depositing it in the tree that became its tomb.

any, have never been discovered. Still, over the past two decades many fascinating fossils have been found.

Determining the Age of a Fossil

An organism represented by a fossil can be localized in the history of life either relatively or absolutely. A **relative date** is based on how far beneath the surface the rock layer lies in which the fossil is found. This is an application of the principle of superposition. However, because different rock strata are not formed at the same rate, assigning fossils to particular layers cannot offer a precise date.

Arriving at a more meaningful date requires tracking a phenomenon that has occurred at a constant and measurable rate for a very long time, so that fossils hundreds of millions of years old can be dated. With the discovery of radioactive elements in the late 1800s, a method of more accurately dating fossils was eventually developed.

Isotopes of certain elements are naturally unstable, causing them to emit radiation. As the isotopes release radiation (or "radioactively decay"), they change into different isotopes of the same element, or isotopes of a different element. (Recall that an isotope is an alternate form of an element distinguished by a different number of neutrons.) Each radioactive isotope decays to its alternate form at a characteristic and unalterable rate, called its **half-life.** The half-life is the time it takes for half of the isotopes in a sample of the original element to decay into the second form. If the half-life of a radioactive isotope and the amounts of its "before" and "after" forms in a rock or tissue sample are known, the time of formation of the sample can be deduced.

Using natural radioactivity as a "clock" is called **radiometric dating.** A date obtained in this way is absolute because it is expressed in a number of years, although it is not exact. Two radioactive isotopes are often used to assign dates to fossils—potassium 40 and carbon 14. Potassium 40 radioactively decays to argon 40 with a half-life of 1.3 billion years, making it valuable in dating old rocks containing traces of both isotopes (fig. 35.3). Chemical methods can detect amounts of argon 40 small enough to correspond to fossils that are about 300,000 years old. However, many sedimentary (layered) rocks, the source of most fossils, contain

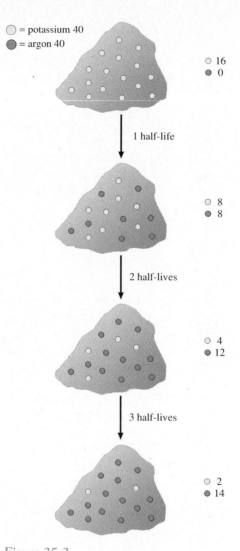

Figure 35.3

Radiometric dating. An approximate age in years can be assigned to some fossils by determining the proportion of potassium 40 to argon 40 in the rock. After a half-life of 1.3 billion years, half of the potassium 40 in a sample has decayed to argon 40. After two half-lives, a quarter of the potassium 40 remains, and after three half-lives, one-eighth of the original isotope is left.

argon 40 that was actually part of much older rock. A potassium 40 date for these rocks would not correspond to the age of the fossils within them.

Fossils up to 40,000 years old are radiometrically dated by measuring the proportion of carbon 12 to the rarer carbon 14. Carbon 14 is a radioactive isotope that forms naturally in the atmosphere when the nonradioactive form, carbon 12, is bombarded with cosmic rays (radiation from space).

Organisms accumulate a certain proportion of carbon 14 as they assimilate carbon during photosynthesis or by eating organic matter. When an organism dies, however, its intake of carbon 14 stops, and from then on, carbon 14 decays to the more stable carbon 12 with a half-life of 5,710 years. The Grand Canyon vultures have about one-fourth the ratio of carbon 14 to carbon 12 seen in a living organism. Therefore, about two half-lives, or about 11,420 years, have passed since the animals died.

A limitation of potassium-argon and carbon 14 dating is that they leave a gap. That is, carbon dates extend back to 40,000 years ago, but potassium-argon dates do not begin reliably until 300,000 years ago. Several new techniques cover the missing years, which include the time of human origin.

Electron-spin resonance and **thermoluminescence** are physical techniques that measure tiny holes made in crystals over time due to exposure to ionizing radiation. Each method counts the holes differently and works on samples up to 1 million years old. Another approach, **amino acid racemization,** chronicles the rate at which amino acids in biological matter alter to mirror-image chemical structures called isomers. It is used for dating eggs and shells up to 100,000 years old.

The fact that electron-spin resonance and thermoluminescence values are perturbed by natural deposits of radioactive substances, and that amino acid racemization is affected by temperature and moisture, means that results must be corrected for these influences. Still, relative dating, radiometric dating, and these newer methods can be used together to pinpoint more accurately when organisms lived.

KEY CONCEPTS

A fossil is evidence of past life in which biological matter is slowly replaced with minerals or in which organisms are buried rapidly and preserved in a low-oxygen environment. The fossil record is incomplete because not all species had hard parts, were buried rapidly, were widespread, or lived long enough to be sampled. A fossil is relatively dated by the rock layer it is in or absolutely dated by isotope ratios, altered crystal structures, and amino acid isomer ratios.

Comparing Structures in Modern Species

Comparative Anatomy

In general, the more similar two living species are, the more recently they diverged in their lineage from a common ancestor. The structures and organization of the vertebrate skeleton are often cited as evidence of a common ancestor to this familiar group of animals. All vertebrate skeletons are built of the same component parts and provide support (fig. 35.4). An ancestor to modern vertebrates must have originated this skeletal organization, which was then modified in more recent organisms (amphibians, reptiles, birds, fishes, and mammals) for their particular modes of life.

Similarly built structures with the same general function that are inherited from a common ancestor, such as the vertebrate skeleton, are termed **homologous.** However, unrelated organisms can evolve structures in response to the same environmental challenge. Such structures that are similar in function, but not in architecture, are termed **analogous.** Birds and insects, for example, each have wings that enable them to fly, but the bird's wing is a modification of vertebrate limb bones, whereas the insect's wing is an outgrowth of the cuticle that covers its body in an exoskeleton. Analogous structures do not offer evidence for evolution (see fig. 33.6*b*).

Determining whether particular body parts are homologous or analogous can be difficult. In general, though, analogous structures tend to resemble one another only superficially, whereas the similarities in body parts between two species related by common descent—homologies—tend to be complex and numerous.

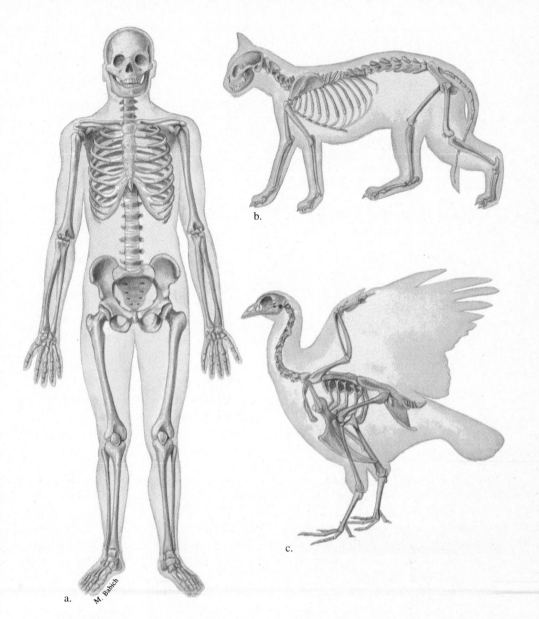

Figure 35.4
Vertebrate skeletal organization reflects common ancestry. Although a human walks erect (*a*), a cat walks on all fours (*b*), and a bird flies (*c*), all have a similar skeletal organization of a skull, shoulder, spine, hips, and limbs. An examination of the forelimbs of these animals accentuates the skeletal similarities.

Vestigial Organs

Evolution is not a perfect process, and as new structures are selected by environmental change, older ones are sometimes retained. A structure that seems not to have a function in an organism, yet resembles a functional organ in another type of organism, is termed **vestigial.** Darwin compared vestigial organs to letters in a word that are not pronounced but offer clues to the word's origin.

Human vestigial organs include wisdom teeth and the appendix, both of which may have been useful to distant ancestors who ate different foods than we do today. Our lowest and smallest vertebrae, the "tailbone," may be a vestige of a monkeylike ancestor who had a tail. In snakes and whales, leg bones are vestigial, perhaps retained from vertebrate ancestors who used their legs (fig. 35.5). A horse has two tiny leg bones that it apparently does not use, but these bones were probably useful to the horse's ancestor, which had a different gait because it had three toes on each foot instead of the modern-day one.

Comparative Embryology

Embryos of a human, monkey, dog, cat, rabbit, and mouse look very much alike. Darwin suggested that the striking similarity between vertebrate embryos reflects adaptations to their similar environments—

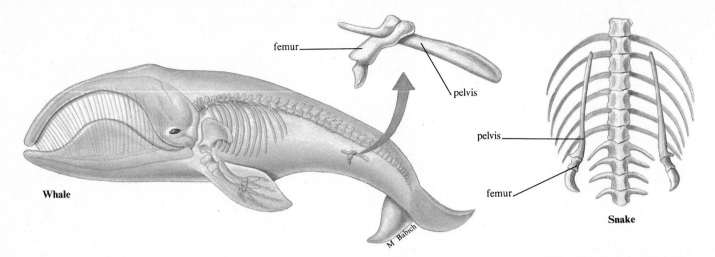

Figure 35.5
Vestigial organs. The whale and the snake have tiny femurs (leg bones), which are apparently of no use to them. These femurs are vestigial organs.

floating in a watery bubble, either in the mother's uterus or in an egg. These embryos may express the same sets of ancestral genes, and as the embryos mature into fetuses, they begin to express other genes and take on the characteristics of their particular species. Shared early genes might explain prenatal similarities, such as the gill slits and rudimentary tail seen in a 7-week-old human embryo.

KEY CONCEPTS

Homologous structures are similar in structure and function, reflecting shared ancestry. Analogous structures are similar in function but not architecture and do not reflect common ancestry. Vestigial organs have no obvious function, resemble structures in other species, and may have had a function in an ancestor. Vertebrate embryos appear similar because of shared, early acting genes.

Molecular Evolution

Large-scale evidence for evolution, such as fossils and similar body parts, can be difficult to interpret. Less ambiguous evidence comes from within the cell, in the molecules of life.

The reasoning behind **molecular evolution** is that genes and proteins are composed of many bits of information. It is highly unlikely that two unrelated species would happen to evolve precisely the same

order of chromosome bands, nucleotides, or amino acids simply by chance. As with larger structures, the greater the molecular similarities between two modern species, the closer their evolutionary relationship. Even more direct evidence is found in preserved DNA from extinct species, which can be amplified and sequenced and compared to DNA from its descendants (fig. 35.6).

Several types of molecular evidence for evolution are used to confirm or challenge lineages proposed on the basis of fossil or comparative anatomy evidence.

Comparing Chromosomes

The number, shape, and banding patterns of stained chromosomes can be compared as a measure of relatedness. The chromosomes of humans, chimpanzees, gorillas, and orangutans are very similarly organized. If human chromosome 2 is broken in half, we would have 48 chromosomes instead of 46, as do the three species of apes. Human chromosome banding patterns match closest those of chimpanzees, then gorillas, and then orangutans. Some differences are inversions of band sequences, rather than missing or extra genetic material. Chromosome patterns can be compared between less closely related species as well. All mammals, for example, have identically banded X chromosomes.

Chromosome evidence has settled a long-standing debate—is the giant panda a bear or a raccoon? Although most children

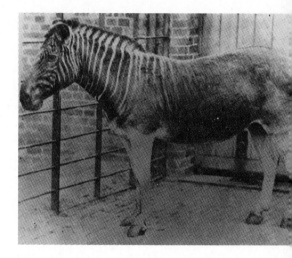

Figure 35.6
Probing the molecules of extinct organisms. The last quagga, a relative of the horse and zebra, died in captivity in Amsterdam in 1883. DNA extracted from this preserved quagga is now being deciphered to see how closely related the extinct animal was to its descendants.

would answer "bear," many biologists have placed the panda with raccoons, based on its resemblance to a relative of the raccoon called the red lesser panda. Bears have 74 short chromosomes, with the constrictions near the tips. Pandas have 42 chromosomes, most of them long and with centrally located constrictions. Several pairs of the small bear chromosomes, if fused, would very closely resemble particular chromosomes of the giant panda. As for the red lesser panda, only 2 of its chromosomes match those in giant pandas or bears, but 14 of them are found in raccoons (fig. 35.7). According to its chromosomes, the panda is a bear after all.

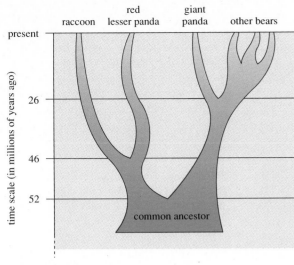

Giant Panda

Raccoon

Bear

Lesser Panda

Figure 35.7

The giant panda finds its place in life history. Is the giant panda a bear or a raccoon? It looks most like a bear, but the similar-looking red lesser panda is in the raccoon family. Molecular studies place the giant panda closer to the bears.

Comparing Protein Sequences

The fact that all species utilize the same genetic code to build proteins argues for a common ancestry to all life on earth. In addition, many different types of organisms use the same proteins, with only slight variations in amino acid sequence. One of the most ancient and well-studied proteins is cytochrome C, which is involved in cellular respiration. Twenty of its 104 amino acids occupy identical positions in the cytochrome C of all eukaryotes. The closer related two species are, the more alike their cytochrome C amino acid sequence is (fig. 35.8). Human cytochrome C and chimpanzee cytochrome C are identical.

The amino acid sequences of dozens of proteins have now been deciphered in many species to track lineages, and quite often the results are consistent with fossil or anatomical evidence. The similarities in amino acid sequences between the proteins of humans and chimpanzees are astounding—many proteins are alike in 99% of their amino acids. Several are virtually identical. Chapter 3 discusses two highly conserved proteins—hemoglobin and albumin.

Organism	Number of Amino Acid Differences from Humans
chimpanzee	0
rhesus monkey	1
rabbit	9
cow	10
pigeon	12
bullfrog	20
fruit fly	24
wheat germ	37
yeast	42

a.

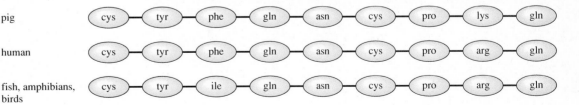

pig   cys — tyr — phe — gln — asn — cys — pro — lys — gln

human   cys — tyr — phe — gln — asn — cys — pro — arg — gln

fish, amphibians, birds   cys — tyr — ile — gln — asn — cys — pro — arg — gln

b.

Figure 35.8

a. Amino acid sequence similarities are a measure of evolutionary relatedness. Similarities in amino acid sequence for the respiratory protein cytochrome C between humans and other species parallel our degree of relatedness to them. *b.* Antidiuretic hormone is a peptide hormone eight amino acids long that signals the kidneys to conserve water. Its sequence differs only slightly between major groups of vertebrates.

Comparing DNA Sequences

Similarities in DNA sequences between two species can be assessed for the total genome or for a single gene or piece of DNA. Examining genomic similarity relies on complementary base pairing. DNA double helices from two species are unwound and mixed together. The rate at which hybrid DNA double helices reform—that is, DNA molecules containing one helix from each species—is a direct measure of how similar they are in sequence. The faster the DNA from two species forms hybrids, the more closely related the two species are. Using this approach of **DNA hybridization,** researchers have shown that human DNA differs in 1.8% of its base pairs from chimpanzee DNA; by 2.3% from gorilla DNA; and by 3.7% from orangutan DNA.

DNA sequence similarity can be used to estimate the time when two species diverged from a common ancestor if the rate of base substitution mutation is known. For example, if the DNA from two species differs in 5% of its bases, and substitutions occur at a rate of 1% per 1 million years, then 5 million years must have passed since the species diverged. The rate of base change in DNA is used as a "molecular clock," just as the rate of radioactive decay of an isotope is used as a natural clock in radiometric dating. The information from DNA sequencing is represented in **evolutionary tree diagrams,** which indicate on a time scale the "branching points" when two species diverged from a common ancestor (fig. 35.9). Mitochondrial DNA provides an even better molecular clock, because it mutates about 5 to 10 times faster than nuclear DNA (Reading 35.1).

KEY CONCEPTS

Evolutionary trees are constructed by considering how alike chromosome bands or gene or protein sequences are between species. This evidence indicates that humans are most closely related to chimpanzees.

The History of Life on Earth

The tantalizing clues to past life offered by fossils, comparative anatomy, and biochemistry have made possible one of the most fascinating pursuits a biologist can follow—piecing together the sequence in which species arose, flourished, and died out on the earth. Of course, we can only glimpse brief moments of life's history.

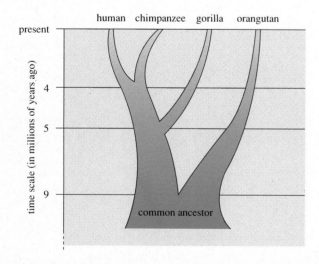

Figure 35.9
Identifying our closest relatives. One way to decipher the evolutionary relationship between humans and apes is to compare the number of chemical building block differences in the sequences of the same gene between pairs of species. This information is then superimposed upon a time scale to estimate when the species diverged from common ancestors by considering the number of years it takes for mutations to accumulate. The resulting "molecular clock" shows the most recent ancestor we have in common with chimpanzees lived about 4 million years ago. According to this theory, the common ancestor of humans and chimps evolved from a common ancestor with gorillas about 5 million years ago, and a common ancestor of all four species lived about 9 million years ago.

The Geological Time Scale

The backdrop for life history is geological history, which began before life debuted yet continues today. The **geological time scale** was developed in the late nineteenth century. It is divided into major **eras** of biological and geological activity lasting vast stretches of time, then **periods** within these eras, and finally **epochs** within some of the periods (table 35.1).

Because evidence of evolution tends to represent accidents, such as mudslides or glaciers, and the more spectacular biological events, the history of life reads like a dramatic series of extinctions followed by adaptive radiation (species entering new habitats and diversifying) of the survivors. Some of the "main events" of evolution include the origin of life (chapter 3), the debut of eukaryotic cells (chapter 4), and mass extinctions (chapter 34). In actuality, the parade of life has probably been continuous since the earliest cell-like collections of organic chemicals formed more than 3 billion years ago.

Following is a probable sequence of events that led from those first cells to the dawn of modern humans. This is a very narrow peek. If the history of life is represented as a vast bush, with each branch representing a type of organism, then those branches leading to humans are but the tiniest of twigs. That is, for each branch leading toward humans, many others led in other directions.

Precambrian Life

Fossil evidence before 600 to 700 million years ago is sparse. This earliest part of earth history, called the **Precambrian era,** accounts for five-sixths of earth's existence so far (fig. 35.10). The oldest rocks to be radiometrically dated come from western Greenland, and they are about 3.8 billion years old. Unfortunately, these rocks were exposed to such high temperatures and pressures that any fossils that might have been in them were undoubtedly destroyed.

Some of the earliest and most intriguing fossils are from the Fig Tree sediments of South Africa, which date back 3.4 billion years. The size and intricate folds of these structures resemble more recent fossils and modern prokaryotes (bacteria and cyanobacteria) (fig. 35.11). Fossils from Rhodesia from 2.8 billion years ago contain

Table 35.1
The Geological Time Scale

Era	Period	Epoch	Millions of Years Ago	Important Events
Cenozoic (Age of Mammals)	Quaternary	Recent	0.01	Modern humans
		Pleistocene	2	Early humans
	Tertiary	Pliocene	6	Radiation of apes
		Miocene	23	Abundant grazing mammals
		Oligocene	38	Angiosperms dominant
		Eocene	54	Mammalian radiation
		Paleocene	65	First placental mammals
Mesozoic (Age of Reptiles)	Cretaceous		135	Climax of reptiles; first angiosperms; extinction of ammonoids
	Jurassic		180	Reptiles dominant; first birds; first mammals
	Triassic		225	First dinosaurs; cycads and conifers dominant
Paleozoic	Permian		275	Widespread extinction of marine invertebrates; expansion of primitive reptiles
	Carboniferous*		345	Great swamp trees (coal forests); amphibians prominent
	Devonian		395	Age of fishes; first amphibians
	Silurian		435	First land plants; eurypterids prominent
	Ordovician		500	Earliest known fishes
	Cambrian		600	Abundant marine invertebrates; trilobites and brachiopods dominant; algae prominent
Precambrian			>3000	Soft-bodied primitive life

*The early Carboniferous is often referred to as the "Mississippian" and the late Carboniferous as the "Pennsylvanian."
From E. Peter Volpe, *Understanding Evolution*, 5th ed. Copyright © 1985, Wm. C. Brown Publishers, Dubuque, Iowa. All Right Reserved. Reprinted by permission.

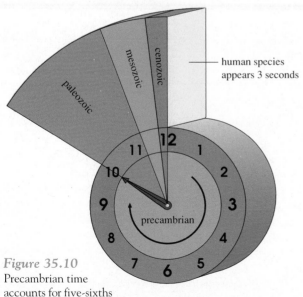

Figure 35.10
Precambrian time accounts for five-sixths of earth's history. The time during which we think life on earth has been abundant—the Paleozoic, Mesozoic, and Cenozoic eras—accounts for only one-sixth of the planet's history.

Figure 35.11
Stromatolites represent very ancient life. Between 2.5 billion years ago and 600 million years ago, bacteria flourished in the shallow seas. Cyanobacteria aggregated into huge colonies, forming great submerged mats that became infiltrated with sediments, which hardened to preserve replicas of these most ancient organisms. These fossils, called stromatolites, are found today in only a few places, such as Shark Bay in Western Australia, where these came from.

Reading 35.1 *The Search for Mitochondrial "Eve"*

A CLOCK MEASURES THE PASSAGE OF TIME BY MOVING ITS HANDS THROUGH A CERTAIN DEGREE OF A CIRCLE IN A SPECIFIC AND CONSTANT INTERVAL OF TIME—A SECOND OR MINUTE. Similarly, a polymeric molecule can be used as a clock if its building blocks are replaced at a known and constant rate. DNA from a cell's nucleus is used as a molecular clock because the rate of base change mutation is known, and a ratio can be set up using the number of base differences in the nuclear DNA of two organisms to estimate passage of time.

DNA in mitochondria (mtDNA) can also be used as a molecular clock. Recall that mitochondria are organelles that house the reactions of cellular respiration. Mitochondria in human cells contain 16,569 base pairs. This genetic material is sometimes referred to as our 24th chromosome. DNA in the mitochondria is valuable to the charting of evolutionary time because this clock ticks 5 to 10 times faster than the nuclear DNA clock—that is, mtDNA mutates this much faster than nuclear DNA. The mtDNA clock can be used to chart more recent evolutionary events.

Like other measures of evolutionary relatedness, the more similar the mtDNA sequence is between two individuals, the more recently they are assumed to be descended from a common ancestor. But following the inheritance of mtDNA presents an interesting quirk, because mtDNA is maternally inherited. That is, mitochondria are passed from mothers only and received by egg cells when they form in meiosis. The part of the sperm cell that enters the egg at fertilization, in contrast,

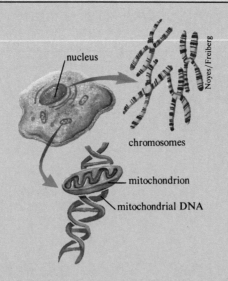

Figure 1
The human mitochondrial genome consists of about 17,000 base pairs.

usually does not contain any mitochondria. Theoretically, if a particular sequence of mtDNA can be identified that could have given rise, by mutation, to mtDNA sequences in modern humans, then that ancestral sequence may represent a very early human or humanlike female—a mitochondrial "Eve," or first woman.

The search for mitochondrial Eve began in 1986, when Wesley Brown, a graduate student at the University of California at Berkeley, cut mtDNA from 21 living people of diverse ethnic backgrounds with a variety of restriction enzymes. A particular restriction enzyme cuts DNA at a specific base sequence. If the DNA of two individuals

differs at a restriction site, and the DNA is cut with an enzyme that cuts at that site, then their DNA will be snipped into a different number of pieces. The similarity of restriction fragment patterns, then, is a measure of relatedness (time of descent from a shared ancestor).

Wesley Brown found that his 21 subjects had very similar mtDNA patterns. The next question—how long would it have taken the differences he did see to accumulate, assuming all the mtDNA types were descended from a single ancestral sequence? By multiplying the rate of mtDNA mutation by the average number of sequence differences between the people's mtDNA, Brown estimated that the ancestral mtDNA came from a woman (or small group of women) who lived about 200,000 years ago.

Where might this figurative first woman have dwelled? Most fossil evidence points to Africa, but some anthropologists maintain that modern peoples came from Asia as well. To answer this question, Berkeley researchers led by Allan Wilson cut mtDNA from 147 people from Africa, Asia, Australia, New Guinea, and Europe with a dozen restriction enzymes. The 133 people who had different mtDNA patterns fell into two groups of similar sequences. One group consisted of all Africans. Because this group had greater sequence diversity within it, the African group is the older of the two. More time must have elapsed from when the ancestral mtDNA existed to produce the present African population than the non-African group. The prevailing view of an African origin is therefore supported by the mtDNA clock.

---

breakdown products of chlorophyll, suggesting that microbes of the time may have photosynthesized. The Gunflint rock formation from the north shore of Lake Superior in Ontario, Canada, has yielded a diverse assortment of Precambrian life forms, including cyanobacteria, early eukaryotes, red algae, and fungi. A billion years ago algae and fungi left their mark in the Bitter Springs formation in Australia.

Between 700 and 600 million years ago, a profound biological change took place—multicellular life appeared. Signs

of worms, jellyfish, and soft corals are evident in the rocks of southern Australia and the Canadian Arctic. Exactly how life proceeded from the single-celled to the many-celled is a mystery. Unicellular organisms may have formed colonies and then undergone a division of labor, with certain cells specializing in certain functions, to eventually form a coordinated multicellular organism. Alternatively, an ancestral, large, single-celled organism may have developed partitions and then undergone division of labor.

The Paleozoic Era

Abundant evidence of life appears quite suddenly in the fossil record of the **Cambrian period** about 600 million years ago—a time quite aptly called the Cambrian explosion. Ancestors of all modern animal phyla debuted in the Cambrian period, plus many now-extinct life forms. Although confined to the seas, life was diverse and plentiful. The ancient oceans were home to abundant soft-bodied organisms, including algae, sponges, jellyfish, and worms, and the earliest known

a.

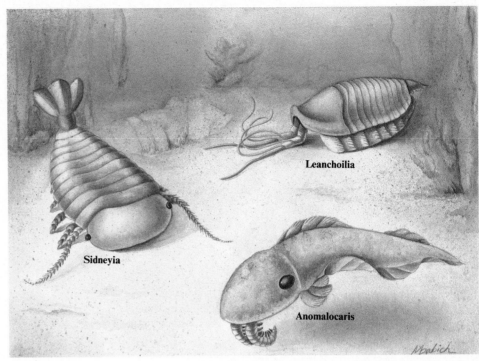

Leanchoilia

Sidneyia

Anomalocaris

b.

Figure 35.12

The Cambrian seas were home to an explosion of life forms. *a.* This piece of shale was once part of the bottom of a Cambrian period sea. These trilobites were distant forerunners of arthropods, and they ranged in size from that of a pea to an automobile. They left behind many fossils because of their abundance, wide geographical distribution, and hard parts. *b.* The Burgess shale in British Columbia revealed fossils of many soft-bodied invertebrates not seen anywhere else in the world. They were apparently fossilized when they were buried by a mudslide.

Figure 35.13

The oldest vertebrate fossils are from the Ordovician period. Several complete fossils of jawless fishes dating back to this period were recently found in Bolivia. Shown here is the reconstruction.

organisms with hard parts, such as shellfish, the insectlike **trilobites, nautiloids,** scorpionlike **eurypterids,** and **brachiopods,** which looked like clams and left many fossils (fig. 35.12). The biological blooming at this time is a major puzzlement in the study of life history.

The **Ordovician period** followed the Cambrian 500 to 435 million years ago. The seas continued to support vast communities of algae and invertebrates. Organisms abundant at this time were the **graptolites,** so-named because their fossilized remains resemble pencil markings. The first vertebrates to leave fossils date from the Ordovician. In 1988, complete fossils of 10 jawless fishes dating from 470 million years ago were found in Bolivia, which was then under an ocean (fig. 35.13). These very early animals with backbones were about 18 inches (46 centimeters) long and 6 inches (15 centimeters) wide and were covered by small scales and had bony plates on their round heads.

At the end of the Ordovician period and during the **Silurian period** (435 to 395 million years ago), organisms first ventured onto the land. These pioneers were odd-looking plants called **psilophytes.** They had bare stems from which spores were scattered and underground branches but no leaves or roots. The first animals to leave fossils on the land resembled scorpions.

The **Devonian period** of 395 to 345 million years ago was the "Age of Fishes." The seas continued to support most life, including the now well-established invertebrates, as well as fishes with skeletons built of cartilage or bone. Corals were abundant, as well as animals called crinoids that resembled flowers. The land was still relatively barren, home to scorpions and millipedes.

The **crossopterygians,** or lobe-finned fishes, lived in the Devonian period and were probably ancestral to amphibians. They could gulp air and use its oxygen, and fleshy fins allowed them to haul themselves along the

land that separated shallow pools (fig. 35.14). These adaptations probably appeared by chance, but once organisms could spend extended periods of time on land, they thrived in the presence of vast, unused resources. Gradually amphibians evolved as those transitional fishes with the strongest fleshy fins and best ability to breathe air were naturally selected.

By 345 million years ago, the beginning of the **Carboniferous period,** or "Age of Amphibians," the descendants of the lobe-finned fishes were prominent on the land. Like modern amphibians, these animals were

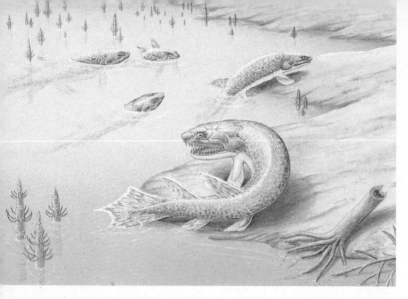

Figure 35.14
From fish to amphibian—how it might have happened. The lobe-finned fish called crossopterygians lived in the Devonian period and had fleshy, powerful fins and the ability to breathe air. These adaptations allowed them to survive on land for short periods of time. By the late Carboniferous period, primitive amphibians appeared that may have descended from the lobe-finned fishes.

a.

b.

Figure 35.15
a. The great forests of the Coal Age. The forests of the Carboniferous period were spectacular and so lush that their remains were preserved in massive coal beds. The fernlike plants in the foreground are very ancient seed-bearing gymnosperms. The thin tree on the right is an extinct ancestor of the modern horsetail, and the thicker trunks on the left, also extinct, gave rise to modern club mosses and ground pines. b. In Indiana and Illinois, a piece of coal will occasionally contain the imprint of a fern.

not entirely land-dwelling. Their legs were not strong enough to support full-time walking, their skin needed frequent moisturizing, and their eggs had to be laid in the water in order for the developing embryos to receive sufficient moisture and nutrients. Toward the end of the Carboniferous period about 275 million years ago, some amphibians had evolved eggs that contained water and nutrients and could be laid on land. Fossil evidence of these early reptiles has not been found, but their existence is inferred from organisms appearing over the following several million years that had traits of both amphibians and reptiles.

When the amphibians of the Carboniferous period crawled onto the swampy land, they must have seen fernlike plants at eye level and majestic conifers towering 130 feet (40 meters) above. By the end of the period, many of these plants had died, buried beneath the swamps to form, over the coming millennia, coal beds (fig. 35.15). Because of these bountiful reminders of the ancient first forests, the Carboniferous period is also called the "Coal Age." Today, a piece of coal split in half will sometimes reveal a perfect impression of an ancient fern.

The Paleozoic era ended rather dramatically with the **Permian period** (275 to 225 million years ago), when half the families of vertebrates and more than 90% of species dwelling in the shallow seas became extinct. Permian lands still supported amphibians, but reptiles were becoming more prevalent.

The reptile introduced a new biological structure, the **amniote egg,** in which an embryo could develop completely, without the need to be laid in water. An amniote egg contains nutrient-rich yolk and extraembryonic membranes, which protect and help to nourish the embryo. The amnion encloses the embryo in a sac of fluid that is chemically very similar to seawater, which nurtured so many early life forms. The amniote egg's prepackaged nutrient stores and protection proved so successful that it persists today in the eggs of reptiles, birds, and mammals.

Cotylosaurs were early Permian reptiles that gave rise to the dinosaurs, as well as to modern reptiles, birds, and mammals. They coexisted with their immediate descendants, the **pelycosaurs,** or sailed lizards. The pelycosaurs were distant ancestors of mammals.

KEY CONCEPTS

The geological time scale is divided into eras, periods, and epochs. Most fossils date since the Cambrian period of 600 to 700 million years ago, although the Precambrian period accounts for five-sixths of the planet's existence. The earliest Precambrian fossils are remains of vast bacterial colonies. Life exploded in the Cambrian period as multicellular forms, including many invertebrates, appeared, flourished, and diversified in the seas. During the following Ordovician period, vertebrates joined the invertebrates and algae. Life came to the land during the Silurian period. Bony fishes evolved during the Devonian period, including a forerunner of amphibians. During the Carboniferous period amphibians and the first reptiles dwelled in forests of ferns and conifers. Reptiles were well established by the Permian period.

The Mesozoic Era

When the Age of Reptiles dawned during the **Triassic period** 225 million years ago, small ancestors of the great dinosaurs flourished. These were the **thecodonts,** descendants of the Permian cotylosaurs. Fossil evidence of thecodonts is scant. One of the earliest known is Staurikosaurus, which stood about 6.5 feet (2 meters) tall and weighed about 70 pounds (32 kilograms). It stood upright, with short forearms and strong hind limbs, and held its tail out, much like the carnivorous dinosaurs that would soon appear.

The thecodonts shared the forest of seed-forming gymnosperms (cycads, ginkgos, and conifers) with other animals called **therapsids.** These were reptiles, but they held their limbs and heads in a position more like those of mammals, and their teeth were more mammalian than reptilian (fig. 35.16). By the end of the Mesozoic era, the therapsids would evolve into small, hair-covered animals, most of whom lived on the forest floor—the first mammals. At the close of the Triassic period, about 190 to 185 million years ago, the numbers of both thecodonts and therapsids were dwindling as much larger animals began to infiltrate a wide range of habitats. These new, well-adapted animals were the dinosaurs, and they would dominate for the next 120 million years. Although the dinosaurs have been traditionally classified as reptiles, evidence is accumulating that they may actually be most closely related to birds (Reading 35.2).

By the **Jurassic period** of 185 to 135 million years ago, the dinosaurs had invaded nearly all habitats, from the **ichthyosaurs** in the seas, to **archaeopteryx** in the air, to the familiar **apatosaurs** (brontosaurs), **stegosaurs, diplodocus,** and **allosaurs** that dwelled in the second half of the period. The first flowering plants (angiosperms) appeared, but forests still consisted mostly of tall ferns and conifers, club mosses, and horsetails.

The **Cretaceous period** (135 to 65 million years ago) was a time of great biological change. Angiosperms spread in spectacular diversity, and the number of dinosaur species declined. Although this was the beginning of the end for the dinosaurs, many species soared to quite healthy numbers. Duck-billed **maiasaurs** traveled in herds of thousands in what is now Wyoming. The plains of Alberta supported huge herds of apatosaurs that migrated to the Arctic, northern Europe, and Asia, landmasses that were then connected. By the end of the period, triceratops were so widespread that some paleontologists call them the "cockroaches of the Cretaceous."

The reign of the great dinosaurs ended about 65 million years ago, and each paleontologist seems to have a favorite theory as to how it happened (chapter 34). Whatever

Figure 35.16
The dawn of the Mesozoic era saw many small animals that had characteristics of reptiles and mammals.

sparked the mass extinctions that marked the end of the Mesozoic era, it is clear that the demise of the dinosaurs opened up habitats for many other species, including the primates that eventually gave rise to our own species.

KEY CONCEPTS

By 225 million years ago, during the Triassic period, thecodonts shared the gymnosperm forests with therapsids, ancestors of mammals. During the Jurassic period, dinosaurs reigned and angiosperms debuted. During the Cretaceous period, some dinosaur species declined while others rose, and the number of angiosperm species continued to increase. At the end of the Mesozoic era, many species became extinct.

Reading 35.2 A New View of Dinosaurs

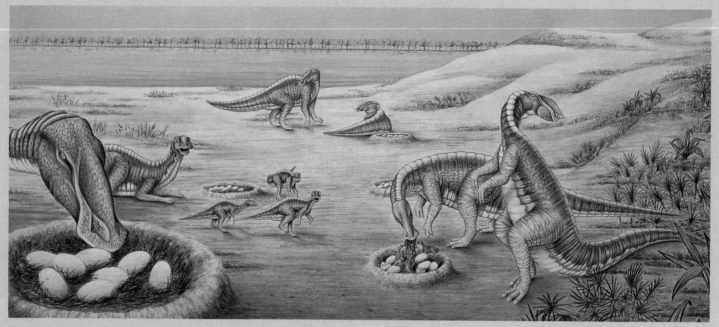

Figure 1
Dinosaur families on egg mountain.

ABOUT 80 MILLION YEARS AGO, A SEAWAY STRETCHING FROM THE BEAUFORT SEA IN NORTHERN CANADA TO THE GULF OF MEXICO DIVIDED NORTH AMERICA. The Rockies jutted up from western America; the Appalachians formed the highlands of the east. Between the Rockies and the mid-American sea lay a coastal plain, rich in sediments washed down from the mountains.

Egg Mountain was a hill about 150 feet (46 meters) high in the middle of a seasonal lake in what is now Choteau, Montana. In 1979, paleontologist John Horner, curator of the Museum of the Rockies in Bozeman, Montana, found in this hill a most spectacular fossil assemblage—nine dinosaur nests, complete with eggs and bones from both adult and juvenile dinosaurs. They were part of a huge dinosaur community preserved in time by a sudden volcanic eruption.

Many of the residents of Egg Mountain were **maiasaurs,** duck-billed dinosaurs that stood about 20 feet (6 meters) high and resembled ostriches. The eggs seemed to have been carefully placed in the nests so that they did not touch one another, deposited pointed-end down. The exposed ends were covered with vegetation. The tops were missing from some of the eggs, and nearby were found bones of baby dinosaurs. The presence of beetle egg cases, fossilized

cocoons, and what Horner believes is "dinosaur upchuck" suggests that a parent dinosaur fed the young. Grooves in the teeth of the young indicate that they ate seeds and berries. Horner X-rayed the unbroken eggs and found dinosaur embryos, "the flesh rotted around prepackaged bundles of bone." The scene looked very much like groupings of families, with carefully guarded nests and adults who nurtured their young. It was a life-style more like that of birds than reptiles.

The dinosaurs resembled birds in their anatomy and physiology as well. The dinosaur egg shells look like those of birds when viewed under a scanning electron microscope. The fast rate of growth and the blood vessel pattern of maiasaurs are more like those of birds than reptiles, findings consistent with the theory of Robert Bakker, curator of the University of Colorado Museum, that dinosaurs were warm-blooded (endothermic), like modern birds and mammals. Bakker examined the spacing between dinosaur footprints, the length of their leg bones, and the structure of the feet and hypothesized that dinosaurs were very active and agile migrants.

This new view of the dinosaur as a swift, warm-blooded social animal led to a reexamination of the evidence that had labeled the dinosaurs as reptiles. The first dinosaur fossils were footprints found in England in 1802, but

they were dismissed as the tracks of giant turkeys. Then in 1822, a woman accompanying her physician and fossil-collector husband on a house call in rural England spied a large tooth jutting out of a rock. The tooth reminded the doctor of a tooth from an iguana lizard, so he named the animal that once possessed it Iguanodon. He thought it was from a giant lizard.

By the 1840s, other large fossils had been found. French anatomist George Cuvier concluded that the fossils were from animals that were about the size of rhinoceroses but resembled reptiles. British anatomist Richard Owen coined the term "Dinosauria," meaning "terrible lizards." In museums, curators arranged fossils into typical reptilian poses, the front ends spread out and bent at the elbows like lizards, the hind legs together, and the tails dragging behind.

In the 1960s, Yale University paleontologist John Ostrom ssuggested that fossilized dinosaur foot bones more closely resembled feet of an agile, predatory bird than a plodding lizard. Ostrom's work sent Bakker in search of additional evidence among fossils, and Bakker's controversial view of the dinosaur helped send Horner to the ancient coastal plain of Montana, and the tribute to the dinosaurian way of life revealed at Egg Mountain.

The Cenozoic Era

At the start of the **Cenozoic era** 65 million years ago, a great variety of hoofed mammals grazed upon the grassy Americas. Many were **marsupials** (pouched mammals) or egg-laying **monotremes,** ancestors of the platypus. Both marsupials and monotremes were more prevalent than they are today. Young marsupials and monotremes were quite helpless. The tiny, hairless, and blind offspring of marsupials, for example, crawled from the mother's reproductive tract along her fur to her chest, where they drank from tiny nipples leading to sweat glands modified to secrete milk.

Gradually a new type of mammal evolved whose young were better protected and therefore more likely to survive, reproduce, and perpetuate their species. These newcomers were the **placental mammals.** The young remain within the female's body for a relatively long time, where they are nurtured by a specialized organ, the placenta. Placental mammals have well-developed mammary glands.

The placental mammals eventually replaced most of the marsupials in North America. Changing geography had much to do with their invasion of South America. Until 2 to 3 million years ago, South America was an island continent. Throughout the Tertiary period, several orders of large marsupials thrived there because the placental mammals, which had originated in North America, could not reach the enormous southern island. (Today placental mammals brought to Australia by human settlers threaten several marsupial species.)

Then about 2 to 3 million years ago, the Bering land bridge rose, connecting Asia to North America, and many mammals, including our ancestors, probably journeyed from what is now the Soviet Union to Alaska and southward through what is now Canada and the continental United States. The isthmus of Panama formed, providing a passageway for the placental mammals of the north to invade the marsupial communities of the south. The first animals to arrive, rodents and ground sloths, crossed when the land bridge was only a string of islands. The overwhelming majority of South American marsupials (23 of 25 orders) were driven to extinction by the arrival of the placental mammals, who successfully competed for the

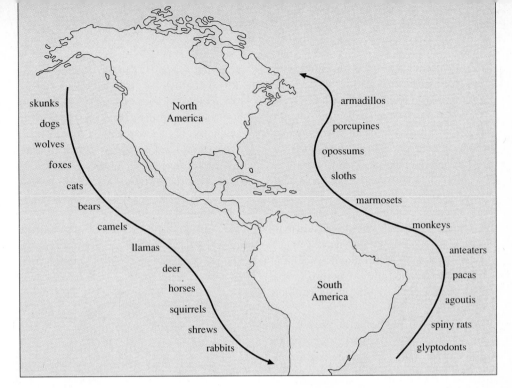

Figure 35.17

Geographical changes alter species distributions. About 3 million years ago, the appearance of the Panama land bridge between the separate continents of North and South America provided a route for the migration of animals between the two huge landmasses. Many species wandered in both directions. The southward invasion of placental mammals drove to extinction many marsupial species living in the former island continent.

same resources. Many of the species found in South America today, including peccaries, llamas, alpacas, deer, tapirs, and jaguars, are descendants of immigrants from the north. A few species, including the opossum, armadillo, and porcupine, traveled in the opposite direction (fig. 35.17).

KEY CONCEPTS

The Cenozoic era has been dominated by mammals, first by marsupials and monotremes and then by placental mammals. Migrations as land bridges formed altered the geographical distribution of species and led to extinctions as arriving species outcompeted resident ones.

The Evolution of Humans

Our species, *Homo sapiens* (the wise human), probably first appeared during the Pleistocene epoch, about 200,000 years ago. Our ancestry reaches farther back within the order Primates, to the early Tertiary period, about 60 million years ago. The ancestral primates were rodentlike insectivores. Like many mammals, these first primates underwent extensive adaptive radiation. Their ability to grasp and to perceive depth provided the flexibility and coordination needed to dominate the treetops.

About 30 to 40 million years ago, a monkeylike animal about the size of a cat, *Aegyptopithecus*, dwelled in the lush tropical forests of Africa. Although most of the animal's time was probably spent in the trees, fossilized remains of limb bones indicate that it could run on the ground as well. Fossils of different individuals have been found together, indicating that they were social animals. *Aegyptopithecus* had fangs that might have been used for defense, and the large canine teeth seen only in males suggest that males might have provided food for their smaller female mates. *Propliopithecus* was a monkeylike contemporary of *Aegyptopithecus*. Both animals are possible ancestors of gibbons, apes, and humans.

About 20 to 30 million years ago, Africa was inhabited by the first **hominoids,** animals ancestral to only apes and humans. This primate was called *Dryopithecus*, meaning "oak ape," because fossilized bones were found with oak leaves (fig. 35.18). The way that the bones fit together suggests that this animal lived in the trees but could swing and walk farther than *Aegyptopithecus*. Because of the large primate population in the forests, selective pressure to venture onto the grasslands must have been intense. Many primate species probably vanished as the protective forests shrank.

By 15 million years ago, an apelike animal, *Ramapithecus*, had evolved in Africa. Fossilized jawbones and teeth are remarkably humanlike. The small canine teeth and massive molars suggest that *Ramapithecus* ate hard nuts and seeds. The animal lived in the treetops but traveled and ate on the ground. *Ramapithecus* became extinct about 7 million years ago.

Hominoid and **hominid** (ancestral to humans only) fossils from 4 to 8 million years ago are scarce. This is thought to be the time when the stooped, large-brained ape gradually became the upright, smaller-brained ape-human. By 4 million years ago, an animal known as *Australopithecus* had ventured forth from the treetops of the shrinking African forests to walk on his knuckles and use tools. The angle of preserved pelvic bones, plus the fact that *Australopithecus* fossils have been found with those of animals that grazed, indicate that this ape-human had left the forest. *Australopithecus* stood about 4 or 5 feet (1.2 to 1.5 meters) tall and had a brain about the size of a gorilla's but teeth that were very much like those of humans (fig. 35.19*a*).

Four species of *Australopithecus* existed by 3.6 million years ago, and paleontologists are still not certain how they are related to one another. A form called *A. afarensis*, represented by the famous fossil "Lucy" (fig. 35.19*b*), may have been our direct ancestor. Her skull was shaped more like that of a human, with a less prominent face and larger brain than her predecessors. These animals probably lived a hunter-gatherer life-style during the Pleistocene ice age.

By 2 million years ago, *Australopithecus* coexisted with *Homo habilis*, a more human-like primate who lived communally in caves and cared for young intensely. "Habilis" means handy, and this primate is the first for whom we have evidence of extensive tool use. *H. habilis* may have descended from a group of *Australopithecines*, who ate a greater variety of foods than other ape-humans, allowing them to adapt to a wider range of habitats.

H. habilis coexisted with and was followed by *H. erectus*, who left fossil evidence of cooperation, social organization, and tool use, including the use of fire. Fossilized teeth and jaws of *H. erectus* suggest that he was a meat eater. The fossils are widespread, found in China, tropical Africa, and southeast Asia, indicating that these animals could migrate farther than earlier primates. The distribution of fossils suggests that *H. erectus* lived in families of male-female pairs (most primates have harems). The male hunted and the female nurtured young for long times.

H. erectus lived from the end of the Australopithecine reign some 1.6 million years ago to as recently as 200,000 years ago and probably coexisted for a time with the very first of our own species. Some paleontologists believe that a species intermediate between *H. erectus* and *H. sapiens*, with a big brain and robust build, lived from 50,000 to 30,000 years ago. Several pockets of ancient peoples may have been dispersed throughout the world at this time. Such fossils have been found in Swanscombe, England, Steinheim, Germany, and sites in the Middle East.

a.

b.

c.

d.

Figure 35.18
Some forerunners of humans. *a.* The "oak ape" *Dryopithecus* lived from 20 to 30 million years ago and was more dextrous than his predecessors. *b.* Four species of *Australopithecus* lived from 2 to 4 million years ago. These hominids walked upright on the plains. *c.* *Homo erectus* made tools out of bone and stone, used fire, and dwelled communally in caves from 1.6 million to 200,000 years ago. *d.* The Neanderthals were a rugged group of *Homo sapiens* who valued family life and religious ritual.

About 75,000 years ago, Europe and Asia were home to the **Neanderthals,** members of *Homo sapiens*. A fossilized crippled skeleton buried with flowers in Shanidar Cave in Iraq reveals that the Neanderthals may have been religious hunter-gatherers clever enough (or lucky enough) to have survived a brutal ice age. The Neanderthals had once been thought to be hunched brutes because the first fossil was from an individual stooped from arthritis. So closely related are the Neanderthals to us that some of them may have been physically indistinguishable from ourselves.

The Neanderthals mysteriously vanished about 40,000 years ago, just as the lighter-weight, finer-boned, and less hairy **Cro-Magnons,** known for their intricate cave art, appeared. The Cro-Magnons may have arisen from a small group of individuals who happened, perhaps by chance mutations, to have high foreheads over well-developed frontal brain regions. It was this group that ultimately flourished and led, over the millennia, to our own kind. The first fossils of modern humans date from about 40,000 years ago.

Telling the story of life has traditionally depended upon the scattered and woefully inadequate clues in rocks. With the new views being offered by physical dating techniques and molecular measurements, scientists will be increasingly able to fill in more of the missing pages of natural history. We will learn more about where we came from, as well as what other organisms have dwelled on this planet in ages past. But perhaps the most compelling questions lie ahead—where will the course of evolution take life on earth in the future?

a.   b.

Figure 35.19

Fossils of two *Australopithecines*—the Taung child and Lucy. In 1925 Australian anatomist Raymond Dart discovered the remarkably well-preserved skull of an ancient child in an outcropping of limestone in the South African village of Taung. The fossil was about 2 million years old; the child it came from was about 6 years old when she died. The skull had several humanlike characteristics—lack of brow ridges, an upright vertebral column suggesting the child may have walked erect, and teeth shaped like our own. However, in 1987 researchers at the Washington University in St. Louis used a CT scan (a multidirectional X-ray) on the skull, which revealed the order in which the different teeth had erupted from the jaw. The dental pattern was more like that of apes than humans. Tooth eruption is an important clue to evolutionary relationships because the slower the teeth appear, the longer the period of infancy. Humans have much longer infancies than apes, and many anthropologists attribute our intelligence to this longer nurturing period. The conclusion about the Taung child? Like many early hominids, she is a little of both—ape and human. *b.* About 3.6 million years ago, a small-brained ancestor of the human walked upright in the grasses along a lake in the Afar region of Ethiopia. She skimmed the shores for crabs, turtles, and crocodile eggs to eat. She died at the age of 20, with severe arthritis in the backbone. Nearly 40% of her skeleton was discovered in 1974, and she was named "Lucy," from the Beatles song "Lucy in the Sky with Diamonds," which Donald Johanson of the Cleveland Museum of Natural History and Timothy White of the University of California at Berkeley were listening to when they found her.

KEY CONCEPTS

Aegyptopithecus lived about 30 to 40 million years ago and was a monkeylike animal ancestral to gibbons, apes, and humans. The first hominoid, Dryopithecus, dwelled 20 to 30 million years ago and may have walked onto grasslands. Ramapithecus lived 15 million years ago and had humanlike teeth and jaws. He lived in the trees but ate on the ground. Australopithecus lived about 4 million years ago, walked on his knuckles, and used tools. By 2 million years ago, Australopithecus coexisted with Homo habilis, who was more humanlike in appearance and social structure. Later on, H. Habilis coexisted with H. erectus, who used tools more extensively and was more social. H. sapiens coexisted with or arose from H. erectus about 75,000 years ago. The Neanderthals preceded the Cro-Magnons, and, about 40,000 years ago, modern humans appeared.

SUMMARY

Evidence for evolution comes directly from extinct organisms and from observation of similarities among modern species. A *fossil* may be once-living matter that has been replaced by mineral, formed gradually or after a sudden catastrophe, or indirect evidence such as footprints. Rarely, actual remains are preserved in ice. Microscopes reveal cellular details in fossils. The rock layer in which a fossil is found provides a *relative date*. The proportion of a stable radioactive isotope to its breakdown product and calculating from this how many *half-lives* have passed provides an *absolute date*. Potassium 40 is used to date fossils older than 300,000 years, and carbon 14 dating is used on fossils younger than 40,000 years. New dating techniques are being developed. The fossil record is incomplete. Geographical upheavals destroy much evidence, and some species existed for too short a time or in too restricted an area to leave many fossils.

Homologous structures are similar in architecture and function in two species because they are inherited from a common ancestor.

Analogous structures reflect a common response by unrelated species to the same environmental challenge. *Vestigial* organs and similar prenatal structures may reflect genes retained from an ancestor.

Techniques of *molecular evolution* include comparing chromosome band patterns, protein, and gene sequences. Each of these consists of many bits of information, and it is far more likely that two species are alike by common descent than by chance.

The *geological time scale* charts earth history, divided into eras, periods, and epochs. According to the fossil record, life debuted in *Precambrian* time and exploded in diversity in the *Cambrian period,* about 600 million years ago. The *Paleozoic* oceans were home to diverse algae, invertebrates, and fishes. Plants appeared on land during the *Ordovician* and *Silurian* periods, and the lobe-finned fishes, forerunners of amphibians, conquered the land for parts of

their life cycles during the *Devonian* period. By the *Carboniferous* period, the land was lush with conifers and fernlike plants, many now extinct. Terrestrial animal life was still scarce. The evolution of the amniote egg allowed animals to live on land for the entire life cycle. By the *Permian* period, the first reptiles had appeared.

The *Mesozoic era* was the age of reptiles. *Cotylosaurs* gave rise to dinosaurs, modern reptiles, and *therapsids,* forerunners of mammals. The dinosaurs radiated during the *Triassic* and *Jurassic* periods, then began to decline in numbers during the *Cretaceous* period, when flowering plants flourished. The mass extinctions of dinosaurs at the end of the Cretaceous period, about 65 million years ago, opened up many habitats for mammals, which flourished during the *Tertiary period* of the *Cenozoic era.* South America was then home to many marsupial species that were driven to extinction

when the isthmus of Panama formed, which allowed the placental mammals of the north to invade the south.

The first primate ancestral to humans, an insectivore, lived about 60 million years ago in Africa. By 40 million years ago, *Aegyptopithecus* had evolved, a monkeylike social animal. By 30 million years ago, the *hominoid Dryopithecus* had appeared. *Ramapithecus* fossils date from 15 million years ago. This apelike animal had humanlike teeth and jaws. *Australopithecus,* the first *hominid,* lived from about 4 million to 2 million years ago. *Homo habilis* coexisted with *Australopithecus.* Later, *Homo erectus* displayed a more complex social structure. Between 500,000 and 75,000 years ago, the first *Homo sapiens* appeared. Groups of early humans included the *Neanderthals* and *Cro-Magnons.* Fossils of modern humans date from about 40,000 years ago.

QUESTIONS

1. Why are a preserved dinosaur bone, a ripple in a rock made by an ancient worm's movements, limestone built from the shells of crustaceans, and insects preserved in amber all fossils?

2. Why don't we have evidence of all extinct forms of life?

3. What type of absolute dating would be useful in dating a fossil of a lobe-finned fish?

4. An elephant uses its trunk to bring food to its mouth; a human uses his hand to do this. Are an elephant's trunk and a human's hand analogous or homologous structures?

TO THINK ABOUT

1. Cytochrome C is a protein that is very similar in all species. Twenty of its 104 amino acids are identical in all eukaryotes. How does the fact that differences among these 20 amino acids are not seen demonstrate that natural selection is operating at the molecular level?

2. What information in this chapter supports the idea, expressed in chapter 1, that the scientific method is a cycle of inquiry?

3. What assumptions underlie the following:
  a. Relative dating by placement in rock strata
  b. Absolute dating by radiometric data
  c. The mitochondrial clock

4. Fossils of horn corals, brachiopods, and trilobites are abundant in Ohio. How can fossils of sea life be found in the middle of a continent?

5. What may have happened in human evolution between 4 and 8 million years ago?

6. How were the development of the following structures or abilities adaptive, and how did they affect evolution?
  a. Strong, fleshy fins in the lobe-finned fish
  b. The amniote egg
  c. The placenta
  d. The ability of primates to walk on the ground

7. What environmental conditions of today might preserve organisms to form the fossils of tomorrow?

SUGGESTED READINGS

Cohn, Jeffrey P. March 1990. Genetics for wildlife conservation. *BioScience.* Molecular techniques reveal the likely lineage of the giant panda.

Gibbons, Ann. February 22, 1991. Systematics goes molecular. *Science,* vol. 251. Molecular analysis is increasingly used to study evolution.

Gould, Stephen Jay. 1989. *Wonderful life.* New York: W.W. Norton. The Burgess shale reveals a slice of Cambrian life.

Horner, John R., and David B. Weishampel. December 1989. Dinosaur eggs: The inside story. *Natural History.* Were dinosaurs birdlike, caring parents?

Johanson, Donald, and James Shreeve. 1989. *Lucy's child.* New York: William Morrow. How paleontologists pieced together our beginnings from scattered 2-million-year-old preserved bones.

Lewis, Ricki. April 1991. An intron in cyanobacteria stirs evolutionary debate. *The Journal of NIH Research.* Clues in modern gene sequences suggest a world based on RNA led to life.

Marshall, Eliot. February 16, 1990. Paleoanthropology gets physical. *Science,* vol. 247. Three new methods may help assign dates to fossils.

Monastersky, Richard. September 22, 1990. Swamped by climate change? *Science News.* The earth was covered in wetlands 315 million years ago.

Palca, Joseph. September 7, 1990. The human genome. *Science,* vol. 249. Mitochondrial genes may hold clues to human disease and origins.

Stolzenberg, William. August 25, 1990. When life got hard. *Science News.* Diverse exoskeletons evolved rapidly in the Cambrian period.

Appendix A
Microscopy

As the study of life has progressed steadily from observing organisms to probing the molecules of life, the technology to view living things has grown accordingly. Today's biologist has a range of microscope types to choose from, and the instrument used depends upon the nature of the biological material being observed (table 1). An *ultraviolet microscope* might be used to highlight stained chromosomes; a *polarizing microscope* to focus in on protein arrays of a cytoskeleton; a *phase contrast microscope* to view cells while they are still alive. A *scanning electron microscope* reveals the topography of cell and organelle surfaces. A *confocal microscope* presents startlingly clear peeks at biological structures in action, and a *scanning probe microscope* reveals surfaces of individual atoms.

All microscopes provide two types of power—*magnification* and *resolution* (also called resolving power). A microscope produces an enlarged, or magnified, image of an object. Magnification is defined as the ratio between the image size and the object size. Resolution refers to the smallest degree of separation at which two objects are viewed as distinct from one another, rather than as a blurry, single image. Resolution is important in distinguishing structures from one another. A *compound microscope* commonly used in college biology teaching laboratories can resolve objects that are 0.1 to 0.2 micrometers (4 to 8 millionths of an inch) apart. The resolving power of an electron microscope is 10,000 times greater than this.

Table 1
Compound Microscopes

Method	Basis	Advantages	Disadvantages
Phase contrast microscopy	Converts differences in the velocity of light through different parts of specimen into observable contrasts	Can be used on live cells	Not all subcellular structures are visible; halos seen around structures
Interference microscopy	Two beams of light hit specimen and join in image plane	No halos on structures; fine detail	Cumbersome to use; expensive
Differential-interference (Nomarski-optics) microscopy	Detects localized differences in velocities at which light passes through specimen	Fine transparent detail visible	
Polarizing microscopy	Ray of plane-polarized (i.e., unidirectional) light hits specimen, splits into two directions, at two different velocities, creating image of ordered molecular detail	Highlights detail at molecular level	Works best on highly oriented, crystalline or fibrous structures
Fluorescence microscopy	Light of one wavelength is selectively absorbed by certain molecules that reemit light of a longer wavelength		Only creates image of structures that absorb the wavelength of light used
Ultraviolet (uv) microscopy	Ultraviolet light used with lens made of quartz	High resolving power; excellent for viewing proteins and nucleic acids	

The Light Microscope

The compound light microscope focuses visible light through a specimen. Different regions of the object scatter the light differently, producing an image. In modern microscopes, three sets of lenses contribute to the generation of an image (fig. 1). The *condenser lens* focuses light through the specimen. The *objective lens* receives light that has passed through the specimen, generating an enlarged image. The *ocular lens*, or eyepiece, magnifies the image further. Total magnification is calculated by multiplying the magnification of the objective lens by that of the ocular lens. The coarse and fine adjustment knobs are manipulated to bring the magnified image into sharp focus. The mirror directs the light into the condenser lens, and the *diaphragm* controls the amount of light to which the specimen is exposed.

A limitation of a light microscope is that only one two-dimensional plane of the specimen can be observed at a time. Thus, when a light microscope is focused on the top of a specimen, different structures are visible than when it is focused at a deeper level. It can be difficult to envision the three-dimensional nature of the specimen from the two-dimensional views afforded by the light microscope. The problem is like focusing on particular parts of a scene with a camera. If the photographer focuses on his children in the foreground of a shot, he may miss entirely the antics of a cat and mouse that are several feet behind the children. Similarly, light microscope views at different depths within a cell can reveal different structures.

Electron Microscopes

Electron microscopes provide greater magnification, better resolution, and a better sense of depth than light microscopes. Instead of visible light, the *transmission electron microscope* (TEM) sends a beam of electrons through the specimen, using a magnetic field to focus the beam rather than a glass lens (fig. 2). Different parts of the specimen absorb different numbers of

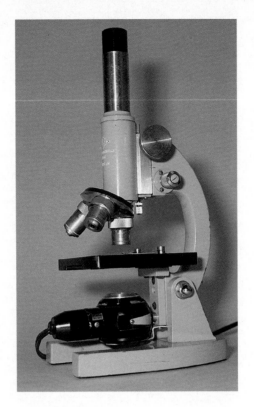

Figure 1
Light Microscope

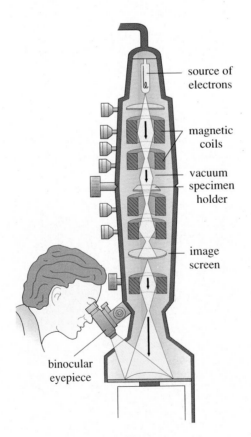

source of electrons

magnetic coils

vacuum specimen holder

image screen

binocular eyepiece

Figure 2
Electron Microscope

electrons. These contrasts are rendered visible to the human eye by a fluorescent screen coated with a chemical that gives off visible light rays when excited by electrons from the specimen.

Although the TEM has provided some spectacular glimpses into the microscopic structures of life, it does have limitations. For the TEM, the specimen must be killed, treated with chemicals, cut into very thin sections, and placed in a vacuum. This treatment can distort natural structures. A close cousin of the TEM eliminates these drawbacks. The *scanning electron microscope* (SEM) bounces electrons off of a three-dimensional specimen, generating a three-dimensional image on a device similar to a television screen. The resulting depth of field highlights crevices and textures. Although many SEM specimens are coated with a heavy metal to highlight their surfaces, some specimens (such as fruit flies) can be examined while alive, with no apparent harm.

A variation of the electron microscope is the *photoelectron microscope* (PEM), originally used to probe metal surfaces but now used to examine cells as well. The PEM bombards a specimen with ultraviolet light, ejecting the valence shell electrons of molecules on a cell or organelle surface. These electrons are accelerated and focused by an electron lens system. The excited electrons are quite sensitive to the surface detail of the specimen, and their deflection pattern provides a high-resolution view of minute surface details. The PEM is especially useful to zero in on specific molecules that have been labeled with fluorescent antibodies. PEM is an electron-based version of fluorescence microscopy.

While the SEM highlights large surface features, the PEM provides a closer look. It is like comparing a topographic map of a mountain (SEM) to a picture of a bump in the terrain of the mountain (PEM). A light microscope and all three electron microscopes can be used in conjunction to paint a detailed portrait of biological structures, which can clarify functions at the organelle or even the molecular level.

The Confocal Microscope

A limitation of light microscopy is that light reflected from regions of the sample near the object of interest interferes with the image, making it blurry or hazy. A *confocal microscope* avoids interference and enhances resolution by passing white or laser light through a pinhole and a lens to the object (fig. 3). The light is then reflected through a beam splitter and then through another pinhole, a detector, and finally a photomultiplier. The result is a scan of highly focused light on one tiny part of the specimen at a time, usually an area 0.25 µm in diameter and 0.5 µm deep. The microscope is called "confocal" because the objective and the condenser lenses are both focused on the same small area.

The idea of a confocal microscope was patented by Marvin Minsky in 1961, but it was not developed until the mid 1980s, when computers enabled many scans of different sites and at different depths to be integrated and translated into a dynamic image. By using fluorescent dyes that label specific cell parts and are activated by the incoming light, different structures can be distinguished. The first division of a fertilized sea urchin egg, for example, can be captured: the spindle fibers appear green, and the chromosomes being pulled in opposite directions are a vibrant blue. Confocal microscopy has also revealed changing concentrations of calcium ions in a neuron receiving a biochemical message; the cytoskeleton in action; platelets aggregating at the scene of an injury to form a clot; sperm fertilizing an ovum; and nerve cells infiltrating the developing brain of an embryo. When teamed with a tool borrowed from the physical sciences called Raman spectroscopy, confocal microscopy reveals details of chromosome structure, and can distinguish between the chemical bonds of a protein or nucleic acid.

Scanning Probe Microscopes

The world of microscopy was again revolutionized in 1981, with the invention of the *scanning tunneling microscope* (STM) by Gerd K. Binnig and Heinrich Rohrer. This device reveals detail at the atomic level. A very

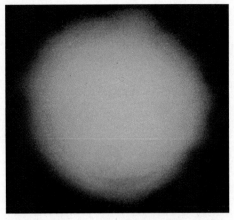

a.

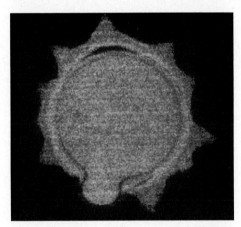

b.

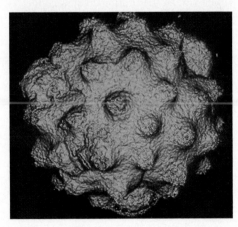

c.

Figure 3

a. Sea urchin embryo at first division stained with fluorescently labeled anti-tubulin antibody, taken with a conventional fluorescence microscope. *b.* Sea urchin embryo at first division stained with fluorescently labeled anti-tubulin antibody, taken with a confocal laser scanning microscope. *c.* Sea urchin embryo at first division, double stained to show tubulin in green and DNA in blue, taken with a tandem-scanning microscope.

sharp metal needle, its tip as small as an atom, is scanned over a molecule's surface. Electrons "tunnel" across the space between the sample and the needle, thereby creating an electrical current. The closer the needle, the greater the current. An image is generated as the scanner continually adjusts the space between needle and sample, keeping the current constant over the topography of the molecular surface. The needle's movements over the microscopic hills and valleys are expressed as contour lines, which in turn are converted and enhanced by computer into a colored image of the surface.

Electrons do not pass readily from many biological samples, limiting use of STM. However, the same principle of adjusting a probe over a changing surface is used in *scanning ion-conductance microscopy* (SICM), developed by Paul K. Hansma and Calvin Quate. It uses ions instead of electrons—useful in the many biological situations where ions travel between cells. The probe is made of hollow glass filled with a conductive salt solution, which is also applied to the sample. When voltage is passed through the sample and the probe, ions flow to the probe. The rate of ion flow is kept constant, and a portrait is painted by the compensatory movements of the probe. SICM is useful in studying cell membrane surfaces and muscle and nerve function.

Another type of scanning probe microscope, the *atomic force microscope* (AFM), was developed in 1986 by the inventors of the SICM. It uses a diamond-tipped probe that resembles the stylus on a phonograph but that presses a molecule's surface with a force millions of times gentler. As the force is kept constant, the probe moves, generating an image. AFM is especially useful for recording molecular movements, such as those involved in blood clotting and cell division.

New and improved microscopes do not always replace existing models but complement the information that they provide. Many researchers today create their own versions of microscopes to suit their particular experiments. All modern microscopes though, some of them quite technologically sophisticated, support the cell theory advanced by the early microscopists, who had only very crude light microscopes with which to work.

Appendix B
Units of Measurement Metric/English Conversions

Length

1 meter = 39.4 inches = 3.28 feet
= 1.09 yard
1 foot = 0.305 meters = 12 inches
= 0.33 yard
1 inch = 2.54 centimeters
1 centimeter = 10 millimeter = 0.394 inch
1 millimeter = 0.001 meter = 0.01
centimeter = 0.039 inch
1 kilometer = 1,000 meters = 0.621 miles
= 0.54 nautical miles
1 mile = 5,280 feet = 1.61 kilometers
1 nautical mile = 1.15 mile

Area

1 square centimeter = 0.155 square inch
1 square foot = 144 square inches = 929
square centimeters
1 square yard = 9 square feet = 0.836
square meters
1 square meter = 10.76 square feet = 1.196
square yards = 1 million square
millimeters
1 hectare = 10,000 square meters = 0.01
square kilometers = 2.47 acres

1 acre = 43,560 square feet = 0.405
hectares
1 square kilometer = 100 hectares = 1
million square meters = 0.386 square
miles = 247 acres
1 square mile = 640 acres = 2.59 square
kilometers

Volume

1 cubic centimeter = 1 milliliter = 0.001
liter
1 cubic meter = 1 million cubic centimeters = 1,000 liters
1 cubic meter = 35.3 cubic feet = 1.307
cubic yards = 264 U.S. gallons
1 cubic yard = 27 cubic feet = 0.765 cubic
meters = 202 U.S. gallons
1 cubic kilometer = 1 million cubic meters
= 0.24 cubic mile = 264 billion gallons
1 cubic mile = 4.166 cubic kilometers
1 liter = 1,000 milliliters = 1.06 quarts =
0.265 U.S. gallons = 0.035 cubic feet
1 U.S. gallon = 4 quarts = 3.79 liters = 231
cubic inches
1 quart = 2 pints = 4 cups = 0.94 liters

Mass

1 microgram = 0.001 milligram = 0.000001
gram
1 gram = 1,000 milligrams = 0.035 ounce
1 kilogram = 1,000 grams = 2.205 pound
1 pound = 16 ounces = 454 grams
1 short ton = 2,000 pounds = 909 kilograms
1 metric ton = 1,000 kilograms = 2,200
pounds

Temperature

Celsius to Fahrenheit $°F = (°C \times 1.8) + 32$
Fahrenheit to Celsius $°C = (°F − 32) ÷ 1.8$

Energy and Power

1 kilocalorie = 1,000 calories

Appendix C
Metric Conversion

	Metric Quantities	Metric to English Conversion	English to Metric Conversion
Length	1 kilometer (km) = 1,000 (10^3) meters 1 meter (m) = 100 centimeters 1 centimeter (cm) = 0.01 (10^{-2}) meter 1 millimeter (mm) = 0.001 (10^{-3}) meter 1 micrometer* (μm) = 0.000001 (10^{-6}) meter 1 nanometer (nm) = 0.000000001 (10^{-9}) meter *formerly called micron	1 km = 0.62 mile 1 m = 1.09 yards = 39.37 inches 1 cm = 0.394 inch 1 mm = 0.039 inch	1 mile = 1.609 km 1 yard = 0.914 m 1 foot = 0.305 m = 30.5 cm 1 inch = 2.54 cm
Area	1 square kilometer (km^2) = 100 hectares 1 hectare (ha) = 10,000 square meters 1 square meter (m^2) = 10,000 square centimeters 1 square centimeter (cm^2) = 100 square millimeters	1 km^2 = 0.3861 square mile 1 ha = 2.471 acres 1 m^2 = 1.1960 square yards = 10.764 square feet 1 cm^2 = 0.155 square inch	1 square mile = 2.590 km^2 1 acre = 0.4047 ha 1 square yard = 0.8361 m^2 1 square foot = 0.0929 m^2 1 square inch = 6.4516 cm^2
Mass	1 metric ton (t) = 1,000 kilograms 1 metric ton (t) = 1,000,000 grams 1 kilogram (kg) = 1,000 grams 1 gram (g) = 1,000 milligrams 1 milligram (mg) = 0.001 gram 1 microgram (μg) = 0.000001 gram	1 t = 1.1025 ton (U.S.) 1 kg = 2.205 pounds 1 g = 0.0353 ounce	1 ton (U.S.) = 0.907 t 1 pound = 0.4536 kg 1 ounce = 28.35 g
Volume (solids)	1 cubic meter (m^3) = 1,000,000 cubic centimeters 1 cubic centimeter (cm^3) = 1,000 cubic millimeters	1 m^3 = 1.3080 cubic yards = 35.315 cubic feet 1 cm^3 = 0.0610 cubic inch	1 cubic yard = 0.7646 m^3 1 cubic foot = 0.0283 m^3 1 cubic inch = 16.387 cm^3
Volume (liquids)	1 liter (l) = 1,000 milliliters 1 milliliter (ml) = 0.001 liter 1 microliter (μl) = 0.000001 liter	1 l = 1.06 quarts (U.S.) 1 ml = 0.034 fluid ounce	1 quart (U.S.) = 0.94 l 1 pint (U.S.) = 0.47 l 1 fluid ounce = 29.57 ml
Time	1 second (sec) = 1,000 milliseconds 1 millisecond (msec) = 0.001 second 1 microsecond (μsec) = 0.000001 second		

Appendix D
Taxonomy

The millions of living and extinct species that have dwelled on earth can be grouped according to many schemes. Taxonomists group organisms to reflect both anatomical similarities and descent from a common ancestor. Two, three, four, five, and most recently, six kingdom classifications have been proposed. The five-kingdom scheme is outlined here with all phyla described briefly. Short statements explaining the rationale behind groupings of phyla are given wherever possible, and indented subheadings reflect these groupings. Scientific names are followed by more familiar names of organisms. Figures from the text accompany the listing to help you visualize and recall the wide diversity of life forms discussed in chapter 2.

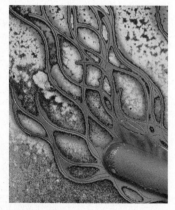

Salmonella

Stromatolites

Kingdom Monera The monerans are unicellular prokaryotes that obtain nutrients by direct absorption or by photosynthesis or chemosynthesis. Most monerans reproduce asexually, but some can exchange genetic material in a primitive form of sexual reproduction. (The six-kingdom classification system divides the monerans into two kingdoms, whose members are distinguished by genetic differences and by whether or not they produce methane as a metabolic by-product. The methane-producing bacteria are thought to be the most primitive organisms, having evolved before the atmosphere contained oxygen.)

Phylum Schizophyta   The bacteria.

Phylum Cyanobacteria   Photosynthetic bacteria, formerly called blue-green algae.

Kingdom Protista Protists are the structurally simplest eukaryotes, and they can be unicellular or multicellular. They can absorb or ingest nutrients or photosynthesize. Reproduction is asexual or sexual. Some forms move by ciliary or flagellar motion, and others are nonmotile. The protists' early development differs from that of the fungi, plants, and animals. The kingdom includes the protozoans, algae, and the water molds and slime molds.

Protozoans   Unicellular, nonphotosynthetic, lack cell walls.

   Phylum Sarcomastigophora   Locomote by flagella and/or pseudopoda and includes the familiar *Amoeba proteus*.

   Phylum Labyrinthomorpha   Aquatic, live on algae.

   Phylum Apicomplexa   Parasitic, with characteristic twisted structure on anterior end at some point in life cycle.

   Phylum Myxozoa   Parasitic on fish and invertebrates.

   Phylum Microspora   Parasitic on invertebrates and primitive vertebrates.

   Phylum Ciliophora   Cilia present at some stage of the life cycle.

Algae   Unicellular or multicellular, photosynthetic, some have cell walls. Distinguished by pigments.

   Phylum Euglenophyta   Unicellular and photosynthetic, with a single flagellum and contractile vacuole.

   Phylum Chrysophyta   Diatoms, golden-brown algae, and yellow-green algae. Unicellular and photosynthetic.

   Phylum Pyrrophyta   Dinoflagellates. Unicellular and photosynthetic.

   Phylum Chlorophyta   Green algae. Unicellular or multicellular, photosynthetic.

   Phylum Phaeophyta   Brown algae (kelps). Multicellular and photosynthetic.

   Phylum Rhodophyta   Red algae. Multicellular and photosynthetic.

Water and Slime Molds

   Phylum Oomycota   The water molds. Unicellular or multi-nucleate, with cellulose cell walls. Live in fresh water.

   Phylum Chytridiomycota   The chytrids. Multicellular, with chitinous cell walls. Aquatic.

   Phylum Myxomycota   Multinucleated, "acellular" slime molds.

   Phylum Acrasiomycota   Multicellular "cellular" slime molds.

Morel mushroom

Fossel ferns

Hydra

Kingdom Fungi   With the exception of the yeasts, fungi are multicellular eukaryotes that decompose organisms to obtain nourishment. Chitinous cell walls. Phyla are distinguished by mode of reproduction.

Phylum Zygomycota   Reproduce with sexual resting spores.

Phylum Ascomycota   Yeasts, morels, truffles, molds, lichens. Reproduce with sexual spores carried in asci. Some ascomycetes cause food spoilage and some plant diseases; others are used in the production of certain foods, beverages, and antibiotic drugs.

Phylum Basidiomycota   Mushrooms, toadstools, puffballs, stinkhorns, shelf fungi, rusts, and smuts. Reproduce by spore-containing basidia.

Kingdom Plantae   Plants are multicellular, land dwelling, photosynthetic, and reproduce both asexually and sexually in an alternation of generations. Cellulose cell walls. Plants have specialized tissues and organs but lack nervous and muscular systems.

Nonvascular Plants (Bryophytes)   Lack specialized conducting tissues and true roots, stems, and leaves. The gamete-producing reproductive phase predominates.

Division Bryophyta   Liverworts, hornworts, mosses.

Vascular Plants (Tracheophytes)   Xylem and phloem transport water and nutrients, respectively, throughout the plant body of roots, stems, and leaves. The spore-producing reproductive phase predominates.

Primitive Plants   Sperm cells travel in water to meet egg cells.

Division Pterophyta   Ferns.

Division Psilophyta   Whisk ferns.

Division Lycophyta   Club mosses and others.

Division Spenophyta   Horsetails.

Seed Plants   Sperm cells and egg cells enclosed in protective structures.

Gymnosperms (naked seed plants)   Male and female cones produce pollen grains and ovules.

Division Coniferophyta   Conifers.

Division Cycadophyta   Cycads.

Division Ginkgophyta   Ginkgos.

Division Gnetophyta   Gnetophytes.

Angiosperms (seeds in a vessel)   The flowering plants.

Division Anthophyta   Flowering plants.

Kingdom Animalia   The animals are multicellular with specialized tissues and organs, including nervous and locomotive systems. No cell walls. Animals obtain nutrients from food. Phyla are distinguished largely on the basis of body form and symmetry, characteristics that are generally established in the early embryo.

Mesozoa   Simplest animals.

Phylum Mesozoa   Very simple, wormlike parasites of marine invertebrates. Consist of only 20 to 30 cells.

Parazoa   A separate branch from the evolution of protozoa to metazoa.

Phylum Placozoa   A single species, *Trichoplax adhaerens*, characterized by two cell layers with fluid in between them.

Phylum Porifera   The sponges. Specialized cell types organized into canal system to transport nutrients in and wastes out.

Eumetazoa   Animal phyla descended from protozoa.

Radiata   Radially symmetric body plan. Sedentary, saclike bodies with two or three cell layers and a diffuse nerve net.

Phylum Cnidaria   Hydroids, sea anemones, jellyfish, horny corals, hard corals.

Phylum Ctenophora   Sea walnuts, comb jellies.

Bilateria   Bilaterally symmetric body plan.

Protostomia (first mouth)   Embryonic characteristics:

1. Mouth forms close to area of initial folding inward in very early embryo.
2. Spiral cleavage: At third cell division, second group of four cells sits atop first group of four cells but rotated by 45°.
3. Determinate cleavage: Cell fates determined very early in development. If a cell from a four-celled embryo is isolated, it will divide and differentiate to form only one-quarter of an embryo.
4. The protostomes are further grouped by the way in which the body cavity (coelom) forms. A true coelom is a body cavity that develops within mesoderm, the middle layer of the embryo.

Acoelomates   No coelom.

Phylum Platyhelminthes   Flatworms.

Phylum Nemertina   Ribbonworms.

Phylum Gnathostomulida   Jawworms.

Pseudocoelomates   Body cavity derived from a space in the embryo between the mesoderm and endoderm. The body cavity is called "pseudo" because it does not form within mesoderm. In the adult, the pseudocoelom is a cavity but it is not lined with mesoderm-derived peritoneum (seen in more advanced forms).

Phylum Rotifera   The rotifers. Small (40μm–3mm), intricately shaped organisms that have a structure on their anterior ends that resembles rotating wheels. The rotifers occupy a variety of habitats.

Octopus   Sea urchin   Boobies and people

Phylum Gastrotricha Aquatic, microscopic, flattened organisms with a scaly outer covering.

Phylum Kinorhyncha Marine worms less than 1 mm long.

Phylum Nematoda Roundworms. Found everywhere, many parasitic.

Phylum Nematomorpha Horsehair worms. Juveniles are parasitic in arthropods; adults are free-living.

Phylum Acanthocephala Spiny-headed worms. Spiny projection from anterior end used to attach to intestine of host vertebrate. Range in size from 2 mm to more than a meter.

Phylum Entoprocta Nonmotile, sessile, mostly marine animals that look like stalks that are anchored to rocks, shells, algae, or vegetation on one end, with a tufted growth on the other.

Eucoelomates Coelom forms in a schizocoelous fashion, in which the body cavity forms when mesodermal cells invade the space between ectoderm and endoderm, and then proliferate so that a cavity forms within the mesoderm.

  Major Eucoelomate Protostomes Three phyla, with many species.

   Phylum Mollusca Snails, clams, oysters, squids, octopuses.

   Phylum Annelida Segmented worms.

   Phylum Arthropoda Spiders, scorpions, ticks, mites, crustaceans, millipedes, centipedes, insects.

  The Lesser Protostomes Seven phyla, including many extinct species. Little-understood offshoots of annelid-arthropod line.

   Phylum Pripulida Bottom-dwelling marine worms.

   Phylum Echiurida Marine worms.

   Phylum Sipunculida Bottom-dwelling marine worms.

   Phylum Tardigrada "Water bears." Less than 1 mm, live in water film on mosses and lichens.

   Phylum Pentastomida Tongue worms. Parasitic on respiratory system of vertebrates, mostly reptiles.

Phylum Onychophora Velvet worms. Live in tropical rain forest and resemble caterpillars, with 14 to 43 pairs of unjointed legs and a velvety skin.

Phylum Pogonophora Beard worms. Live in mud on ocean bottom.

Lophophorates Three phyla distinguished by a ciliary feeding structure called a lophophore.

  Phylum Phoronida Small, wormlike bottom-dwellers of shallow, coastal temperate seas. Live in a tube that they secrete.

  Phylum Ectoprocta Bryozoa, or "moss animals." Aquatic, less than 1/2 mm long, live in colonies but each individual lives within a chamber secreted by the epidermis. Bryozoa look like crust on rocks, shells, and seaweeds.

  Phylum Brachiopoda Lampshells. Attached, bottom-dwelling marine animals that have two shells and resemble mollusks, about 5 to 8 mm long.

Deuterostomia (second mouth) Embryonic characteristics:

1. Mouth forms far from area of initial folding inward in very early embryo.
2. Radial cleavage: At third cell division, second group of four cells sits directly atop first group.
3. Indeterminate cleavage: Cell fates of very early embryo not detmined. If a cell from a four-cell embryo is isolated, it will develop into a complete embryo.
4. Coelom formation is enterocoelous. Body cavity forms from outpouchings of endoderm that become lined with mesoderm.

Phylum Echinodermata Sea stars, brittle stars, sea urchins, sea cucumbers, sea lilies. Radial symmetry in adult but larvae are bilaterally symmetric. Complex organ systems, but no distinct head region.

Phylum Chaetognatha Arrow worms. Marine-dwelling with bristles surrounding mouth.

Phylum Hemichordata Acorn worms and others. Aquatic, bottom-dwelling, nonmotile, wormlike animals.

Phylum Chordata Tunicates, lancelets, hagfishes, lampreys, sharks, bony fishes, amphibians, reptiles, birds, mammals. Chordates have a notochord, dorsal nerve cord, gill slits, and a tail. Some of these characteristics may only be present in embryos.

Glossary

A

abscisic acid *ab-SIS-ik AS-id* A plant hormone that inhibits growth. 588

abscission zone *ab-SCISZ-on ZONE* A region at the base of the petiole from which leaves are shed. 562

abyssal zone *ah-BIS-el ZONE* The part of the bottom of the ocean where light does not reach. 737

acclimation *AK-klah-MA-shun* Changes in a plant in preparation for winter. 599

accommodation *ah-KOM-o-DAY-shun* Changes in the shape of the lens to suit the distance of the object being viewed. 356

acetyl CoA formation *AS-eh-til FOR-MAY-shun* The first step in aerobic respiration, occurring in the mitochondrion. Pyruvic acid loses a carbon dioxide and bonds to coenzyme A to form acetyl CoA. 122

acid *AS-id* A molecule that releases hydrogen ions into water. 46

acquired immune deficiency syndrome (AIDS) *ak-KWY-erd im-MUNE dah-FISH-en-see SIN-drome* Infection by the human immunodeficiency virus (HIV), which kills a certain class of helper T cells, causing profound immune suppression and resulting in opportunistic infections and cancer. 211

acromegaly *AK-ro-MEG-eh-lee* Abnormal thickening of bones in an adult due to excess growth hormone. 374

acrosome *AK-ro-som* A protrusion on the anterior end of a sperm cell containing digestive enzymes that enable the sperm to penetrate the protective layers around the oocyte. 163

actin *AK-tin* A type of protein in the thin myofilaments of skeletal muscle cells. 407

action potential *AK-shun po-TEN-shel* The measurement of an electrochemical change caused by ion movement across the cell membrane of a neuron. The message formed by this change is the nerve impulse. 317

active immunity *AK-tiv im-MUNE-eh-tee* Immunity generated by an organism's production of antibodies. 522

active site *AK-tiv SITE* The portion of an enzyme's conformation that directly participates in catalysis. 56

active transport *AK-tiv TRANZ-port* Movement of a molecule through a membrane against its concentration gradient, using a carrier protein and energy from ATP. 102

adaptation *AD-ap-TAY-shun* An inherited trait that enables an organism to survive a particular environmental challenge. 40

adaptive radiation *ah-DAP-tiv RAID-ee-AY-shun* The divergence of several new types of organisms from a single ancestral type. 626

adenine *AD-eh-neen* One of two purine nitrogenous bases in DNA and RNA. 57, 253

adenosine triphosphate *(ATP)* *ah-DEN-o-seen tri-FOS-fate* A molecule whose three high-energy phosphate bonds power many biological processes. 101, 109

adipose cell *ADD-eh-pos SEL* A cell filled almost entirely with lipid. 51

adrenal cortex *ad-REE-nal KOR-tex* The outer part of the adrenal glands. 377

adrenal glands *ad-REE-nal GLANZ* Paired, two-part glands that sit atop the kidneys and produce catecholamines, mineralocorticoids, glucocorticoids, and sex hormones. 377

adrenal medulla *ad-REE-nal mah-DUEL-ah* The inner part of the adrenal glands. 377

adrenocorticotropic hormone (ACTH) *ah-DREEN-o-KOR-tah-ko-TROP-ik HOR-moan* A hormone made in the anterior pituitary that stimulates secretion of hormones from the adrenal cortex. 375

adventitious roots *AD-ven-TISH-shus ROOTZ* Roots that form on stems or leaves, replacing the first root (the radicle). 563

aerial roots *AIR-ee-al ROOTZ* Adventitious roots that form and grow in the air. 564

afferent arterioles *AF-fer-ent are-TEAR-ee-olz* Branches of the renal artery approaching the proximal portion of a nephron. 506

agonist *AG-o-nist* A drug that activates a receptor, triggering an action potential, or helps a neurotransmitter to bind to the receptor. 325

agriculture *AG-rah-CUL-tur* The domestication of animals and the planting and cultivation of plants used as crops. 540

AIDS-related complex (ARC) *AIDS re-LAY-tid KOM-plex* The early stages of AIDS, characterized by weakness, swollen glands in the neck, and frequent fever. 523

alcoholic fermentation *AL-ko-HALL-ik FER-men-TAY-shun* An anaerobic step following glycolysis utilized by yeast. Pyruvic acid is converted to ethanol and carbon dioxide. 121

aldosterone *al-DOS-ter-own* The major mineralocorticoid hormone produced by the adrenal cortex. It maintains the level of Na^+ in the blood by altering the amount reabsorbed in the kidneys. 378, 510

aleurone *AL-ah-roan* A protective layer of a seed. 541

algae *AL-gee* Photosynthetic eukaryotes, including the unicellular diatoms, euglenoids, and dinoflagellates and the multicellular red, brown, and green algae. 25

alkaloids *AL-kah-loids* Plant biochemicals that are used to treat cancer and to relieve pain. 547

allele *ah-LEEL* An alternate form of a gene. 159, 220

allergens *AL-er-gens* Substances that provoke an allergic response. 525

allergy *AL-er-gee* An inappropriate response of the immune system against a nonthreatening substance, caused by IgE antibodies binding to mast cells and releasing their allergy mediators. 525

allergy mediators *AL-er-gee MEED-ee-A-terz* Biochemicals, such as histamine and heparin, that are released from mast cells when an allergen is encountered and that cause the symptoms of an allergy. 525

allopatric *AL-o-PAT-rik* Two populations that are geographically isolated from one another. 638

allopatric speciation *AL-o-PAT-rik SPE-she-A-shun* The formation of new species initiated by geographic isolation. 638

allopolyploid *AL-lo-POL-ee-ploid* An organism with multiple chromosome sets resulting from fertilization of an individual of one species by an individual of a different species. 639

allosaurs *AL-lo-SORZ* Carnivorous dinosaurs that stood upright. 659

alternation of generations *ALL-ter-NAY-shun JEN-er-AY-shunz* The existence of a gamete-producing and a spore-producing phase in the life cycle of a plant. 28, 573

altruism *AL-tru-iz-um* A behavior that harms the individual performing it but helps another organism. 692

alveolar ducts *AL-vee-O-ler DUCTS* The narrowed ending of bronchioles, opening into clusters of alveoli. 451

alveoli *AL-vee-O-li* A microscopic air sac in the lung. 451

amaranth *AM-ah-RANTH* A tall plant that can supply many types of food. 547

amino acid *ah-MEEN-o AS-id* An organic molecule built of a central carbon atom bonded to a hydrogen atom, an amino group, a carboxylic acid, and an R group. A polymer of amino acids is a peptide. 19, 52

amino acid racemization *ah-MEEN-o AS-id RACE-eh-mah-ZA-shun* A technique that measures the rate at which amino acids in biological matter alter to isomeric forms. This measurement is used in absolute dating of fossils and remains up to 100,000 years old. 650

ammonia *ah-MOAN-ee-ah* The chemical compound NH₃, which is a nitrogenous waste generated by the deamination of protein. 502

amniocentesis *AM-nee-o-cen-TEE-sis* A prenatal diagnostic procedure, performed during the fourth month of pregnancy. Fetal cells and biochemicals are sampled and then examined to reveal certain abnormalities. 180, 300

amniote egg *AM-nee-oat EGG* An egg in which an embryo could develop completely, without the requirement of being laid in water. 659

ampullae *AM-pew-li* The enlarged bases of the semicircular canals in the inner ear, lined with hair cells that detect fluid movement and convert it into action potentials. 362

amygdala *ah-MIG-dah-lah* A part of the cerebrum involved in encoding factual memory. 341

anabolism *eh-NAB-o-liz-um* Synthetic metabolic reactions, using energy. 110

anal canal *AAN-al kah-NAL* The final section of the digestive tract. 477

analgesic *AN-al-JEE-sik* A pain-relieving treatment. 459

analogous *ah-NAL-eh-ges* Structures similar in function but not in structure that have evolved in unrelated organisms in response to a similar environmental challenge. 651

anaphase *AN-ah-faze* The stage of mitosis when centromeres split and the two sets of chromosomes move to opposite ends of the cell. In anaphase of meiosis I, homologs separate. 134

anaphylactic shock *AN-ah-fah-LAK-tik SHOCK* A potentially life-threatening allergic reaction in which mast cells release allergy mediators throughout the body, causing apprehension, rash, and a closing of the throat. 528

androecium *an-DREE-see-um* The innermost whorl of a flower's corolla, consisting of male reproductive structures. 574

aneuploid *AN-you-ploid* A cell with one or more extra or missing chromosomes. 280

angina pectoris *an-GINE-ah pek-TORE-is* A gripping, viselike pain in the chest. 436

angiosperms *AN-gee-o-spermz* The flowering plants. 29

Animalia *AN-ah-MAIL-ee-ah* Kingdom including eukaryotes that derive energy from food and have nervous systems. 22

anorexia nervosa *AN-eh-REX-ee-ah ner-VO-sah* An eating disorder characterized by self-imposed starvation due to a psychological problem involving self-image. 490

antagonist *an-TAG-o-nist* A drug that binds to a receptor, blocking the docking of a neurotransmitter. 325

antagonistic muscles *an-TAG-o-NIS-tik MUS-selz* The two muscles or muscle groups that flank a movable bone and move it in opposite directions. 414

anthers *an-THERZ* Oval bodies at the tips of stamens that produce pollen. 574

anthocyanins *AN-tho-CY-ah-ninz* Pigments produced in senescent plant cells. 599

antibodies *AN-tah-BOD-eez* Proteins secreted by B cells that recognize and bind to foreign antigens, disabling them or signaling other cells to do so. 518

anticodon *AN-ti-ko-don* A three-base sequence on one loop of a transfer RNA molecule that is complementary to an mRNA codon and therefore serves to bring together the appropriate amino acid and its mRNA instructions. 258

antidiuretic hormone (ADH) (vasopressin) *AN-ti-DI-yur-RET-ik HOR-moan* A hormone made in the hypothalamus and released from the posterior pituitary that acts on the kidneys and smooth muscle cells of blood vessels to maintain the composition of body fluids. 375, 510

antigen *AN-tah-gen* The specific parts of cells or chemicals that elicit an immune response. 517

antigen binding site *AN-tah-gen BIND-ing SITE* Specialized ends of antibodies that bind specific antigens. 519

antihistamines *AN-ti-HIS-tah-meens* Drugs that decrease mucus secretion and alleviate watery eyes and sneezing. 459

antisense strand *AN-ti-sense strand* The side of the DNA double helix for a particular gene that is not transcribed into mRNA. 257

anus *A-nus* The opening to the anal canal. 477

anvil *AN-vil* One of the bones in the middle ear. 359

aorta *a-OR-tah* The largest artery that leaves the heart. 432, 435

aortic semilunar valve *a-OR-tik SEM-i-LOON-er VALVE* The valve between the left ventricle and the aorta. 435

apatosaurs *ah-PAT-o-SORZ* Huge, land-dwelling, herbivorous dinosaurs, also called brontosaurs. 659

apical meristems *A-pik-el MER-eh-STEMZ* Unspecialized cells that divide; found in plants near the tips of roots and shoots. 552

apneustic center *ap-NUS-tik CEN-ter* The part of the brain controlling the ability to take a deep breath. 458

appendicular skeleton *AP-en-DIK-u-lar SKEL-eh-ten* In a vertebrate skeleton, the limb bones and the bones that support them. 397

appendix *ap-PEN-diks* A thin tube from the cecum. 475

aqueous humor *AWK-kwee-es U-mer* A nutritive, watery fluid between the cornea and the lens of the eye that focuses incoming light rays and maintains the shape of the eyeball. 356

archaeopteryx *AR-kee-OP-ter-iks* A type of dinosaur that could fly. 659

arteries *ARE-teh-reez* Large, elastic blood vessels that leave the heart and branch into arterioles. 428

arterioles *are-TER-ee-olz* Small, elastic blood vessels that arise from arteries and lead into capillaries. 428

arthritis *arth-RI-tis* Inflammation of the joints. 401

artificial insemination *AR-teh-FISH-el in-SEM-eh-NAY-shun* Placing donated sperm in a woman's reproductive tract to start a pregnancy. 205

artificial seed *ARE-tah-FISH-al SEED* A somatic embryo placed in a transparent polysaccharide gel containing nutrients and hormones, with an outer, biodegradable polymer coat. 606

artificial selection *AR-tah-FISH-al sah-LEK-shun* Influencing the genetic makeup of a population, as occurs in agriculture and selective breeding of domesticated animals. 540, 626

ascending limb *as-SEN-ding LIM* The distal portion of the loop of Henle, which ascends from the kidney's medulla. Cells here are impermeable to water, and they actively transport Na⁺ into the medullary space. 508

ascomycete *AS-ko-my-seat* A fungus with asci as sexual structures, such as the organism that causes athlete's foot. 27

asexual reproduction *A-sex-yu-al re-pro-DUK-shun* A cell's doubling its contents and then splitting in two to yield two identical cells. 42, 158

association areas *ah-SOC-ee-A-shun AIR-ee-ahs* Little-understood parts of the cerebral cortex that control learning and creativity. 337

asthma *AS-mah* Spasm of the bronchial muscles. 451

atherosclerosis *ATH-ee-ro-skle-RO-sis* The accumulation of fatty plaques inside coronary arteries. 436

atom *AT-um* A chemical unit, composed of protons, neutrons, and electrons, that cannot be further broken down by chemical means. 44

atria *A-tree-ah* The paired uppermost chambers of the heart, which receive blood returning to the heart and pump it to the ventricles below. 434

atrial natriuretic factor (ANF) *A-tree-al NAY-tre-yu-RET-ik FAK-ter* A hormone produced in the heart atria of mammals that regulates blood pressure and volume and the excretion of K⁺, Na⁺, and water. 383

atrioventricular node (AV node) *A-tre-o-ven-TRIK-yu-lar NOOD* Specialized muscle cells that branch into a network of Purkinje fibers, which conduct electrical stimulation

six times faster than other parts of the heart. 438

atrioventricular valves *A-tree-o-ven-TRIK-ku-ler VALVZ* Flaps of tissue between each atrium and ventricle that move in response to the pressure changes accompanying the contraction of the ventricle. 434

atrophy *AH-tro-fee* Muscle degeneration resulting from lack of use or immobilization. 417

auditory nerve *AWD-eh-tore-ee NERV* Nerve fibers carrying action potentials from the cochlea in the inner ear to the cortex of the brain. 360

autoantibodies *AW-to-AN-tah-BOD-eez* Antibodies produced by an organism that attack tissue of the body, resulting in an autoimmune disease. 525

autonomic nervous system *AW-toe-NOM-ik NER-ves SIS-tum* Part of the motor pathways of the peripheral nervous system that leads to smooth muscle, cardiac muscle, and glands. 344, 439

autopolyploid *AW-toe-POL-ee-ploid* An organism with multiple chromosome sets derived from the same species. 639

autosome *AW-toe-soam* A non-sex chromosome. 225

autotroph(ic) *AW-toe-trof* An organism that manufactures nutrient molecules using energy harnessed from the environment. 22, 114

auxin *AWK-zin* A type of plant hormone that causes cell elongation in seedlings, shoot tips, embryos, and leaves. 580, 588

axial skeleton *AX-ee-al SKEL-eh-ten* In a vertebrate skeleton, the skull, vertebral column, ribs, and breastbone. 397

axil *AX-el* The regions between a leaf stalk and stem. 557

axon *AX-on* An extension from a neuron that conducts information away from the cell body toward a receiving cell. 315

B

B cells *B SELZ* A class of lymphocytes that produce antibodies. 518

bacteria *BACK-TEAR-ee-ah* Single-celled prokaryotic organisms. 22

balanced polymorphism *BAL-anced POL-ee-MORF-iz-um* A form of stabilizing selection that allows a genetic disease to remain in a population because heterozygotes enjoy a selective advantage. 637

bark *BARK* All of the tissues outside of the vascular cambium. 568

Barr body *bar BOD-ee* The dark-staining body seen in the nucleus of a cell from a female mammal, corresponding to the inactivated X chromosome. 239

basal ganglia *BASE-el GANG-lee-ah* Masses of nerve cell bodies in the cerebrum involved in forming memories required to perform certain skills. 341

basal metabolic rate *BA-sal MET-ah-BALL-ik RATE* The energy required by an organism to stay alive. 112

base *BASE* A molecule that releases hydroxide ions into water. 46

basidiomycete *bah-SID-ee-o-my-SEAT* A fungus with spore-containing basidia, including hallucinogenic mushrooms. 28

basilar membrane *BAY-seh-ler MEM-brane* The membrane beneath the hair cells in the cochlea of the inner ear that vibrates in response to sound. 360

behavioral isolation *be-HAAV-yu-ral I-so-LAY-shun* When members of two populations do not crossbreed because they perform different courtship rituals. 638

benthic zone *BEN-thik ZONE* The bottom of the ocean. 737

bicuspid valve *BI-kus-pid VALVE* The valve between the left atrium and the left ventricle. 435

bile *BILE* A substance produced by the liver and stored in the gallbladder that emulsifies fats. 472

binary fission *BI-nair-ee FISH-en* A type of asexual reproduction in which a cell divides into two identical cells. 22, 131

biofeedback *BI-o-FEED-bak* A technology giving people information on physiological processes they wish to control. 673

biogeochemical cycles *BI-o-GEE-o-KEM-ik-el SI-kelz* The pathways of chemicals between the atmosphere, the earth's crust, water, and organisms. 721

biogeography *BI-o-gee-OG-grah-fee* The physical distribution of organisms. 638

biological clock *BI-o-LOG-ik-kal CLOCK* An internal timing mechanism in an organism that controls its circadian rhythms. 600, 674

biomagnification *BI-o-MAG-nah-fah-KA-shun* The increasing concentration of a substance at higher trophic levels in a food chain. 721

biomass *BI-o-mass* The total dry weight of organisms in an area. 719

biome *BI-oam* A group of interacting terrestrial ecosystems characterized by a dominant collection of plant species, or a group of interacting aquatic ecosystems with similar salinities. 717

biosphere *BI-o-sfer* All of the parts of the earth that support life. 717

biotechnology *BI-o-tek-NAL-eh-gee* The alteration of cells or biological molecules with a specific application, including monoclonal antibody technology, genetic engineering, and cell culture. 268, 603

biotherapy *BI-o-THER-ah-pee* Use of body chemicals as pharmaceuticals. 534

biotic potential *bi-OT-ik po-TEN-shal* The maximum number of offspring an individual is physiologically capable of producing. 701

blade *BLADE* The flattened region of a leaf. 559

blastocyst *BLAS-toe-cyst* The preembryonic stage of human development when the organism is a hollow, fluid-filled ball of cells. 173

blastomere *BLAS-toe-mere* A cell in a preembryonic organism resulting from cleavage divisions. 172

blood *BLOOD* A complex fluid consisting of formed elements (blood cells and platelets) suspended in a watery plasma, in which are dissolved a variety of proteins and other biochemicals. 421

blood-brain barrier *BLOOD BRANE BARR-ee-er* Capillaries in the brain whose endothelial cells are so closely packed that many substances cannot cross from the blood to the brain tissue. 342

blood pressure *BLOOD PRESH-yur* The force exerted outward on blood vessel walls by the blood. 432

blood vessels *BLOOD VES-selz* Conduits that conduct blood throughout the body, including arteries, arterioles, capillaries, venules, and veins. 421

body *BOD-ee* The midsection of the stomach. 470

bolus *BO-lus* Food rolled into a lump by the tongue. 469

bomb calorimeter *BOMB KAL-or-IM-ah-ter* A chamber surrounded by water that is used to measure the caloric content of a food. 484

bone *BONE* A connective tissue consisting of bone-building osteoblasts, stationary osteocytes, and bone-destroying osteoclasts, embedded in a mineralized matrix infused with spaces and canals (lacunae, canaliculi, and Haversian canals). 86

Bowman's capsule *BOW-manz KAP-sul* The cup-shaped proximal end of the renal tubule which surrounds the glomerulus. 506

braced framework *BRACED FRAME-work* A skeleton built of solid structural components that are strong enough to resist pressure without collapsing. 390

brachiopods *BRAK-ee-o-PODZ* Clamlike organisms that appeared in the seas of the Cambrian period. 657

bracts *BRAKS* Floral leaves that protect developing flowers. 561

bronchi *BRON-ki* Two tubules that branch from the trachea as it reaches the lungs. 450

bronchioles *BRON-ki-olz* Microscopic branches of the bronchi within the lungs. 450

bronchitis *bron-KI-tis* Inflammation of the mucous membrane of the bronchi. 459

bryophytes *BRY-o-FIGHTS* Primitive plants that lack specialized tissues to conduct water and nutrients. 29, 571

bulimia *bu-LEEM-ee-ah* An eating disorder characterized by binging and purging. 492

bursae *BUR-si* Small packets within synovial joints that store synovial fluid, which helps to reduce friction between bones and nearby structures. 401

bursitis *bur-SI-tis* Inflammation of the bursae, possibly due to calcium deposits. 401

C

calcitonin *KAL-sah-TOE-nin* A thyroid hormone that decreases blood calcium levels. 375, 396

callus *KAL-lus* An undifferentiated white lump that grows from a cultured plant explant. 605

Calorie *CAL-o-ree* The amount of energy needed to raise the temperature of 1 kilogram of water by 1°C. 112

calyx *KA-liks* One of two outermost whorls of a flower, with no direct role in sexual reproduction. 574

Cambrian period *KAB-ree-an PER-ee-od* The time in earth history about 600 million years ago when many new types of organisms appeared. 656

canaliculi *kah-NAL-ku-LI* Narrow passageways in bone that connect spaces housing osteocytes. 393

cancer *CAN-sir* A group of disorders resulting from the loss of normal control over mitotic rate and number of divisions. 141

capacitation *cah-PASS-eh-TAY-shun* Activation of sperm cells in the human female reproductive tract. 171

capillaries *KAP-ah-lair-eez* The smallest blood vessels, with a lining one cell thick. 428

carbohydrases *KAR-bo-HI-dra-sez* Enzymes that chemically break down certain disaccharides into monosaccharides. 472

carbohydrate loading *KAR-bo-HI-drat LOAD-ing* A regimen of following a high-carbohydrate diet in the week before an endurance athletic event in an attempt to maximize muscle glycogen.

carbohydrates *CAR-bo-HIGH-drates* Compounds containing carbon, hydrogen, and oxygen, with twice as many hydrogens as oxygens. Carbohydrates include the sugars and starches. 49

carbonic anhydrase *kar-BON-ik an-HI-draze* An enzyme in red blood cells that catalyzes the conversion of carbon dioxide to carbonic acid. 457

Carboniferous period *KAR-bah-NIF-er-es PER-ee-od* The time from 345 to 275 million years ago, when the first amphibians and reptiles appeared on the land. 657

cardia *KAR-dee-ah* The neck of the stomach. 470

cardiac cycle *KAR-dee-ak SI-kel* The sequence of a contraction and relaxation that comprises the heartbeat. 438

cardiac muscle *CAR-dee-ak MUS-sel* Striated, involuntary, single-nucleated contractile cells found in the mammalian heart. 87, 405

cardioaccelerator area *KAR-dee-o-ak-SEL-er-ay-ter AIR-ee-ah* Part of the brain's vasomotor center that stimulates circulation by speeding the heart. 439

cardioinhibition area *KAR-de-o-IN-hah-BISH-un AIR-ee-ah* Part of the brain's vasomotor center that slows the heart. 439

carotenoid pigments *KAIR-et-teh-noid PIG-mentz* Yellow and orange plant pigments that become visible in autumn when chlorophyll production declines. 599

carpel *KAR-pel* Leaflike structures in a flower that enclose ovules. 574

carpels *KAR-pelz* The wrist bones. 400

carrying capacity *KARR-e-ing kah-PAS-eh-tee* The maximum number of individuals that can be supported by the environment for an indefinite time period. 705

cartilage *CAR-teh-lij* A supportive connective tissue consisting of chondrocytes embedded in collagen and proteoglycans. 84

Casparian strip *kas-PAHR-ee-an STRIP* The single layer of tightly packed cells comprising the endodermis of a plant. 564

catabolism *cah-TAB-o-liz-um* Metabolic reactions of degradation, releasing energy. 110

catecholamines *KAT-eh-KOL-ah-meenz* A class of hormones, including epinephrine and norepinephrine. 377

cecum *SEE-cum* A pouch at the entrance to the large intestine. 475

cell *SEL* The structural and functional unit of life. 40, 67

cell body *SEL BOD-ee* The central, rounded portion of a neuron from which an axon and dendrites extend. 315

cell cycle *SEL CY-kel* The life of a cell, in terms of whether it is dividing or in interphase. 131

cell membrane (plasmalemma) *SEL MEM-brane* An oily structure built of proteins embedded in a lipid bilayer, which forms the boundary of cells. 92

cell population *SEL POP-u-LAY-shun* A group of cells with characteristic proportions in particular stages of the cell cycle. 139

cell theory *SEL THER-ee* The ideas that all living matter is built of cells, cells are the structural and functional units of life, and all cells come from preexisting cells. 71

cellular respiration *SEL-u-ler RES-pir-AY-shun* Biochemical reactions involved in energy extraction in the mitochondrion. 119

cell wall *SEL WALL* A rigid boundary built of peptidoglycans in prokaryotic cells and cellulose in plant cells. 72

cementum *sah-MEN-tum* An outer layer of the tooth, anchoring it to the gum and jawbone. 469

Cenozoic era *CEN-o-ZO-ik ER-ah* The time from 65 million years ago, including the present. 661

central nervous system (CNS) *SEN-tral NER-vous SIS-tum* The brain and the spinal cord. 331

centrioles *CEN-tre-olz* Paired, oblong structures built of microtubules and found in animal cells, where they organize the mitotic spindle. 81

centromere *CEN-tro-mere* A characteristically located constriction in a chromosome. 133

cereals *SER-ee-alz* Members of the grass family Poaceae, which have seeds that can be stored for long periods of time. 541

cerebellum *SER-eh-BELL-um* A grooved area behind the brain stem and connected to the cerebrum above that receives impulses from the cerebral cortex and the peripheral nervous system and then unconsciously adjusts muscular responses so that they are smooth and coordinated. 335

cerebral cortex *sah-REE-bral KOR-tex* Gray matter comprising the outer layer of the cerebrum that integrates incoming information. 350, 458

cerebrospinal fluid *sah-REE-bro-SPI-nal FLU-id* Fluid similar to blood plasma that bathes and cushions the central nervous system. 342

cerebrum *seh-REE-brum* The higher region of the brain, controlling intelligence, learning, perception, and emotion. 337

cervical vertebrae *SER-vah-kel VER-tah-bray* Seven vertebrae in the neck. 398

cervix *SIR-viks* In the female human, the opening to the uterus. 157

chlorenchyma *klor-REN-kah-mah* Chloroplast-containing parenchyma cells. 553

chlorofluorocarbons (CFCs) *KLOR-o-FLOR-o-KAR-bunz* Compounds containing carbon, chlorine, and fluorine that destroy atmospheric ozone, which filters out ultraviolet radiation. 751

chlorophyll *KLOR-eh-fill* A green pigment used by plants to harness the energy in sunlight. 28, 81, 115

chloroplast *KLOR-o-plast* A plant cell organelle housing the reactions of photosynthesis. 81, 116

chlybrid *KLI-brid* A cell into which a chloroplast from another cell is introduced. 610

cholecystokinin (CCK) *KOL-e-sis-TOE-kah-nin* A hormone produced in the small intestine that signals the release of substances needed for fat digestion. 473

chorionic villi *KOR-ee-ON-ik VIL-i* Fingerlike projections extending from the chorion to the uterine lining. 179

choroid coat *KOR-oid KOAT* The middle layer of the human eyeball, containing many blood vessels. 354

chromatid *CRO-mah-tid* A continuous strand of DNA comprising an unreplicated chromosome or one-half of a replicated chromosome. 133

chromosome *KRO-mo-soam* A dark-staining, rod-shaped structure in the nucleus of a eukaryotic cell built of a continuous molecule of DNA, wrapped in protein. 76, 218

chyme *KIME* Semisolid food in the stomach. 470

chymotrypsin *KEE-mo-TRIP-sin* A pancreatic enzyme that participates in protein digestion in the small intestine. 472

cilia *SIL-ee-ah* Protein projections from cells. Cilia beat in unison, moving substances. 83, 104

ciliary body *SIL-ee-AIR-ee BOD-ee* A highly folded, specialized structure in the center of the choroid coat of the human eye that houses the ciliary muscle, which controls the shape of the lens. 354

ciliary muscle *SIL-e-AIR-ee MUS-sel* A muscle at the center of the choroid coat in the human eye that alters the shape of the lens. 354

circadian rhythms *sir-KA-dee-en RITH-umz* Regular, daily rhythms of particular biological functions. 600

circalunadian *SIR-kah-lu-NAY-di-an* A biological rhythm that repeats approximately every day. 677

circannual *SIR-kah-AN-u-al* A biological rhythm that repeats approximately every year. 677

classical conditioning *KLAS-ik-kal kon-DISH-on-ing* A form of learning in which an animal responds in a familiar way to a new stimulus. 673

cleavage *KLEV-ij* A period of rapid cell division following fertilization but before embryogenesis. 172

climax community *KLI-max kom-MUUN-eh-te* A community that remains fairly constant if the land and climate are undisturbed. 722

clonal propagation *KLO-nel PROP-ah-GAY-shun* Uniform plants grown from cells or protoplasts cultured in the laboratory. 607

clones *KLONZ* Genetically identical individuals. 584

closed behavior program *CLOZED bee-HAIV-yur PRO-gram* A behavior that is largely genetically determined and rigid and not easily influenced by the environment. 667

closed circulatory system *CLOZED SIR-ku-lah-TORE-ee SIS-tum* A circulatory system in which the blood is contained in blood vessels. 422

coagulation *ko-AG-u-LAY-shun* Clotting of blood. 427

coccyx *COK-six* The final four vertebrae, which are fused to form the tailbone. 399

cochlea *COKE-lee-ah* The spiral-shaped, hindmost portion of the inner ear, where vibrations are translated into nerve impulses. 359

cochlear implant *COKE-lee-ar IM-plant* A device that delivers an electronic stimulus directly to the auditory nerve, bypassing the function of hair cells to provide an awareness of sound. 361

codominant *KO-DOM-eh-nent* Alleles that are both expressed in the heterozygote. 225

codon *KO-don* A continuous triplet of mRNA that specifies a particular amino acid. 258

coelom *SEE-loam* A central body cavity in an animal. 31

coevolution *KO-ev-eh-LU-shun* The interdependence of two types of organisms for survival. 619

coleoptile *KOL-ee-OP-tile* A sheathlike structure covering the plumule in monocots. 578

collateral circulation *ko-LAT-er-al SIR-ku-LAY-shun* Rerouting of blood in the heart into different arteries following damage to the heart. 436

collecting duct *ko-LEK-ting DUCT* A structure in the kidney into which nephrons drain urine. 509

collenchyma *kol-LEN-kah-mah* Elongated, living cells that differentiate from parenchyma and support the growing regions of shoots. 553

colon *KOL-en* The large intestine. 475

color blind *KUL-er BLIND* A condition in which one or more types of cone cells in the retina are missing. The individual cannot distinguish among all colors. 358

colorectal cancer *KOL-ah-REK-tal KAN-cer* Cancer of the large intestine and rectum. 477

colostomy *ko-LOS-toe-mee* Surgery that attaches the large intestine to an opening leading to a bag worn outside the body, where fecal matter collects. 477

commensalism *kom-MEN-sah-liz-um* A symbiotic relationship where one partner benefits and the other is unaffected. 14

community *kom-MUN-nah-tee* All of the organisms in a given area. 713

compact bone *KOM-pact BONE* A layer of solid, hard bone covering spongy bone. 393

complement system *KOM-plah-ment SIS-tum* A group of proteins that assist other immune defenses. 515

complementary *kom-ple-MENT-ah-ree* The tendency of adenine to hydrogen bond to thymine and guanine to cytosine in the DNA double helix. 253

complex carbohydrates *KOM-plex kar-bo-HI-drates* The polysaccharides, which are chains of sugars. Polysaccharides include starch, glycogen, cellulose, and chitin. 50

compound *KOM-pound* A molecule consisting of different atoms. 45

compound microscope *KOM-pound MI-kro-scope* A microscope built of two lenses. 70

concentration gradient *KON-sen-TRA-shun GRAY-dee-ent* The phenomenon of ions passively diffusing from an area in which they are highly concentrated to an area where they are less concentrated. 318

concordance *KON-KOR-dance* A measure of the inherited component

of a trait, consisting of the number of pairs of either monozygotic or dizygotic twins in which both members express a trait, divided by the number of pairs in which at least one twin expresses the trait. 292

conditioned stimulus *kon-DISH-ond STIM-u-lus* A new stimulus that is coupled to a familiar, or unconditioned, stimulus, so that an animal can learn an association between the two. 673

conductive deafness *kon-DUK-tiv DEF-nes* Hearing loss resulting from blocked transmission of sound through the middle ear. 360

cones *KONZ* Specialized neurons found in the central portion of the retina that detect colors. 355

cones *KONZ* The reproductive structures of pines. 583

conformation *KON-for-MAY-shun* The three-dimensional shape of a protein. 53

confusion effect *kon-FUZ-yun E-fekt* The confusion faced by a predator in the presence of a school of fish. 687

congestive heart failure *kon-JES-tiv HART FAIL-yur* A weakening of the heart, impairing circulation. 436

connective tissue *kon-NECK-tiv TISH-u* Tissues consisting of cells embedded or suspended in a matrix, including loose and fibrous connective tissues, cartilage, bone, and blood. 81

constant regions *KON-stant REE-genz* The sequence of amino acids comprising the lower portions of heavy and light antibody chains, which is very similar in different antibody types. 518

constipation *KON-stah-PAY-shun* The infrequent passage of hard feces, caused by abnormally slow movement of fecal matter through the large intestine. 476

contact inhibition *KON-tact IN-heh-BISH-un* The tendency of a cell to cease dividing once it touches another cell. 138

contest competition *KON-test KOM-pah-TISH-un* Indirect competition of individuals in a population for a limited resource, such as acquiring a territory that provides access to resources. 705

contractile vacuole *KON-tract-till VAK-u-ol* An organelle in paramecium that pumps water out of the cell. 100

convergent evolution *KON-ver-gent EV-o-LU-shun* Organisms that have evolved similar adaptations to a similar environmental challenge but are not related by descent. 625

cork cambium *KORK KAM-bee-um* The lateral meristem that produces the periderm, the outer protective covering on mature stems and roots. 568

cork cells *KORK SELZ* Waxy, densely packed cells covering the surfaces of mature stems and roots. 568

cornea *KOR-nee-ah* A modified portion of the human eye's sclera that forms a transparent curved window admitting light. 353

corolla *kah-ROLE-ah* One of two outermost whorls of a flower, with no direct role in sexual reproduction. 574

corona radiata *kah-ROAN-ah RAID-ee-AH-tah* Cells surrounding the secondary oocyte and the zona pellucida. 171

coronary arteries *KOR-eh-nair-ee AR-ter-eez* Paired arteries that diverge from the aorta and surround and enter the heart. 439

coronary circulation *KOR-eh-nair-ee SIR-ku-LA-shun* The network of blood vessels that supplies blood to the heart. 439

coronary heart disease *KOR-eh-nair-ee HART DIS-eez* Disease of the coronary arteries. 436

corpus callosum *KOR-pes ka-LAWS-um* Tracts of myelinated nerve fibers that form a bridge between the cerebral hemispheres. 340

corpus luteum *KOR-pis LU-te-um* A gland formed from an ovarian follicle from which an oocyte has recently been ovulated that produces estrogen and progesterone. 381

cortex *KOR-teks* In plants, the ground tissue that fills the area between the epidermis and vascular tissue in stems. 558

cortex *KOR-teks* The outermost part of the kidney, consisting of glomeruli, Bowman's capsules, and proximal and distal convoluted tubules of nephrons. 505

cortisol *KOR-teh-sol* A major glucocorticoid hormone produced in the adrenal cortex that helps enable the body to cope with prolonged stress. 378

cotyledons *KOT-ah-LEE-donz* Embryonic leaves in flowering plants that store energy used for germination. 562, 578

cotylosaurs *KOT-el-o-SORZ* Animals living in the early Permian period that were ancestors of the dinosaurs and modern reptiles, birds, and mammals. 659

countercurrent flow *COUNT-er-CURR-ent FLO* A system in which fluid flows in a continuous tubule in opposite directions, which maximizes the amount of a particular substance that diffuses out of the tubule. 447

countercurrent multiplier system *KAUN-ter-CUR-ent MUL-tah-PLI er SIS-tum* The movement of Na⁺ and water between the limbs of the loop of Henle and the medullary space in the kidney. The concentration of Na⁺ in the medullary space forces water to leave the descending limb, and it then reenters the bloodstream. 509

courtship ritual *KOURT-ship RIT-u-al* A stereotyped, elaborate, and conspicuous behavior that overcomes aggressive tendencies long enough for mating to occur. 696

covalent bond *KO-va-lent bond* The sharing of electrons between atoms. 47

cranial nerves *CRANE-e-al NERVZ* Twelve pairs of somatic nerves that arise from the brain. 344

creatine phosphate *KRE-ah-tin FOS-fate* A molecule stored in muscle fibers that can donate its high-energy phosphate to ADP to regenerate ATP.

Cretaceous period *kra-TAY-shus PER-ee-od* The time from 135 to 65 million years ago when angiosperms were abundant and the number of dinosaur species declined. 659

cretinism *KRE-tin-iz-um* A child who is physically and mentally retarded due to a thyroid gland underactive since birth.

cristae *KRIS-ty* The folds of the inner membrane of a mitochondrion along which many of the reactions of cellular respiration occur. 79, 122

critical period *KRIT-eh-kel PER-ee-od* The time during prenatal development when a specific structure can be altered by a gene or an external influence. 202

critical period *KRIT-eh-kel PER-ee-od* The time in an animal's life when it performs a particular imprinting behavior. 673

Cro-Magnons *kro-MAG-nonz* Lightweight, fine-boned, less hairy members of *Homo sapiens* who lived about 40,000 years ago in Europe and Asia. 663

crossing over *KROS-ing O-ver* The exchange of genetic material between homologous chromosomes during prophase of meiosis I. 159, 237

crossopterygians *cros-SOP-ter-REEG-ee-anz* The lobe-finned fishes, which first appeared in the Devonian period and were probably ancestral to amphibians. 657

cuticle *KU-tah-kal* A covering tissue over all of a plant except the roots. 554

cutin *KU-tin* A fatty material produced by a plant's epidermal cells that forms the cuticle. 554

cyanobacteria *si-AN-o-bak-TEAR-ee-ah* Prokaryotic organisms that contain pigments and can photosynthesize. Also called blue-green algae. 22

cybridization *SI-brid-di-ZAY-shun* The production of a cell having cytoplasm derived from two cells but containing a single nucleus. 610

cyclic ovulator *SI-klik OV-u-LAY-ter* A female mammal that undergoes a monthly cycle of fertility. 382

cyclosporin *SI-klo-SPOR-in* A fungus-derived drug that suppresses immunity and is of great value in assisting transplant recipients in accepting a new organ. 529

cystic fibrosis *SIS-tik fi-BRO-sis* An inherited condition in which excess mucus plugs up the lungs and pancreas. 460

cytokinesis *SI-toe-kin-E-sis* Distribution of cytoplasm, organelles, and macromolecules into two daughter cells in cell division. 131

cytokinins *SI-toe-KI-ninz* A class of plant hormones that promote cytokinesis (division of a cell following division of the genetic material) in seeds, roots, young leaves, and fruits. 588

cytoplasm *SI-toe-PLAZ-um* The jellylike fluid in which organelles are suspended in eukaryotic cells. 75

cytosine *SI-toe-seen* One of the two pyrimidine nitrogenous bases in DNA and RNA. 57, 253

cytoskeleton *SI-toe-SKEL-eh-ten* A framework built of arrays of protein rods and tubules found in animal cells. 75, 92

D

dark reactions *DARK re-AK-shuns* Reactions of photosynthesis that do not require light and that use the products of the light reactions (NADPH and ATP) to synthesize organic molecules. 117

day-neutral plants *DAY NU-trel PLANTZ* Plants that do not rely on photoperiod to flower. 596

dead space *DEAD SPACE* The air in the pharynx, trachea, and the upper third of the lungs, which is not used in gas exchange. 455

deciduous trees *dah-SID-u-us TREEZ* Trees that shed their leaves at the end of a growing season. 562

decomposers *DEE-kom-POZ-erz* Organisms that consume dead organisms and feces. 718

decongestants *DE-kon-JES-tentz* Drugs that shrink nasal membranes, easing breathing. 459

defibrillator *de-FIB-rah-LAY-ter* A device that sends an electric shock to the heart to restore a normal heartbeat. 436

degenerate *de-JEN-er-at* Different codons specifying the same amino acid. 261

dehydration synthesis *DE-hi-DRA-shun SYN-theh-sis* Formation of a covalent bond between two molecules by the loss of water. 50

dendrites *DEN-dritz* Short, branched, numerous extensions from a neuron that usually receive information from other neurons and transmit it toward the neuron cell body. 315

denitrifying bacteria *DE-ni-trah-FI-ing bak-TER-ee-ah* Bacteria that convert ammonia, nitrite, and nitrate to nitrogen gas. 721

density dependent factors *DEN-seh-tee DE-pen-dent FAK-terz* Factors that kill a greater percentage of a population as population size increases. 705

density independent factors *DEN-seh-tee IN-deh-PEN-dent FAK-terz* Factors that kill a certain percentage of a population regardless of population size, such as natural disasters. 705

dentine *DEN-tin* The bonelike material beneath a tooth's enamel. 469

deoxyhemoglobin *DE-OX-ee-HEEM-o-GLO-bin* Hemoglobin that is deep red after releasing its oxygen to tissues. 426

deoxyribonucleic acid (DNA) *de-OX-ee-RI-bo-nu-KLAY-ic AS-id* A double-stranded nucleic acid built of nucleotides containing a phosphate group, a nitrogenous base (A, T, G, or C), and the sugar deoxyribose. 57, 217

depolarized *DE-pol-er-ized* When the charge of the interior of a neuron at rest becomes less negative by the influx of Na⁺. 319

dermal tissue *DER-mal TISH-u* Tissue covering a plant's body. 554

descending limb *de-SEN-ding LIM* The proximal portion of the loop of Henle, which descends into the kidney's medulla. Cells here are permeable to water, which passively diffuses into the kidney's medulla in response to the Na⁺ that collects there after leaving the ascending limb. 508

desensitization *de-SEN-sah-teh-ZA-shun* Periodic injection of allergens under the skin in an attempt to plug receptors on mast cells with IgG so that allergy mediators are not released upon encountering the allergen. 526

Devonian period *deh-VOAN-ee-an PER-ee-od* The time following the Silurian period, 395 to 345 million years ago, when fishes first became abundant. 657

diabetes insipidus *DI-ah-BEE-teez IN-sip-eh-dis* A disruption of the synthesis or release of antidiuretic hormone, producing intense thirst and copious, watery urine. 375

diabetes mellitus *DI-ah-BEAT-es MEL-eh-tis* A medical condition in which the body does not produce sufficient insulin or cannot react to the insulin present. 379

diaphragm *DI-ah-fram* A broad sheet of muscle separating the thoracic cavity from the abdominal cavity. 453

diarrhea *DI-ah-REE-ah* The frequent and too-rapid passage of loose feces, caused by abnormally fast movement of fecal matter through the large intestine. 476

diastole *di-AS-toll-ee* The heart's relaxation. 438

diastolic pressure *DI-ah-stol-ik PRESH-yur* The blood pressure at its lowest, when the ventricles relax. 432

dicots *DI-kotz* Flowering plants that have two seed leaves. 557, 578

dihybrid *DI-HI-brid* An individual heterozygous for two particular genes. 222

dilution effect *dah-LU-shun E-fekt* A behavior in which ostriches with mates sit on eggs of females lacking permanent mates, which decreases the chances of their own eggs being eaten. 687

diplodocus *DIP-lo-DOE-kus* Huge, land-dwelling, herbivorous dinosaurs. 659

diploid *DIP-loid* A cell with two copies of each chromosome. 157

directional selection *dah-REK-shun-al sah-LEK-shun* When a previously prevalent characteristic of the individuals of a population is altered in response to a changing environment as the number of better-adapted individuals increases. 637

disaccharide *DI-SAK-eh-ride* A sugar built of two bonded monosaccharides, including sucrose, maltose, and lactose. 50

disruptive selection *dis-RUP-tiv sah-LEK-shun* When either of two extreme expressions of a trait are the most fit. 637

distal convoluted tubule *DIS-tel KON-vo-LU-tid TU-bule* The region of the kidney distal to the loop of Henle and proximal to a collecting duct where Na⁺ is reabsorbed into the peritubular capillaries by active transport, blood pH is maintained, and wastes are secreted. 509

diverticulosis *DI-ver-TIK-ku-LO-sis* A weakening of parts of the large intestinal wall. 476

DNA hybridization *HI-brid-i-ZAY-shun* Determining the relatedness of two types of organisms by observing how rapidly separated strands of their DNA form hybrids. 654

DNA polymerase *po-LIM-er-ase* A type of enzyme that participates in DNA replication by inserting new bases and correcting mismatched base pairs. 257

DNA replication *REP-leh-KAY-shun* Construction of a new DNA double helix using the information in parental strands as a template. 253-54

dominance hierarchy *DOM-eh-nance HI-er-AR-kee* A social ranking of members of a group of the same sex, which distributes resources with a minimum of aggression. 695

dominant *DOM-eh-nent* An allele that masks the expression of another allele. 220

dormant *DOR-mant* A period of decreased metabolism that often enables an organism to survive harsh climatic conditions. 599

double-blind *DUB-el BLIND* An experimental protocol where neither the participants nor the researchers know which subjects have received a placebo and which have received the treatment being evaluated. 5

double fertilization *DUB-el FER-til-i-ZAY-shun* The fertilization of both the egg and the polar nuclei in a flowering plant. 578

duodenum *DO-o-DEE-num* The first section of the small intestine. 472

dystrophin *DIS-tro-fin* A protein comprising only 0.002% of the total protein in skeletal muscle but vital for this tissue's function. Lack of dystrophin leads to muscular dystrophy. 412

E

ecological isolation *E-ko-LOG-eh-kel I-so-LAY-shun* When members of two populations do not crossbreed because they prefer to mate in different habitats. 638

ecological succession *E-ko-LODG-ik-el suk-SESH-un* The process of change in an ecological community. 722

ecology *e-KOL-o-gee* The study of the relationships between organisms and their environments. 713

ecosystem *E-ko-SIS-tum* A unit of interaction among organisms and between organisms and their physical environments, including all living things within a defined area. 713

ecotones *E-ko-tonz* Bridges between ecosystems, such as marshes and meadows. 753

ectoderm *EK-TOE-derm* The outermost embryonic germ layer, whose cells become part of the nervous system, sense organs, outer skin layer, and its specializations. 175

ectopic pregnancy *ek-TOP-ik PREG-nan-see* The implantation of a zygote in the wall of a fallopian tube rather than in the uterus. 201

ectotherms *EK-toe-THERMZ* Animals that lose or gain heat to their surroundings by moving into areas where the temperature is suitable. 499

edema *eh-DEEM-ah* Swelling of a body part due to fluid buildup. 441

effector *E-fek-ter* A muscle or gland that receives input from a neuron. 315

efferent arterioles *EF-fer-ent are-TEAR-ee-olz* Branches of the renal artery leaving the proximal portion of a nephron. 506

electrical gradient *e-LEK-trik-el GRAY-dee-ent* The phenomenon of like charges repelling one another and opposite charges attracting one another. 318

electric discharge particle acceleration *e e-LEK-trik DIS-charge PAR-te-kel ak-SEL-er-AY-shun* A gunlike device that shoots tiny metal particles coated with DNA into cells. 612

electron *e-LEK-tron* A subatomic particle carrying a negative electrical charge, and a negligible mass, that orbits the atomic nucleus. 44

electron-spin resonance *e-LEK-tron SPIN REZ-o-nence* A technique that measures the formation of tiny holes in crystals over time, caused by exposure to ionizing radiation. This measurement is used in absolute dating of fossils up to 1 million years old. 650

electron-transport chain *ee-LEK-tron TRANZ-port CHANE* Linked oxidation-reduction reactions. 116

electroporation *ee-LEK-tro-por-AY-shun* Applying a brief jolt of electricity to open up transient holes in cell membranes, allowing foreign DNA to be introduced. 612

element *EL-eh-ment* A pure substance, consisting of atoms containing a characteristic number of protons. 44

embolus *EM-bo-lis* A blood clot that travels in the bloodstream to another location. 428

embryo *EM-bree-o* The stage of prenatal development when organs develop from a three-layered organization. 155

embryonic induction *EM-bree-ON-ik in-DUK-shun* The ability of a group of specialized cells to stimulate neighboring cells to specialize. 180

embryo sac *EM-bree-o SAK* A mature megagametophyte, containing an egg. 574

emphysema *EM-fah-ZEE-ma* Impaired breathing caused by an inherited enzyme deficiency or smoking. The lung's alveoli become overinflated and burst. 459

enamel *ee-NAM-el* The hard covering of a tooth.

endocrine glands *EN-do-crin GLANZ* Structures that secrete hormones directly into the circulatory system. 368

endocytosis *EN-doe-si-TOE-sis* The engulfing of an extracellular substance by the cell membrane. 81, 102

endoderm *EN-doe-derm* The innermost embryonic germ layer, whose cells become the organs and linings of the digestive, respiratory, and urinary systems. 175

endodermis *EN-do-DER-mis* The innermost region of a root's cortex. 564

endogenous pyrogen *en-DODGE-eh-nes PIR-o-gen* A protein secreted by some white blood cells that stimulates the hypothalamus to spike a fever. 516

endometrium *EN-doe-MEE-tree-um* The inner uterine lining. 173

endoplasmic reticulum *EN-doe-PLAZ-mik reh-TIK-u-lum* A maze of interconnected membranous tubules and sacs, winding from the nuclear envelope to the cell membrane, along which proteins are synthesized (in the rough ER) and lipids synthesized (in the smooth ER). 77

endorphins *en-DORF-inz* Peptides produced in the human body that influence mood and the perception of pain. 326

endoskeleton *EN-do-SKEL-eh-ten* An internal scaffolding type of skeleton in vertebrates. 390

endosperm *EN-do-sperm* A triploid tissue that provides nutrients to the embryo in a seed. 541, 578

endosymbiont theory *EN-doe-SYM-ee-ont THER-ee* The idea that eukaryotic cells evolved from large prokaryotic cells that engulfed once free-living bacteria. 87

endotherms *EN-doe-THERMZ* Animals that regulate their temperatures by using metabolic heat. 499

energy nutrients *EN-er-gee NU-tre-entz* Dietary fats, carbohydrates, and proteins. 482

energy pyramid *EN-er-gee PIR-ah-mid* A depiction of trophic levels, with each level represented by a bar whose length is proportional to the number of kilocalories available from that food for growth and development. 719

energy RDA *EN-er-gee* The recommended dietary allowance for the energy nutrients, which are carbohydrates, proteins, and fats. 485

entrainment *en-TRANE-ment* The resynchronization of a biological clock by the environment. 600, 674

environmental resistance *en-VIR-on-MEN-tal ree-SIS-tance* All factors that reduce birth rate or increase death rate in a population. 704

enzyme *EN-zime* A protein that catalyzes a specific type of chemical reaction. 54

epicotyl *EP-eh-KOT-el* The stemlike region above the cotyledons. 578

epidemiology *EP-eh-dee-mee-OL-o-gee* The analysis of data derived from real-life, nonexperimental situations. 7

epidermis *EP-eh-DER-mis* The covering on the primary plant body. 554

epididymis *EP-eh-DID-eh-mis* In the human male, a tightly coiled tube leading from each testis, where sperm mature and are stored. 155

epiglottis *EP-eh-GLOT-is* A piece of cartilage that covers the glottis, routing food to the digestive tract and air to the respiratory tract. 449

epinephrine (adrenaline) *EP-eh-NEF-rin* (*ah-DREN-ah-lin*) A catecholamine hormone produced in the adrenal medulla and sent into the bloodstream, where it raises blood pressure, constricts blood vessels, and slows digestion, as part of the "fight or flight" response to a threat. 377

epiphyseal plates *EP-eh-FEEZ-ee-al PLATZ* In children, thin disks of cartilage at the ends of long bones from which new growth occurs. 395

epistasis *EP-eh-STAY-sis* A gene masking another gene's expression. 231

epithelial tissue *EP-eh-THEL-e-al TISH-u* Tissue built of cells that are packed close together to form linings and boundaries. 81

epithelium *EP-eh-THEL-e-um* Cells that form linings and coverings. 81

epochs *EP-okz* Time periods within periods, which are within eras. 654

equational division *ee-QUAY-shun-el deh-VISZ-un* The second meiotic division, when four haploid cells are generated from the two haploid cells that are the products of meiosis I by a mitosislike division. 157

eras *ER-ahs* Very long periods of time of biological or geological activity. 654

erythropoietin *eh-RITH-ro-PO-eh-tin* A hormone produced in the kidneys when the oxygen supply is insufficient that stimulates red blood cell production in the red bone marrow. 426

esophagus *ee-SOF-eh-gus* A muscular tube leading from the pharynx to the stomach. 469

essential nutrients *e-SEN-shal NU-tree-entz* Nutrients that must be obtained from the diet because the body cannot synthesize them. 484

estrogen *ES-tro-gen* A hormone made in the ovaries that increases the rate of mitosis in the uterine lining. 381

estuary *ES-tu-AIR-ee* The point where the fresh water of a river meets the salty water of an ocean. 735

ethology *ee-THOL-o-gee* The study of how natural selection shapes behavior to enable an animal to survive. 668

ethylene *ETH-eh-leen* A simple organic molecule that functions as a hormone in plants, produced in large amounts by a stigma when a pollen tube begins growing. It hastens fruit ripening. 579, 588

etiolated *E-ti-o-LAY-tid* Seedlings that have abnormally elongated stems, small roots, and leaves and a pale color, because they were grown in the dark. 598

eukaryotic cell *u-CARE-ee-OT-ik SEL* A complex cell containing organelles, which carry out a variety of specific functions. 17

eurypterids *yu-RIP-ter-idz* Scorpionlike organisms that appeared in the seas of the Cambrian period. 657

eusocial *YU-sosh-al* A population of animals that communicate with each other, cooperate in caring for young, has overlapping generations, and demonstrates division of labor. 684

eutrophic *yu-TRO-fik* An aging lake, containing many nutrients and decaying organisms, often tinted green with algae. 734

evolution *Ev-eh-LU-shun* The process by which the genetic composition of a population of organisms changes over time. 621

evolutionary tree diagrams *EV-o-LU-shun-air-ee TREE DI-ah-gramz* A depiction of DNA sequence differences indicating evolutionary relationships between different types of organisms. 654

exchange system *ex-CHANGE SIS-tum* A diet planning system based on classifying foods according to their percentages of carbohydrate, protein, and fat. 487

excitatory synapse *ex-SI-TAH-tore-ee SIN-apse* A synapse across which a particular neurotransmitter travels and depolarizes the postsynaptic membrane. 324

exocytosis *EX-o-si-TOE-sis* The fusing of secretion-containing organelles, which travel to the inside surface of the cell membrane, where

they transport a substance out of the cell. 79, 102

exon *EX-on* The bases of a gene that code for amino acids. 265

exoskeleton *EX-o-SKEL-eh-ten* A braced framework skeleton on the outside of an organism. 390

experimental control *ex-PEAR-eh-MEN-tel KON-trol* An extra test that does not directly address the hypothesis but can rule out causes other than the one being investigated. 5

expiration *EX-spir-AY-shun* Exhalation. 455

explants *EX-plantz* Small pieces of plant tissue grown in a laboratory dish with nutrients and plant hormones. 605

expressivity *EX-pres-SIV-eh-tee* The degree of expression of a phenotype. 227

extinction *ex-TINK-shun* The disappearance of a type of organism. 621

extinction *ex-TINK-shun* The loss of a conditioned response. 673

extracellular digestion *EX-tra-SEL-yu-lar di-JEST-shun* Dismantling of food by hydrolytic enzymes in a cavity within an organism's body. 465

extraembryonic membranes *EX-tra-EM-bree-on-ik MEM-BRANZ* Structures that support and nourish the mammalian embryo and fetus, including the yolk sac, allantois, and amnion. 168

F

facilitated diffusion *fah-SIL-eh-tay-tid dif-FU-shun* Movement of a substance down its concentration gradient with the aid of a carrier protein. 101

facultative photoperiodism *FAK-kel-TAY-tiv FO-toe-PER-ee-o-DIZ-um* Plants for which an inductive photoperiod speeds flowering. 596

fallopian tubes *fah-LO-pee-an TUBES* In the human female, paired tubes leading from near the ovaries to the uterus, where oocytes can be fertilized. 157

fall turnover *FALL TURN-o-ver* The mixing of upper and lower layers in a lake by wind, which mixes nutrients and oxygen. 734

fast twitch-fatigable fibers *FAST TWITCH fah-TEEG-ab-bel FI-berz* Skeletal muscle fibers that contract rapidly but tire easily due to scarce oxygen. 414

fast twitch-fatigue resistant fibers *FAST TWITCH fah-TEEG re-ZIS-tent FI-berz* Skeletal muscle fibers that contract rapidly, do not tire easily, and have abundant oxygen. 413

fats *FATS* Organic compounds containing carbon, hydrogen, and oxygen but with less oxygen than carbohydrates. 51

feedback loop *FEED-bak LOOP* A complex interaction between the

product of a biochemical reaction and the starting material. 370

femur *FE-mer* The thigh bone. 400

fibrillation *FIB-rah-LAY-shun* Wild twitching of the heart muscle. 436

fibroblast *FI-bro-blast* A cell of connective tissue that secretes the proteins collagen and elastin. 83

fibrous root system *FI-bres ROOT SIS-tum* A plant in which the first root (the radicle) is short-lived. 563

fibula *FIB-u-lah* The smaller of the two bones of the lower leg. 400

fixed action pattern (FAP) *FIXED AK-shun PAT-ern* An innate, stereotyped behavior. 668

flagella *fla-GEL-ah* Taillike appendages on prokaryotic cells. 72, 104

flavin *FLA-vin* A yellow pigment in plants that is probably the photoreceptor for phototropism. 592

flowers *FLAU-erz* The reproductive structures of angiosperms. 574

fluid mosaic *FLU-id mo-ZAY-ik* Description of a biological membrane, referring to the arrangement of proteins embedded in the oily lipid bilayer. 97

follicle cells *FOL-ik-kel SELZ* Nourishing cells surrounding oocytes. 155

follicle stimulating hormone (FSH) *FOL-eh-kul STIM-u-la-ting HOR-moan* A hormone made in the anterior pituitary that controls oocyte maturation, the development of ovarian follicles, and their release of estrogen. 374

food chain *FOOD CHANE* A series of organisms in which one eats another. 717

food group plan *FOOD GROUP PLAN* A diet plan based on classifying foods into four groups—meat and meat substitutes, milk and milk products, fruits and vegetables, and grains. 486

food webs *FOOD WEBZ* The interconnection of food chains to form webs. 718

formed elements *FORMED EL-eh-mentz* Blood cells and platelets. 370

fossils *FOS-silz* Evidence of past life. 622

founder effect *FAUN-der ah-FEKT* A type of genetic drift occurring when small groups of people leave their homes to found new settlements, taking with them a subset of the original population's genes. 633

fountain effect *FOUN-ten E-fekt* The splitting in two and regrouping of a school of fish, which confuses a predator. 687

fovea centralis *FO-ve-ah cen-TRAL-is* An indentation in the retina directly opposite the lens containing only cones and important to the acuity of an animal's sight. 355

free nerve ending *FREE NERV EN-ding* A type of receptor in the skin that responds to touch. 363

free radicals *FREE RAD-eh-kelz* Highly reactive by-products of

metabolism that can damage tissue. 188

fruit *FROOT* A ripened plant ovary enclosing a seed. 580

fundamental niche *FUN-dah-MEN-tel NITCH* All the places and ways in which members of a species can live. 707

fundus *FUN-dus* The domelike top of the stomach. 470

Fungi *FUN-ji* The taxonomic kingdom of eukaryotes with chitin cell walls and no nervous systems and distinguished by their reproductive structures. 22, 26

G

G$_1$ phase *FAZE* The stage of interphase when proteins, lipids, and carbohydrates are synthesized. 133

G$_2$ phase *FAZE* The stage of interphase when membrane components are synthesized and stored. 133

gallbladder *GALL-blad-er* A structure leading from the liver and toward the small intestine that stores bile. 477

gamete *GAM-eet* A sex cell. The sperm and ovum. 28

gametoclonal variation *gah-ME-toe-KLON-al VAR-ee-AY-shun* Genetically variant plantlets grown from callus initiated by sex cells. 609

gametophyte *gah-MEE-toe-fight* The part of a plant's life cycle when sex cells are manufactured. 28, 573

ganglia *GANG-lee-ah* Cell bodies of neurons. 331

ganglion cells *GANG-lee-on SELZ* Cells comprising the third layer of the retina in the human eye. 356

gastric juice *GAS-trik JUICE* The fluid secreted by stomach cells; responsible for chemical digestion there. 470

gastric lipase *GAS-trik LI-pace* A stomach enzyme that chemically digests certain lipid molecules. 470

gastrin *GAS-trin* A hormone secreted by stomach cells that stimulates more gastric juice to be secreted. 470

gastrointestinal tract *GAS-tro-in-TES-ti-nal TRAKT* A continuous tube along which food is physically and chemically digested into its constituent nutrients. 467

gene *JEAN* A sequence of DNA that specifies the sequence of amino acids in a particular polypeptide. 217

gene library *JEAN LI-brair-ee* The genome of an organism, cut into pieces that are each cultured in recombinant bacteria. 274

gene pool *JEAN PUL* All the genes in a population. 631

generative nucleus *GEN-er-rah-tiv NU-klee-us* A haploid cell resulting from the mitotic division of a microspore, in male plant reproduction. 574

genetic code *jeh-NET-ik KODE* The correspondence between specific DNA base sequences and the amino acids that they specify. 259

genetic drift *jah-NET-ik DRIFT* Changes in gene frequencies caused by the separation of a small group from a larger population. 632

genetic heterogeneity *jeh-NET-ik HET-er-o-jeh-NE-eh-tee* Different genotypes that have identical phenotypes. 231

genetic load *jah-NET-ik LOAD* The collection of deleterious alleles in a population. 634

genetic marker *jeh-NET-ik MAR-ker* A detectable piece of DNA that is closely linked to a gene of interest, whose precise location is not known. 237, 303

genome *jeh-NOME* All of the DNA in a cell of an organism. 253

genotype *JEAN-o-type* The genetic constitution of an individual. 220

geological time scale *GE-o-LODG-ik-kel TIME SKAL* A division of time into major eras of biological and geological activity, then periods within eras, and finally epochs within some periods. 654

geotropism *GEE-o-TRO-piz-um* A plant's growth response toward gravity. 592

gerontology *JER-on-TOL-o-gee* Study of the biological changes of aging at the molecular, cellular, organismal, and population levels. 187

gibberellins *JIB-ah-REL-linz* A class of plant hormones that promote cell elongation and division in seeds, roots, shoots, and young leaves. 588

globin *GLO-bin* A polypeptide chain that binds iron and forms part of a molecule of hemoglobin. 426

glomerular filtrate *glo-MER-u-ler FIL-trate* In a nephron in the kidney, the material that diffuses from the glomerulus to the Bowman's capsule. 508

glomerulus *glo-MER-u-lus* A ball of capillaries lying between the afferent arterioles and efferent arterioles in the proximal region of a nephron. 506

glottis *GLOT-is* The opening from the pharynx to the larynx. 449

glucagon *GLU-ka-gon* A pancreatic hormone that breaks down glycogen into glucose, raising blood-sugar levels. 378

glucocorticoids *GLU-ko-KOR-tah-koidz* Hormones secreted by the adrenal cortex that enable the body to survive prolonged stress. 378

glycolysis *gli-KOL-eh-sis* A catabolic pathway occurring in the cytoplasm of all cells. One molecule of glucose is split and rearranged into two molecules of pyruvic acid. 119

glycoprotein *GLY-ko PRO-teen* A molecule built of a protein and a sugar. 97

goiter *GOI-ter* A lump in the neck caused by a thyroid gland that swells due to lack of iodine in the diet. 376

Golgi apparatus *GOL-gee AP-ah-rah-tis* A system of flat, stacked, membrane-bound sacs where sugars are polymerized to starches or bonded to proteins or lipids. 77

gonadotropic hormones *go-NAD-o-TRO-pik HOR-moan* Hormones made in the anterior pituitary that affect the ovaries or testes. 374

gout *GOUT* An inborn error of purine metabolism in which uric acid accumulates in the joints. 502

grana *GRAN-ah* Stacks of flattened thylakoid discs comprising the inner membrane of a chloroplast. 81, 116

graptolites *GRAP-toe-litz* Organisms that lived in the Ordovician period, whose fossilized remains resemble pencil markings. 657

gray matter *GRAY MAT-ter* Cell bodies and interneurons that are not myelinated and are often involved in integration. 321

greenhouse effect *GREEN-haus E-fekt* Elevation in surface temperature of the earth by accumulation of carbon dioxide, which allows solar radiation of short wavelengths in but does not release the longer wavelength, infrared heat that the energy is converted to. 749

gross primary production *GROSS PRI-mar-ee pro-DUK-shun* The total amount of energy converted to chemical energy by photosynthesis in a certain amount of time in a given area. 717

ground tissue *GROUND TISH-u* The tissue comprising most of the primary body of a plant, filling much of the interior of roots, stems, and leaves. 552

growth factor *GROWTH FAK-ter* Locally acting proteins that assist in would healing. 137

growth rings *GROWTH RINGZ* Demarcations seen in cross sections of wood, indicating yearly growth. 566

guanine *GWAN-een* One of the two purine nitrogenous bases in DNA and RNA. 57, 253

guard cells *GUARD SELZ* Cells that control the opening and closing of stomata in plants. 554

gymnosperms *JIM-no-spermz* Plants whose sex cells are on cones. 29

gynoecium *gin-NEE-see-um* The second innermost whorl of a flower, consisting of female reproductive structures. 574

H

habitat *HAB-eh-tat* The place where an organism lives. 706

habituation *ha-BIT-ju-AY-shun* The simplest form of learning, in which an animal learns not to respond to certain irrelevant stimuli. 672

hair cells *HAIR SELZ* Mechanoreceptors in the inner ear that lie between the basilar membrane and the tectorial membrane and trigger action potentials in fibers of the auditory nerve. 360

half-life *HAF-life* The time it takes for half of the isotopes in a sample of an element to decay into the second isotopic form. This measurement is used in absolute dating of fossils. 650

hammer *HAM-er* One of the bones in the middle ear. 359

haploid *HAP-loid* A cell with one copy of each chromosome. 157

hardwoods *HARD-woodz* Woods of dicots, such as oak, maple, and ash. 566

Hardy-Weinberg equilibrium *HAR-dee WINE-berg EE-kwah-LEE-BREE-um* Maintenance of the proportion of genotypes from one generation to the next, signifying that for a particular gene, evolution is not occurring. 632

Haversian canal *hah-VER-shun kah-NAL* In bone, a central portal housing blood vessels. 393

heart *HART* A muscular pump that forces blood through conduits throughout the body. 421

heart murmur *HART MUR-mer* A sound heard in the chest when heart valves do not function normally. 434

heartburn *HART-burn* A burning sensation in the upper chest caused by acidic chyme squeezing into the esophagus. 471

heartwood *HART-wood* Wood in the center of a tree, where wastes collect. 566

heavy chain *HEV-ee CHANE* The two larger polypeptide chains comprising a Y-shaped subunit of an antibody. 518

Heimlich maneuver *HEIM-lik mah-NU-ver* A motion of pushing up and in under a choking person's rib cage, which can dislodge the item caught in the throat. 450

helper T cells *HEL-per T SELZ* Lymphocytes that produce lymphokines and stimulate the activities of other T cells and other cell types. 521

heme *HEEM* An iron-containing complex that is the oxygen-binding part of the hemoglobin molecule. 426

hemizygous *HEM-ee-ZY-gus* A gene carried on the Y chromosome in humans. 238

hemoccult test *HEM-ok-kult TEST* An examination of fecal matter for blood, which can indicate a disorder. 477

hepatic portal system *heh-PAH-tik POR-tel SIS-tum* A special division of the circulatory system that enables the liver to harness the chemical energy in digested food rapidly. 432

hepatic portal vein *heh-PAH-tik POR-tel VANE* The vein that leads to the liver. 432

hepatitis *HEP-ah-TI-tis* Inflammation of the liver, usually caused by a viral infection. 478

heterogametic sex *HET-er-o-gah-MEE-tik SEX* The sex with two different sex chromosomes, such as the human male. 245

heterotroph(ic) *HET-er-o-TROF* An organism that obtains nourishment from another organism. 22, 114

heterozygous *HET-er-o-ZI-gus* Possessing two different alleles for a particular gene. 220

hippocampus *HI-po-KAM-pes* A part of the cerebral cortex thought to be involved in forming memories. 341

histamine *HIS-tah-meen* An allergy mediator that widens blood vessels and causes certain allergy symptoms. 515

homeostasis *HOME-ee-o-STA-sis* The ability of an organism to maintain constancy of body temperature, fluid balance, and chemistry. 498

hominid *HAWM-eh-nid* Animals ancestral to humans only. 662

hominoids *HAWM-eh-noidz* Animals ancestral to apes and humans that dwelled in Africa about 20 to 30 million years ago. 661

homogametic sex *HO-mo-gah-MEE-tik SEX* The sex with two identical sex chromosomes, such as the human female. 245

homologous *ho-MOL-eh-gus* Similarly built structures in different organisms that have the same general function, indicating that they are inherited from a common ancestor. 651

homologous pairs *ho-MOL-eh-gus PAIRZ* Chromosome pairs that have the same sequence of genes. 159

homozygous *HO-mo-ZI-gus* Possessing two identical alleles for a particular gene. 220

hormone *HOR-moan* A biochemical manufactured in a gland and transported in the blood to a target organ, where it exerts a characteristic effect. 137, 368

human chorionic gonadotropin *YU-man KOR-ee-on-ik go-NAD-o-TRO-pin* A hormone secreted by the preembryo and embryo that prevents menstruation. 173, 381

human lung surfactant *HU-man LUNG sir-FAK-TANT* A mixture of phospholipid molecules that inflates alveoli in the lungs. 453

humerus *YOOM-eh-ris* The upper arm bone. 400

humoral immune response *HUME-er-al IM-mune ree-SPONZ* The secretion of antibodies by B cells in response to detecting a foreign antigen. 518

hunter-gatherer *HUN-ter GATH-er-er* A person who collects and eats native vegetation. 539

hybridoma *HI-bra-DOE-mah* An artificial cell created by fusing a B cell with a cancer cell that secretes a particular antibody indefinitely. 531

hydrocarbon *HI-dro-kar-bon* A molecule containing carbon and hydrogen. 47

hydrochloric acid *HI-dro-KLOR-ik AS-id* A strong acid found in the stomach, where it provides the pH needed to activate pepsin, which chemically digests protein. 470

hydrogen bond *HI-dro-gen bond* A weak chemical bond between negatively charged portions of molecules and hydrogen ions. 48

hydrolysis *hi-DROL-eh-sis* Splitting of a molecule in two by adding water. 50

hydrophilic *HI-dro-FILL-ik* Attraction of part of a molecule to water. 95

hydrophobic *HI-dro-FOOB-ik* Repulsion of part of a molecule from water. 95

hydrostatic skeleton *HI-dro-STAT-ik SKEL-eh-ten* The simplest type of skeleton, built of a liquid surrounded by a layer of flexible tissue. 390

hyperpolarize *HI-per-POLE-er-ize* The action of an inhibitory neurotransmitter, which causes the postsynaptic neuron's interior to become more negative than the resting potential by admitting Cl⁻. 324

hypertension *HI-per-TEN-shun* Higher than normal blood pressure. 434

hyperthyroidism *HI-per-THY-roid-iz-um* A swelling in the neck (toxic goiter) caused by an overactive thyroid gland, which accelerates metabolism. 377

hypertrophy *hi-PER-tro-fee* An increase in muscle mass, possibly due to exercise. 417

hyperventilation *HI-per-VEN-tah-LAY-shun* An increased breathing rate, which decreases the level of carbon dioxide in the blood. 458

hyphae *HI-fee* Threadlike filaments that are part of the bodies of multicellular fungi. 27

hypocotyl *HI-po-KOT-el* The stemlike region below the cotyledons. 578

hypodermis *HI-po-DER-mis* The outermost, protective layer of the cortex of a plant. 564

hypoglycemia *HI-po-gly-SEEM-ee-ah* A low level of glucose in the blood, producing weakness, anxiety, and shakiness. 379

hypotension *HI-po-TEN-shun* Lower than normal blood pressure. 434

hypothalamus *HI-po-THAL-eh-mus* A small area beneath the thalamus that controls many aspects of homeostasis, including hunger, thirst, body temperature, heartbeat, water balance, blood pressure, sexual arousal, and feelings of pain, pleasure, anger, and fear. The hypothalamus links the nervous and endocrine systems. 335

hypothesis *hy-POTH-eh-sis* An educated guess, based on prior knowledge. 3

hypothyroidism *HI-po-THY-ro-diz-um* A slowing of metabolism and heartbeat and lowering of blood pressure and body temperature resulting from an underactive thyroid gland. 376

I

ichthyosaurs *IK-thee-o-SORZ* Dinosaurs that lived in the seas. 659

idiotype *ID-ee-o-TYPE* The particular parts of an antibody's antigen binding site that are complementary in conformation to the conformation of a particular antigen. 519

ileum *IL-ee-um* The last section of the small intestine. 472

imbibition *IM-bah-BISH-un* The absorption of water by a seed. 580

impact theory *IM-pakt THER-ee* The idea that a meteor or comet crashed to earth, throwing soot into the atmosphere, which blocked the sun and hampered photosynthesis, leading to the extinctions of many types of organisms. 640

imprinting *IM-print-ing* A type of learning that occurs for a limited time, usually early in an animal's life, and is performed usually without obvious reinforcement. Chicks following a parent illustrates imprinting. 673

inborn error of metabolism *IN-born ER-er Mah-TAB-o-liz-um* A disorder caused by a missing or inactive enzyme. 287

inclusive fitness *in-KLU-siv FIT-nes* A definition of fitness including personal reproductive success as well as that of relatives sharing an individual's genes. 692

incomplete dominance *IN-kim-plete DOM-eh-nance* A heterozygote whose phenotype is intermediate between the phenotypes of the two homozygotes. 225

independent assortment *IN-deh-PEN-dent ah-SORT-ment* The random arrangement of homologs during metaphase of meiosis I. 160, 223

indoleacetic acid (IAA) *IN-doe-ah-SEE-tik AS-id* The most active auxin, a type of plant hormone that stimulates growth. 589

induced ovulator *in-DEUCED OV-u-LAY-ter* Inducement of ovulation by the presence of a male. 382

industrial melanism *in-DUS-tree-al MEL-an-iz-um* An adaptive response of insects to pollution, in which coloration that is protective against a sooty background is selected. 635

inferior vena cava *in-FEAR-ee-er VE-nah kah-vah* The lower branch of the largest vein that leads to the heart. 432, 434

infertility *IN-fer-TIL-eh-tee* The inability to conceive a child after a year of trying. 196

inflammation *IN-fla-MA-shun* Increased blood flow and accumulation of fluid and phagocytes at the site of an injury, rendering the area inhospitable to bacteria. 515

inhibitory synapse *in-HIB-eh-tore-ee SIN-apse* A synapse across which a particular neurotransmitter has difficulty depolarizing the postsynaptic membrane. 324

innate *in-ATE* Instinctive. 667

inner cell mass *IN-er SEL MASS* The cells in the blastocyst that develop into the embryo. 173

inner ear *IN-ner EAR* A fluid-filled chamber that houses structures important in providing hearing and maintaining balance. 359

insect-trapping leaves *IN-sect TRAP-ing LEEVZ* Leaves of carnivorous plants that attract, capture, and digest prey. 562

insertion *in-SER-shun* The end of a muscle on a movable bone. 414

insight learning *IN-site LEARN-ing* The ability to apply prior learning to a new situation without observable trial-and-error activity. This is reasoning. 674

insomnia *in-SAWM-nee-ah* A sleep disorder in which a person has difficulty falling or remaining asleep. 676

inspiration *IN-spir-AY-shun* Inhalation. 453

insulin *IN-sel-in* A pancreatic hormone that lowers blood-sugar level by stimulating body cells to take up glucose from the blood and to metabolize or store it. 378

insulin-dependent diabetes *IN-sel-in de-PEN-dent DI-ah-BEAT-es* Diabetes mellitus resulting from insufficient insulin, usually beginning in childhood. Without injecting insulin, this condition causes extreme thirst, blurred vision, weakness, fatigue, nausea, and weight loss. 379

insulin-independent diabetes *IN-sel-in IN-de-PEN-dent DI-ah-BEAT-es* Diabetes mellitus resulting from the body's inability to utilize insulin. It usually begins in adulthood, produces fatigue, itchy skin, blurred vision, slow wound healing, and poor circulation and can often be controlled by diet, exercise, and drugs. 379

intercalary meristems *in-TER-kah-LER-ee MER-eh-stemz* Dividing tissues in grasses between mature regions of stem. 552

intercalated disks *in-TER-kah-LAY-tid DISKS* Tight foldings in cardiac muscle cell membranes that join adjacent cells. 405

interferon *IN-ter-FEAR-on* A polypeptide produced by a T cell infected with a virus that diffuses to surrounding cells and stimulates them to manufacture biochemicals that halt viral replication. 515

intermediate-day plants *IN-ter-MEED-ee-at DAY PLANTZ* Plants that flower only when exposed to days of intermediate length, growing vegetatively at other times. 596

interneuron *IN-ter-neur-on* A neuron that connects one neuron to another to integrate information from many sources and to coordinate responses. 315

internodes *IN-ter-noodz* Portions of stem between nodes. 557

interphase *IN-ter-FAZE* The period when the cell synthesizes proteins, lipids, carbohydrates, and nucleic acids. 131

interstitial cell stimulating hormone (ICSH) *IN-ter-STISH-el STIM-u-la-ting HOR-moan* A hormone made in the anterior pituitary that stimulates late development of sperm cells and the synthesis of testosterone. 375

intertidal zone *IN-ter-TI-dal ZONE* The region bordering an estuary where the tide recedes and returns. 735

intracellular digestion *IN-tra-SEL-yu-lar di-JEST-shun* Digestion within food vacuoles in cells. 465

intron *IN-tron* Bases of a gene that are transcribed but are excised from the mRNA before translation into protein. 265

inversion *in-VER-shun* A chromosome with part of its gene sequence inverted. 280

ion *I-on* An atom that has lost or gained electrons, giving it an electrical charge. 46

ionic bond *i-ON-ik bond* Attraction between oppositely charged ions. 46

iris *I-rus* The thin, opaque, colored region of the choroid coat in the human eye. 354

irritability *IR-eh-tah-BIL-eh-tee* An immediate response to a stimulus. 40

islets of Langerhans *I-lets LANG-er-hanz* Clusters of cells in the pancreas that secrete hormones controlling the body's utilization of nutrients. 378

isotope *I-so-tope* A differently weighted form of an element. 45

J

J-shaped curve *J SHAPED KURV* The mathematical curve resulting from plotting exponential population growth over time. 701

jaundice *JAWN-dis* An overproduction of the bile pigment bilirubin, which causes the skin to turn yellow. 478

jejunum *jah-JU-num* The middle section of the small intestine. 472

Jurassic period *jur-AS-ik PER-ee-od* The time from 185 to 135 million years ago, when dinosaurs were abundant. 659

K

karyokinesis *KAR-ee-o-kah-NEE-sus* Division of the genetic material. 131

karyotype *KAR-ee-o-type* A size-order chart of chromosomes. 298

keystone herbivore hypothesis *Ke-stone ER-bah-vor hi-POTH-eh-sis* The theory that the demise of large herbivores 11,000 years ago led to overgrowth of vegetation, which changed the environment sufficiently to kill many small herbivores. 643

kidney failure *KID-nee FAIL-yur* Damaged renal tubules, which eventually hamper the function of nephrons, resulting in the buildup of toxins in the blood. 511

kidney stones *KID-nee STONZ* Salts that precipitate out of newly formed urine and collect as solid masses in the kidney tubules or the renal pelvis. 511

kidneys *KID-neez* Paired organs built of millions of tubules responsible for excretion of nitrogenous waste and osmoregulation. 504

kilocalories *KIL-o-KAL-o-reez* The energy needed to raise one gram of water one degree Celsius. 484

kwashiorkor *KWASH-ee-OR-ker* Starvation resulting from a switch from breast milk to food deficient in nutrients. 490

L

lactic acid formation *LAK-tik AS-id for-MAY-shun* The conversion of pyruvic acid from glycolysis into lactic acid, occurring in some anaerobic bacteria and tired mammalian muscle cells. 121

lactose intolerance *LAK-tos in-TOLL-eh-rence* Digestive difficulties caused by a deficiency of the enzyme lactase. 472

larynx *LAR-inks* The "voice box" and a conduit for air. 449

latent learning *LA-tent LEARN-ing* Learning without any obvious reward or punishment; not apparent until sometime after the learning experience. 674

lateral meristems *LAT-er-al MER-eh-STEMZ* Actively dividing plant cells that grow outward, thickening the plant. 552

leaf abscission *LEAF ab-SCISZ-on* The shedding of a tree's leaves as a normal part of its life cycle. 562

lean tissue *LEEN-TISH-u* Body weight consisting of muscle, bone, connective tissue, and water. 493

learning *LEARN-ing* A change in behavior as a result of experience. 672

lens *LENZ* The structure in the eye through which light passes and is focused.

lentic system *LEN-tik SIS-tum* Fresh water biomes that have standing water, such as lakes and ponds. 733

lichen *LI-ken* An organism formed by the union of a fungus and a green alga. 16

ligaments *LIG-ah-mentz* Tough bands of fibrous connective tissue that form the joint capsule. 401

light chain *LITE CHANE* The two smaller polypeptide chains comprising a Y-shaped subunit of an antibody. 518

light reactions *LITE re-AK-shunz* The light-requiring reactions of photosynthesis that harness photon energy and use it to convert ADP to ATP. 117

limnetic zone *lim-NET-ik ZONE* The layer of open water in a lake or pond that is penetrated by light. 734

linkage *LINK-ege* The location of genes on the same chromosome. 237

lipases *LI-pay-ses* Enzymes that chemically digest fats. 472

lipid bilayer *LIP-id BI-lay-er* A two-layered structure formed by the alignment of phospholipids, reflecting their hydrophobic and hydrophilic tendencies. 95

lipids *LIP-idz* Organic molecules that are insoluble in water, including the fats. 51

littoral zone *LIT-or-al ZONE* The shallow region along the shore of a lake or pond where light can penetrate to the bottom with sufficient intensity to allow photosynthesis. 734

liver *LIV-er* The largest solid organ in the body, which detoxifies the blood, stores glycogen and fat-soluble vitamins, synthesizes blood proteins, and monitors blood-sugar level, plus other functions. 477

logistic growth curve *lo-JIS-tik GROWTH KURV* An S-shaped mathematical curve reflecting the slowing of population growth as the carrying capacity is reached, in response to environmental resistance. 705

long-day plants *LONG-day PLANTZ* Plants that require light periods longer than some critical length to flower. 596

long-term synaptic potentiation *LONG TERM sin-AP-tik PO-ten-she-A-shun* The hypothesis that long-term memory results from repeated and frequent stimulation of the same neurons, which strengthens their synaptic connections. 341

loop of Henle *LUP HEN-lee* A loop of a nephron, lying between the proximal and distal convoluted tubules, where water is conserved and the urine becomes concentrated by a countercurrent multiplier system that returns water to the blood. 508

lordosis *lor-DOE-sis* An abnormal forward curvature of the spine. 399

lotic system *LO-tik SIS-tum* Fresh water biomes with running water, such as rivers and streams. 733

lumbar vertebrae *LUM-bar VER-tah-bray* The five vertebrae in the small of the back.

lungs *LUNGZ* Paired structures that house the bronchial tree and the alveoli, the sites of gas exchange. 453

luteinizing hormone (LH) *LU-tah-ni-zing HOR-moan* A hormone made in the anterior pituitary that promotes ovulation. 375

luteinizing hormone releasing hormone (LHRH) *LU-ten-I-zing HOR-moan ree-LEAS-ing HOR-moan* A hormone sent from the hypothalamus to the anterior pituitary, where it stimulates release of follicle stimulating hormone and luteinizing hormone. 381

lymph *LIMF* Blood plasma minus some large proteins, which flows through lymph capillaries and lymph vessels. 441

lymphatic system *lim-FAH-tik SIS-tum* A circulatory system consisting of lymph capillaries and lymph vessels that transports lymph, which consists of blood plasma minus large proteins. 441

lymph capillaries *LIMF CAP-eh-LAIR-eez* Dead-ended, microscopic vessels that transport lymph. 441

lymph nodes *LIMF NOODZ* Structures in the lymphatic system that contain white blood cells and protect against infection. 441

lymphocytes *LIM-fo-SITZ* White blood cells that provide immune protection, including the B cells, which secrete antibodies, and the T cells, which secrete lymphokines and control the activities of each other and other cell types. 517

lymphokines *LIM-fo-KINES* Biochemicals secreted by lymphocytes that attack cancer cells or cells coated with viruses. 517

lymph vessels *LIMF VES-selz* Vessels that transport lymph and eventually empty into veins. 441

lysosome *LI-so-soam* A sac in a eukaryotic cell in which molecules and worn-out organelles are enzymatically dismantled. 80

M

macroevolution *MAK-ro-ev-eh-LU-shun* Large-scale evolutionary changes, such as speciation and extinction. 621

macronutrients *MAK-ro-NU-tri-entz* The carbohydrates, fats, and proteins that are obtained from food and required in large amounts. 482

macrophages *MAK-ro-FAH-ges* Very large, wandering phagocytic cells. 515

maiasaurs *MI-ah-SORZ* Duck-billed dinosaurs that lived in Montana about 80 million years ago. 659

major histocompatibility complex (MHC) *MA-jer HIS-toe-kum-PAT-ah-BIL-eh-tee KOM-plex* A family of genes in mammals that specifies cell surface proteins involved in cell-cell recognition. 518

map sense *MAP SENS* A sense that tells an organism its location relative to its home. 681

marasmus *mah-RAS-mus* Starvation due to profound nutrient deficiency. 490

marrow cavity *MAR-o KAV-eh-tee* A space in the shaft of a long bone housing fatty yellow marrow. 393

marsupials *mar-SU-pee-alz* Pouched mammals. 661

mast cells *MAST SELZ* Large cells that are burst by allergens binding to IgE on their surfaces, releasing allergy mediators that cause allergy symptoms. 515

maximum intrinsic rate of increase *MAX-ah-mum in-TRIN-sik RATE IN-krees* The rate of growth of a population when each member produces as many offspring as is possible and the environment does not restrict reproduction. 701

medulla *mah-DUEL-ah* The middle portion of the kidney, consisting of loops of Henle and collecting ducts of nephrons. 505

medulla *mah-DULE-ah* The part of the brain stem closest to the spinal cord; regulates such vital functions as breathing, heartbeat, blood pressure, and certain reflexes. 334

megagametophytes *MEG-ah-gah-MEE-toe-fightz* The large, female egg-producing gametophytes in a plant. 573

megakaryocyte *MEG-ah-KAR-ee-o-site* A huge bone marrow cell that breaks apart to yield platelets. 427

megasporangia *MEG-ah-spor-AN-gee-ah* Structures in which megaspores form. 573

megaspore mother cell *MEG-ah-spor MOTH-er SEL* A cell within an ovule that divides meiotically to produce four haploid cells, three of which degenerate. 574

megaspores *MEG-ah-sporz* Structures in plants that give rise to the female gametophytes. 573

meiosis *Mi-O-sis* Cell division resulting in a halving of the genetic material. 131

melanocyte stimulating hormone (MSH) *mah-LAN-o-site STIM-u-lat-ing HOR-moan* A hormone produced in between the anterior and posterior lobes of the pituitary in some vertebrate species that controls skin pigmentation. 375

melatonin *MEL-ah-TOE-nin* A hormone produced by the pineal gland that may control other hormones by a sensitivity to lightness and darkness. 382, 677

memory cells *MEM-or-ee SELZ* Mature B cells that are specific to an antigen already encountered and respond quickly by secreting antibodies when that antigen is encountered subsequently. 518

meninges *MEN-in-gees* A triple layer of membranes that covers and protects the central nervous system. 342

mesentery *MEZ-en-tear-ee* An epithelial sheet that supports digestive structures in the human.

mesoderm *MEZ-o-derm* The middle embryonic germ layer, whose cells become bone, muscle, blood, dermis, and reproductive organs. 175

messenger RNA (mRNA) *MESS-en-ger* A molecule of ribonucleic acid that is complementary in sequence to the sense strand of a gene. 76, 258

metabolism *meh-TAB-o-liz-um* The biochemical reactions that acquire and utilize energy. 109

metacarpals *MET-ah-KAR-pelz* Bones of the hand. 400

metaphase *MET-ah-faze* The second stage of cell division, when chromosomes align down the center of a cell. In mitosis the chromosomes form a single line. In meiosis I, the chromosomes line up in homologous paris. 134

metastasis *meh-TAH-STAH-sis* The spreading of cancer from its site of origin to other parts of the body. 145

metazoan *MET-ah-ZO-en* An ancient, simple multicellular animal ancestral to modern animals. 31

mibrid *MI-brid* A cell into which a mitochondrion from another cell is introduced. 610

microevolution *MIKE-ro-ev-eh-LU-shun* The more subtle, incremental single-trait changes that underlie speciation. 621

microfilaments *MI-kro-FILL-ah-ment* Tiny rods built of actin found within cells, especially contractile cells. 104

microgametophytes *MIKE-ro-gah-MEE-toe-fightz* The small, male sperm-producing gametophytes in a plant. 573

micronutrients *MIKE-ro-NU-tree-entz* The vitamins and minerals that are obtained from food and required in small amounts. 482

microsporangia *MI-kro-spor-AN-gee-ah* Structures in which microspores form. 573

microspore mother cells *MI-kro-spor MOTH-er SELZ* Cells in pollen sacs that divide meiotically to produce four haploid microspores. 574

microspores *MI-kro-sporz* Structures in plants that give rise to the male gametophytes. 573

microtubules *MI-kro-TO-bules* Long, hollow tubules, built of the protein tubulin, that provide movement within cells. 81, 104

microvilli *MI-kro-VIL-i* Tiny projections on the surfaces of epithelial cells, which comprise intestinal villi. 473

midbrain *MID-brane* The part of the brain stem above the pons where white matter connects with higher brain structures and gray matter contributes to sight and hearing. 335

middle ear *MID-el EAR* The part of the ear consisting of three bones, the hammer, anvil, and stirrup, that transmit and amplify sound. 359

mineralocorticoids *MIN-er-rel-KOR-tah-KOIDZ* Hormones produced in the adrenal cortex that maintain blood volume and electrolyte balance by stimulating the kidneys to return Na⁺ and water to the blood and to excrete K⁺. 378

mitochondria *MI-toe-KON-dree-ah* Organelles within which the reactions of cellular metabolism occur. 79

mitosis *mi-TOE-sis* A form of cell division in which two genetically identical cells are generated from one. 131

molecular evolution *mo-LEK-yu-ler EV-o-LU-shun* The tracing of sequence differences in proteins and nucleic acids between living species to establish degrees of evolutionary relatedness. 652

molecule *MOLL-eh-kuel* A structure resulting from the combination of atoms. 45

Monera *mo-NER-ah* The taxonomic kingdom including the bacteria and the cyanobacteria. 22

monoclonal antibodies *MON-o-KLON-al AN-tah-BOD-eez* Antibodies descended from a single B cell and therefore are identical. B cells are fused with cancer cells to create hybridomas, which are artificial cells that secrete a particular antibody indefinitely. 531

monocots *MON-o-kotz* Flowering plants that have one seed leaf. 557, 578

monogamy *mah-NAUG-o-mee* The formation of a permanent male-female pair. 696

monohybrid *MON-o-HI-brid* An individual heterozygous for a particular gene. 221

monosaccharide *MON-o-SAK-eh-ride* A sugar built of one 5- or 6-carbon unit, including glucose, galactose, and fructose. 49

monosomy *MON-o-soam-ee* A cell missing one chromosome. 280

monotremes *MON-o-tremz* Egg-laying mammals. 661

morula *MORE-u-lah* The preembryonic stage of a solid ball of cells. 172

mosaic catastrophism *mo-ZAY-ik CAT-as-TROF-iz-um* A variation of Neptunism that holds that a series of great floods molded the earth's features and caused various extinctions and speciations. 621

motor areas *MO-ter AIR-ee-ahs* Parts of the cerebral cortex that send impulses to skeletal muscles. 337

motor (efferent) neuron *MO-ter (EF-fer-ent) NEUR-on* A neuron that transmits a message from the central nervous system toward a muscle or gland. It has a long axon and short dendrites. 315

motor pathways *MO-ter PATH-wayz* Nerve tracts in the peripheral nervous system that carry impulses from the central nervous system to muscles or glands. 342

motor unit *MOW-ter U-nit* A nerve cell and all of the muscle fibers it contacts. 411

mucigel *MUUS-eh-gel* A slimy, lubricating substance produced by cells of a root cap. 563

muscle fasciculi *MUS-sel fah-SIK-u-li* Bundles of muscle fibers. 406

muscle spindles *MUS-sel SPIN-delz* Receptors in skeletal muscle that monitor the degree of muscle tone or how many fibers are contracted at a given time. 416

muscle tone *MUS-sel TONE* The contraction of some fibers in skeletal muscle at any given time. 416

muscular tissue *MUS-ku-lar TISH-u* Tissue built of contractile cells, providing motion. 81

mutant *MU-tent* A phenotype or allele that is not the most common for a certain gene in a population. 220

mutant selection *MU-tant sah-LEK-shun* Searching for genetic variants that offer a desired characteristic. 609

mutation *mu-TAY-shun* A change in a gene or chromosome. 232, 261

mutualism *MU-tu-al-iz-um* A symbiotic relationship in which both partners benefit. 14

mycelium *MI-seal-ee-um* An assemblage of hyphae in a fungus. 27

mycorrhizae *MI-ko-RI-zee* A mutualistic association between a plant's roots and fungi that absorb nutrients from soil. 564

myelin sheath *MI-eh-lin SHEATH* A fatty material that insulates some nerve fibers in vertebrates, allowing rapid transmission of nerve impulses. 320

myofibrils *MI-o-FI-brilz* Cylindrical subunits of a muscle fiber. 407

myofilaments *MI-o-FILL-eh-mentz* Actin or myosin "strings" that comprise myofibrils. 407

myosin *MI-o-sin* A type of protein comprising the thick myofilaments of skeletal muscle cells. 407

myxedema *MIX-eh-DEEM-ah* Lethargy, dry sparse hair, and a puffy face, caused by an underactive thyroid beginning in adulthood. 376

N

naked-gene hypothesis *NA-kid JEAN hi-POTH-eh-sis* The theory that nucleic acids evolved before proteins. 62

narcolepsy *NAR-co-LEP-see* A sleep disorder in which a person suddenly falls asleep during the day. 676

nasal conchae *NAZ-al KON-chi* Three shelflike bones in each nasal cavity that partition it into channels. 448

nastic movements *NAS-tic MOVE-mentz* Nondirectional plant motions. 594

natural killer cells *NAT-chu-ral KILL-er SELZ* Lymphocytes that cause infected cells and possibly cancer cells to burst.

natural products chemists *NAT-u-ral PROD-uks KEM-ists* Chemists who examine biochemicals for substances with therapeutic or other value. 547

natural selection *NAT-rul sah-LEK-shun* The differential survival and reproduction of organisms whose genetic traits better adapt them to a particular environment. 626

nautiloids *NAWT-eh-loidz* Organisms that appeared in the seas of the Cambrian period. 657

Neanderthals *nee-AN-der-thalz* Members of *Homo sapiens* who lived about 75,000 years ago in Europe and Asia. 663

negative feedback *NEG-ah-tiv FEED-bak* The turning off of an enzyme's synthesis or activity caused by accumulation of the product of the reaction that the enzyme catalyzes. 111

negative feedback loop *NEG-ah-tiv FEED-bak LOOP* A biochemical pathway in which accumulation of a product inhibits earlier reactions. 370

negative reinforcement *NEG-eh-tiv REE-in-FORC-ment* A painful stimulus given to encourage an animal to avoid a particular behavior. 673

neonatology *NE-o-nah-TOL-eh-gee* The study of the newborn. 204

neoteny *ne-OT-eh-nee* Retaining juvenile features of an ancestral species. 669

nephron *NEF-ron* A microscopic, tubular subunit of a kidney, built of a renal tubule and peritubular capillaries. 505

Neptunism *NEP-tune-iz-um* The idea that a single great flood organized the features of the earth's surface present today. 621

neritic zone *NER-it-ik ZONE* The coastal region of an ocean. 737

nerve fiber *NERVE FI-ber* An axon. 315

nervous tissue *NER-vis TISH-u* A tissue whose cells (neutrons and neuroglia) form a communication network. 81

net primary production *NET PRI-mar-ee pro-DUK-shun* The energy left over for growth and reproduction after an animal has eaten. 717

neural (synaptic) integration *NEUR-el (sin-AP-tik) IN-tah-GRAY-shun* The summing of incoming inhibitory and excitatory messages by a neuron. This information determines whether or not an action potential will occur. 324

neural tube *NEUR-el TUUB* The embryonic precursor of the central nervous system. 181

neuron *NEUR-on* A nerve cell, consisting of a cell body, a long "sending" projection called an axon, and numerous "receiving" projections called dendrites. 86

neurosecretory cells *NUR-o-SEK-rah-tore-ee SELZ* Cells in the hypothalamus that function as neurons at one end but like endocrine cells at the other by receiving neural messages and secreting the hormones ADH and oxytocin. 372

neurotransmitter *NEUR-o-TRANZ-mit-er* A chemical passed from a nerve cell to another nerve cell or to a muscle or gland cell, relaying an electrochemical message. 86, 321

neutron *NEW-tron* A particle in an atom's nucleus that is electrically neutral and has one mass unit. 44

neutrophils *NU-tro-FILLZ* Short-lived phagocytic white blood cells that help combat the initial stages of infection. 515

niche *NITCH* The ways in which an organism interacts with the living and nonliving environment. 706

nitrifying bacteria *NI-trah-FI-ing bak-TER-ee-ah* Bacteria that convert ammonia from dead organisms to nitrite. 721

nitrite bacteria *NI-trit bak-TER-ee-ah* Bacteria that convert nitrite to nitrate.

node of Ranvier *NODE RON-vee-ay* A short region of exposed axon between adjacent Schwann cells on neurons of the peripheral nervous systems of vertebrates. 321

nodes *NOODZ* Areas of leaf attachment. 557

nondisjunction *NON-dis-JUNK-shun* The unequal partition of chromosomes into gametes during meiosis. 280

nonessential nutrients *NON-ee-SEN-shal NU-tree-entz* Nutrients found in food but that can also be synthesized in the body. 484

norepinephrine (noradrenaline) *NOR-EP-eh-NEF-rin (NOR-ah-DREN-ah-lin)* A catecholamine hormone produced in the adrenal medulla and sent into the bloodstream, where it raises blood pressure, constricts blood vessels, and slows digestion, as part of the "fight or flight" response to a threat. 377

notochord *NO-toe-kord* A semirigid rod running down the length of an animal's body. 33, 181

nucleoid *NEW-klee-oid* The part of a prokaryotic cell where the DNA is located. 72

nucleolus *new-KLEE-o-lis* A structure within the nucleus where RNA nucleotides are stored. 76, 134

nucleotide *NEW-klee-o-tide* The building block of a nucleic acid, consisting of a phosphate group, a nitrogenous base, and a five-carbon sugar. 57, 252

nucleus (atomic) *NEW-klee-is* The central region of an atom, consisting of protons and neutrons. 44

nucleus (cellular) *NEW-klee-is* A membrane-bound sac in a eukaryotic cell that contains the genetic material. 22

nutrient *NU-tri-ent* A substance that is obtained from food and used in an organism to promote growth, maintenance, and repair of tissues. 482

nutrient dense *NU-tri-ent DENSE* Foods that offer a maximum amount of nutrients with a minimum number of kilocalories. 487

nyctinasty *NIK-tah-NAS-tee* A nastic (nondirectional) movement caused by daily rhythms of light and dark. 595

O

obese *o-BESE* A person who is 20% above "ideal" weight based on population statistics considering age, sex, and build. 492

obligate photoperiodism *OB-lah-get FO-toe-PER-ee-o-DIZ-um* Plants that will not flower unless they are exposed to the correct photoperiod. 596

oceanic zone *O-she-AN-ik ZONE* The deep, open part of an ocean. 737

olfactory bulb *ol-FAK-tore-ee BULB* A part of the brain that relays a message from olfactory receptor cells. 350

olfactory receptor cells (epithelium) *ol-FAK-tore-ee re-CEP-ter SELZ* Neurons specialized to detect odors, found in a small patch of tissue high in the nostrils. 350

oligotrophic *OL-ah-go-TRO-fik* A lake with few nutrients, usually a sparkling blue. 734

ommatidia *O-mah-TID-ee-ah* The visual units comprising a compound eye. 352

oncogene *ON-ko-jean* A gene that normally controls cell division but when overexpressed leads to cancer. 145

oocyte *O-o-site* The female sex cell before it is fertilized. 155

oogenesis *O-o-GEN-eh-sis* The differentiation of an egg cell, from a diploid oogonium, to a primary oocyte, to two haploid secondary oocytes, to ootids, and finally, after fertilization, to a mature ovum. 165

open behavior program *O-pen bee-HAIV-yur PRO-gram* A behavior that is flexible and easily altered by learning. 667

open circulatory system *O-pen SIR-qu-lah-TORE-ee SIS-tum* A circulatory system in which blood is not always contained in blood vessels. 422

operant conditioning *OP-er-aunt kon-DISH-on-ing* Trial-and-error learning, in which an animal voluntarily repeats any behavior that brings success. 673

operculum *o-PER-ku-lum* A flap of tissue protecting gills. 447

optic nerve *OP-tik NERV* Nerve fibers leading from the retina to the visual cortex of the brain. 356

Ordovician period *OR-do-VEESH-ee-an PER-ee-od* The period following the Cambrian period, 500 to 435 million years ago. 657

organ *OR-gan* A structure built of two or more tissues that functions as an integrated unit. 40

organelles *OR-gan-nellz* Specialized structures in eukaryotic cells that carry out specific functions. 17, 22

organelle transfer *OR-gan-el TRANZ-fer* Engineering combinations of nuclei and organelles in plant cells not seen in nature. 610

origin *ARE-eh-jen* The end of a muscle on an immobile bone. 414

osmoreceptors *OZ-mo-ree-CEP-terz* Specialized cells in the hypothalamus that sense the concentration of water in the blood. 375

osmosis *oz-MO-sis* Passive diffusion of water. 100

ossification *OS-eh-feh-KAY-shun* The process by which cartilage in embryonic bones is replaced with bone tissue. 394

osteocytes *OS-tee-o-sitz* Mature bone cells. 393

osteoporosis *OS-tee-o-por-O-sis* Bones that break easily because calcium is removed from them faster than it is replaced, possibly caused by hyperthyroidism. 377

otolith *O-toe-lith* Calcium carbonate granules in the vestibule of the inner ear whose movements provide information on changes in velocity. 363

outcrossing *OUT-cross-ing* The transfer of pollen grains from one flower to the stigma of another flower. 574

oval window *O-vel WIN-dow* A membrane between the middle ear and inner ear. 359

ovaries *O-var-ees* The paired, female gonads, which house developing oocytes. 155, 374

ovary *O-var-ree* In a flowering plant, the carpels and the ovules they enclose. 574

over dominant *O-ver DOM-en-nant* A heterozygote that is more vigorous that either homozygote. 226

ovulation *OV-u-LAY-shun* The release of an oocyte from the largest ovarian follicle just after the peak of luteinizing hormone in the blood in the middle of a woman's menstrual cycle. 381

ovules *OV-yulz* In flowering plants, a megasporangium containing a megaspore mother cell, which undergoes meiosis to produce four cells, three of which degenerate. 574

oxidation *OX-en-DAY-shun* A chemical reaction in which electrons are lost. 48

oxygen debt *OX-eh-gen DET* The body's need for oxygen to complete the metabolism of lactic acid following heavy exercise that has temporarily shifted metabolism to the anaerobic pathway. 410

oxyhemoglobin *OX-ee-HEEM-o-GLO-bin* Hemoglobin that is bright red because it has just picked up oxygen in the lungs. 426

oxytocin *OX-eh-TOE-sin* A hormone made in the hypothalamus and released from the posterior pituitary that stimulates muscle contraction in the mammary glands and the uterus. 375

P

pacemaker *PACE-may-ker* Specialized cells in the wall of the right atrium that set the pace of the heartbeat. Also called the sinoatrial node. 438

Pacinian and Meissner's corpuscles *pah-SIN-ee-en MICE-nerz KOR-pus-elz* Receptors in the skin that provide information on touch. 363

paleontologist *PAY-lee-on-TOL-ah gist* A scientist who studies evidence of past life. 640, 648

palisade mesophyll *PAL-eh-sade MEZ-o-fil* Long, columnar cells along the upper side of a leaf specialized for light absorption. 561

pancreas *PAN-kre-as* A structure that has an endocrine component, which produces somatostatin, insulin, and glucagon, and a digestive component, which produces a pancreatic juice containing trypsin, chymotrypsin, pancreatic amylase, pancreatic lipase, and nucleases. 477

parasitism *PAR-eh-sah-TIZ-um* A symbiotic relationship where one partner benefits from the other, while harming it. 15

parasympathetic nervous system *PAR-ah-SIM-pah-THE-tik NER-ves SIS-tum* Part of the autonomic nervous system that controls vital functions such as respiration and heart rate when at rest. 344, 439

parathyroid glands *PAR-ah-THY-roid GLANZ* Four small groups of cells embedded in the thyroid gland that secrete a hormone that releases calcium from bones and enhances calcium absorption through the digestive tract and kidneys, actions that regulate calcium level in blood and tissue fluid. 377, 396

parathyroid hormone *PAR-ah-THY-roid HOR-moan* The hormone produced by the parathyroid glands; regulates calcium level in the blood and tissue fluid by releasing calcium from bones and enhancing calcium absorption through the digestive tract and kidneys. 377

parenchyma *pah-REN-kah-mah* Abundant, unspecialized plant cells that can divide. 553

passive immunity *PAS-siv im-MUNE-eh-tee* Immunity generated by an organism's receiving antibodies manufactured by another organism. 522

patella *pah-TEL-lah* The bony part of the kneecap. 400

pectoral girdle *PEC-tor-al GIR-del* The two clavicles and two scapulae bones that form the shoulders. 400

pedigree *PED-eh-gree* A chart showing the relationships of relatives and which ones have a particular trait. 297

pelagic zone *pah-LA-gik ZONE* The water above the ocean floor. 737

pelvic girdle *PEL-vik GIR-del* The two hipbones. 400

pelvis *PEL-vis* The innermost portion of the kidney, which stores urine. 505

pelycosaurs *PEL-eh-ko-SORZ* The sailed lizards, which were distant ancestors of mammals. 659

penetrance *PEN-eh-trance* The percentage of individuals inheriting a genotype who express the corresponding phenotype. 227

pepsin *PEP-sin* A stomach enzyme that chemically digests protein. 470

pepsinogen *pep-SIN-o-jen* A precursor molecule that is split to yield pepsin, a stomach enzyme that chemically digests protein. 470

peptidase *PEP-tah-daze* A type of intestinal enzyme that completes protein digestion. 472

peptide bond *PEP-tide BOND* A chemical bond between two amino acids resulting from dehydration synthesis. 53, 262

peptide hormone *PEP-tide HOR-moan* A hormone composed of amino acids. It is water soluble but fat insoluble so cannot traverse a cell's membrane. Instead, it binds to a cell surface receptor and triggers a second messenger. 369

pericardium *PEAR-eh-KAR-dee-um* The tough, connective tissue sac enclosing the heart. 434

pericarp *PEAR-ah-karp* A protective layer of a seed. 541

perichondrium *PEAR-eh-KON-dree-um* A layer of connective tissue surrounding embryonic, cartilaginous bones. 394

pericycle *PEAR-ah-SI-kel* A ring of parenchyma cells in a root's cortex that produces branch roots that burst through the cortex and epidermis and into the soil. 564

periderm *PEAR-ah-derm* The outer protective covering on mature stems and roots. 568

periodontal membrane *PEAR-ah-DON-tal MEM-brane* An outer layer of the tooth, anchoring it to the gum and jawbone. 469

periods *PER-ee-odz* Time periods within eras. 654

peripheral nervous system (PNS) *per-RIF-er-al NER-vous SIS-tum* Nerves and cell bodies (ganglia) that transmit information to and from the central nervous system. 331

peristalsis *pear-eh-STAL-sis* Waves of muscle contraction along the digestive tract that propel food. 468

peritubular capillaries *pear-eh-TUUB-yu-lar CAP-eh-LAIR-eez* The capillaries that surround the renal tubule of the nephron, in the kidney. 505

permafrost *PER-mah-frost* The permanently frozen part of the ground in the tundra. 733

Permian period *PER-mee-an PER-ee-od* The time from 275 to 225 million years ago, when many species became extinct. Amphibians and reptiles were still abundant. 658

peroxisome *PER-ox-eh-soam* A membrane-bound sac budded off of the smooth ER housing enzymes important in oxygen utilization. 81

petals *PET-alz* Large and often colorful parts of flowers that sometimes help to attract pollinators. 574

petiole *PET-ee-ol* The stalklike portion of a leaf. 559

phagocytes *FAG-o-sitez* Scavenger cells that engulf and digest foreign cells. 515

phalanges *fah-LAN-gees* The finger bones. 400

pharynx *FAHR-inks* The throat. 449, 469

phelloderm *FEL-ah-derm* Living parenchyma cells in secondary growth. 568

phenocopy *FEEN-o-KOP-ee* An environmentally caused trait that resembles an inherited trait. 232

phenotype *FEEN-o-type* The observable expression of a genotype in a specific environment. 220

pheromones *FER-eh-moanz* Biochemicals secreted by an organism that stimulate a physiological or behavioral response in another individual of the same species. 385

phlebitis *flah-BI-tis* Inflammation of a vein wall. 438

phloem *FLO-um* Plant tissue that transports water and food materials. 29, 555

phospholipid *FOS-fo-LIP-id* A molecule built of a lipid and a phosphate that is hydrophobic at one end and hydrophilic at the other end. 94

photolysis *fo-TOL-eh-sis* A photosynthetic reaction in which electrons from water replace electrons lost by chlorophyll a. 116

photoperiodism *FO-toe-PER-ee-o-DIZ-um* A plant's ability to measure seasonal changes by the length of day and night. 596

photophosphorylation *FO-toe-FOS-for-eh-LAY-shun* A photosynthetic reaction in which energy released by the electron transport chain linking the two photosystems is stored in the high-energy phosphate bonds of ATP. 116

photoreceptors *FO-toe-ree-CEP-terz* Neurons that detect light by means of pigment molecules in contact with sensitive membranes. 351

photosynthesis *FO-toe-SIN-the-sis* The series of biochemical reactions that enable plants to harness the energy in sunlight to manufacture nutrient molecules. 24, 81, 113

photosystem *FO-toe-SIS-tum* A cluster of pigment molecules that enable green plants to absorb, transport, and harness solar energy. 116

phototropism *FO-to-TRO-piz-um* A plant's growth towards unidirectional light. 592

pH scale *SKALE* A measurement of how acidic or basic a solution is. 47

phylogenies *fi-LAWG-ah-nees* The evolutionary relationships between organisms. 648

phytochrome *FI-toe-krom* A pale blue plant pigment that exists in two interconvertible forms. The active form promotes flowering of long-day plants and inhibits flowering of short-day plants. 597

pica *PI-kah* A compulsive disorder in which people consume huge amounts of nonnutritive substances. 488

piloerection *PIL-o-ee-REK-shun* The raising of fur or feathers, which traps a layer of air near the body surface, serving as insulation. 500

pilus *PILL-us* A projection from a bacterial cell that transfers genetic information. 24

pineal gland *pin-EEL GLAND* A small oval structure in the brain, near the hypothalamus, that produces melatonin, a hormone that regulates the activities of other hormones, possibly by a sensitivity to patterns of lightness and darkness. 382, 677

pioneer species *PI-o-neer SPE-shez* The first species to colonize an area, such as lichens and mosses that begin soil formation. 722

pistil *PIS-til* The female reproductive structures and their covering in a flower. 574

pith *PITH* Ground storage tissue in the center of the stem in plants having concentric cylinders of xylem and phloem. 558

pituitary *pah-TU-eh-TEAR-ee* A pea-sized gland in the head. The anterior lobe releases growth hormone, thyroid stimulating hormone, adrenocorticotropic hormone, prolactin, and the gonadotropic hormones. The hypothalamus sends antidiuretic hormone and oxytocin to the posterior pituitary, from where they are released. Melanocyte stimulating hormone is secreted from the region of the pituitary between the lobes in some vertebrates. 371

pituitary dwarfism *pah-TU-eh-TEAR-ee DWARF-is-um* Short stature caused by a deficiency of growth hormone in childhood. 373

pituitary giant *pah-TU-eh-TEAR-ee GI-ant* A very tall child whose height results from a tumor that produces excess growth hormone. 374

placebo *pla-SEE-bo* A substance similar in taste and appearance to a substance under investigation, whose effects are known. 4

placenta *pla-CEN-tah* A specialized organ that develops in certain mammals, connecting mother to unborn offspring. 33, 168

placental mammals *plah-CEN-tel MAM-malz* Mammals that nurture the young in the female's body for a relatively long time, where they are nurtured by an organ called a placenta. 661

Plantae *PLAN-tye* Kingdom including land-dwelling multicellular organisms that extract energy from sunlight and have cell walls built of cellulose. 22

plant embryo *PLANT EM-bree-o* A plant after only a few cell divisions, forming part of a seed. 578

plasma *PLAZ-ma* A watery, protein-rich fluid that is the matrix of blood. 83, 424

plasma cells *PLAZ-mah SELZ* Mature B cells that secrete vast quantities of a single antibody type. 518

plasmid *PLAZ-mid* A small circle of double-stranded DNA found in some bacteria in addition to their DNA, commonly used as a vector for recombinant DNA. 270

platelet *PLATE-let* A cell fragment that is part of the blood and orchestrates clotting. 83, 424

plate tectonics *PLATE tek-TAWN-iks* A geological theory that views the earth's surface as several rigid plates that can move. 641

pleiotropic *PLY-o-TRO-pik* A genotype with multiple expressions. 231

Pleistocene overkill hypothesis *PLEIS-toe-seen O-ver-kill hi-POTH-eh-sis* The theory that the disappearance of many species of herbivores in North America 11,000 years ago was caused by humans hunting them. 642

plumule *PLU-mule* The epicotyl plus the first leaves of a young plantlet. 578

polar body *POLE-er BOD-ee* A small cell generated during female meiosis, enabling much cytoplasm to be partitioned into just one of the four meiotic products, the ovum. 165

polarized *PO-ler-ized* The state of a biological membrane when the electric charge inside differs from the electric charge outside. 317

polar nuclei *PO-lar NU-klee-i* The two nuclei in a cell of a plant's megagametophyte. 574

pollen grains *POL-en GRAANZ* Male microgametophytes. 574

pollen sacs *POL-en SAKS* The four microsporangia in an anther, the male part of a flower. 574

pollination *POL-eh-NA-shun* The transfer of pollen from an anther to a receptive stigma. 574

polygamy *pol-IG-ah-mee* A mating system in which a member of one sex associates with several members of the opposite sex. 696

polygyny *pol-IJ-ah-nee* A mating system in which one male mates with several females. 696

polymer *POL-eh-mer* A long molecule built of similar subunits. 50

polyploidy *POL-ee-PLOID-ee* A condition in which a cell has one or more extra sets of chromosomes. 278, 639

pons *PONZ* An oval mass in the brain stem where white matter connects the medulla to higher brain structures and gray matter helps control respiration. 335

population *POP-u-LAY-shun* Any group of interbreeding organisms. 631

population bottleneck *POP-u-LAY-shun BOT-el-nek* A type of genetic drift resulting from an event that kills many members of a population, and the numbers are restored by mating among a small number of individuals, restricting the gene pool compared to the original population. 633

population growth curve *POP-u-LAY-shun GROWTH CURVE* Description of the growth of a group of cells, influenced by nutrient and space availability and waste removal. Includes lag, log, stationary, and decline phases. 139

positive feedback loop *PAHZ-eh-tiv FEED-bak LOOP* A biochemical pathway in which accumulation of a product stimulates its production. 370

positive reinforcement *POS-eh-tiv REE-in-FORC-ment* A reward given for performing a particular behavior. 673

positron emission tomography (PET) *POS-eh-tron ee-MISH-on tah-MOG-rah-fee* A scanning technology that reveals biochemical activity in a living organism. 340

postsynaptic cell *POST-sin-AP-tik SEL* One of two adjacent neurons that are receiving a message. 321

Precambrian era *pre-KAB-ee-an ER-ah* The earliest part of earth history, from which few fossils are known. 654

presynaptic cell *PRE-sin-AP-tik SEL* One of two adjacent neurons that are transmitting a message. 321

primary body *PRI-mer-ee BOD-ee* A plant's axis, consisting of a root and a shoot. 552

primary consumers *PRI-mar-ee kon-SU-merz* Herbivores, which consume primary producers. 718

primary growth *PRI-mer-ee GROWTH* Lengthening of a plant due to cell division in the apical meristems. 552

primary immune response *PRI-mar-ee IM-mune ree-SPONZ* The immune system's response to its first encounter with a foreign antigen. 518

primary motor cortex *PRI-mare-ee MO-ter KOR-tex* A band of cerebral cortex extending from ear to ear across the top of the head that controls voluntary muscles. 337

primary nutrient deficiencies *PRI-mar-ee NU-tri-ent dee-FISH-en-seez* Too little of a particular nutrient due to an inadequate diet. 487

primary producers *PRI-mar-ee pro-DUCE-erz* Organisms that can use inorganic materials and energy to produce the organic material they require. These organisms form the first trophic level of food chains. 717

primary sensory cortex *PRI-mare-ee SEN-sore-ee KOR-tex* A band of cerebral cortex extending from ear to ear across the top of the head that receives sensory input from the skin. 337

primary structure *PRI-mer-ee STRUK-sure* The amino acid sequence of a protein. 53

primary succession *PRI-mar-ee suk-SESH-un* The arrival of life in an area where no community previously existed. 722

primary tissues *PRI-mer-ee TISH-yuz* Groups of cells with a common function. 552

primitive streak *PRIM-eh-tiv STREEK* The pigmented band along the back of a 3-week embryo that develops into the notochord. 181

principle of competitive exclusion *PRIN-sah-pul of kom-PET-ah-tiv ex-KLU-shun* The observation that two competing species will not continue to coexist indefinitely. 706

principle of superposition *PRIN-sah-pul SU-per-po-ZISH-un* The fact that lower rock layers are older than those above them. 621

prions *PRI-onz* Infectious protein particles. 43

profundal zone *pro-FUN-dal ZONE* The deep region of a lake or pond where light does not penetrate. 734

progeria *pro-JER-ee-ah* An inherited, accelerated aging disease. 188

progesterone *pro-JES-ter-own* A hormone produced by the ovaries that controls secretion patterns of other hormones involved in reproduction. 381

prokaryotic cell *pro-CARE-ee-OT-ik SEL* A structurally simple cell, lacking organelles. 22

prolactin *pro-LAK-tin* A hormone made in the anterior pituitary that stimulates milk production. 374

pronuclei *pro-NU-kle-eye* The genetic packages of gametes. 172

prophase *PRO-faze* The first stage of cell division, when chromosomes condense and become visible. During prophase of meiosis I, synapsis and crossing over occur. 134

prostaglandins *PROS-tah-GLAN-dinz* Lipid molecules that are released locally and transiently at the site of a cellular disturbance. They control a variety of body functions and are not well understood. 384

prostate *Pros-STATE* A male gland that produces a milky, alkaline fluid that activates sperm. 164

protein *PRO-teen* A long molecule built of amino acids bonded to each other. 19, 52

proteinoid theory *PRO-teh-noid THER-ee* The idea that proteins evolved before nucleic acids. 60

Protista *pro-TEES-tah* The taxonomic kingdom including the simplest eukaryotes—the protozoans, algae, water molds, and slime molds. 22

proton *PRO-ton* A particle in an atom's nucleus carrying a positive charge and having one mass unit. 44

protoplast fusion *PRO-toe-plast FU-zhun* The creation of new types of plants by combining their cells, from which the cell walls have been removed, and then regenerating a mature plant hybrid from the fused cell. 604

protozoans *PRO-toe-ZO-anz* Single-celled eukaryotes, often classified by their mode of movement, including the familiar amoeba, euglena, and paramecium. 25

proximal convoluted tubule *PROX-eh-mel KON-vo-LU-tid TU-bule* The region of the nephron proximal to Bowman's capsule where selective reabsorption of useful components of the glomerular filtrate occurs. 508

radicle *RAD-eh-sil* The first root to emerge from a seed. 563, 578

psilophytes *SIL-o-FIGHTS* Plants that first ventured onto the land, during the Silurian period 435 to 395 million years ago. 657

pulmonary artery *PULL-mo-NAIR-ee AR-ter-ee* The artery leading from the right ventricle to the lungs. 435

pulmonary semilunar valve *PULL-mo-NAIR-ee SEM-i-LOON-er VALVE* The valve leading from the right ventricle to the pulmonary artery. 435

pulmonary veins *PULL-mo-NAIR-ee VANEZ* Four veins leading from the lungs to the left atrium of the heart. 435

pulp *PULP* The soft inner portion of a tooth, consisting of connective tissue, blood vessels, and nerves. 469

punctuated equilibrium *PUNK-tu-A-tid EE-kwah-LEE-BREE-um* The view that evolution is characterized by long periods of relatively little change interrupted by bursts of rapid evolutionary change.

pupil *PU-pull* The opening in the iris that admits light into the human eye. 354

purine *PURE-een* A type of organic molecule with a double ring structure, including the nitrogenous bases adenine and guanine. 253

Purkinje fibers *per-KIN-gee FI-berz* Muscle fibers that branch from the atrioventricular node and transmit electrical stimulation rapidly. 438

Purkinje system *per-KIN-gee SIS-tum* The sinoatrial node, atrioventricular node, and Purkinje fibers, constituting a network of muscle fibers that triggers contraction of the ventricles. 439

pyloric stenosis *pi-LOR-ik stah-NO-sis* A birth defect in which the pyloric sphincter, which lies between the stomach and the small intestine, fails to open. 471

pylorus *pi-LOR-is* The bottom of the stomach. 470

pyramid of biomass *PIR-ah-mid BI-o-mass* A depiction of trophic levels indicating weight of organisms. 719

pyramid of numbers *PIR-ah-mid NUM-berz* A depiction of the number of organisms at each trophic level in a food chain. 719

pyrimidine *pie-RIM-eh-deen* A type of organic molecule with a single ring structure, including the nitrogenous bases cytosine, thymine, and uracil. 253

Q

quaternary structure *QUAR-teh-nair-ee STRUK-sure* The number and arrangement of polypeptide chains of a protein. 53

quiescent center *kwi-ES-cent CEN-ter* A reservoir of cells behind the root cap that can replace damaged cells in the adjacent meristem. 563

R

radiometric dating *RAD-ee-o MET-rik DA-ting* Using the measurement of natural radioactivity as a clock to date fossils. 650

radius *RAY-dee-is* One of the two lower arm bones. 400

realized niche *RE-ah-lized NITCH* The environment in which a species actually lives, which is restricted from its fundamental niche by competition with other species. 707

receptor *re-CEP-ter* A protein protruding from a cell membrane that forms a dock for other molecules. 321

receptor potential *re-CEP-ter po-TEN-shel* A change in membrane potential in a neuron specialized as a sensory receptor, caused by the redistribution of ions, whose magnitude varies with the strength of the stimulus. 349

recessive *re-CESS-ive* An allele whose expression is masked by the activity of another allele. 220

recombinant DNA technology *re-KOM-bah-nent DNA tek-NAL-eh-gee* Transferring a gene from a cell of a member of one species to the cell of a member of a different species. 270, 610

Recommended Dietary Allowances (RDAs) *REK-o-MEN-ded DI-ah-TEAR-ee ah-LAOW-ance* Guidelines on healthy foods to eat issued by the Unites States government every 5 years. 485

rectum *REC-tum* A storage region leading from the large intestine. 477

red blood cell (erythrocyte) *RED BLOOD SEL* A disc-shaped cell, lacking a nucleus, that is packed with the oxygen-carrying molecule hemoglobin. 83, 424

red marrow *RED MAR-o* Immature blood cells and platelets that reside in cavities in spongy bone. 393

reduction *re-DUK-shun* A chemical reaction in which electrons are gained. 48

reduction division *re-DUK-shun dah-VISH-un* Meiosis I, when the diploid chromosome number is halved. 157

reflex *RE-flex* A rapid, involuntary response to a stimulus from within the body or from the outside environment. 331

reflex arc *RE-flex ARK* A neural pathway linking a sensory receptor and an effector, such as a muscle. 333

relative date *REL-ah-tiv DATE* An estimate of the time at which an organism lived based upon the location of its fossils in sedimentary rock. 650

releaser *rah-LEAS-er* The specific factor that triggers a fixed action pattern, also called a sign stimulus. 669

releasing hormone *re-LEES-ing HOR-moan* A hormone produced by the hypothalamus that influences the secretion of a hormone by another gland. 371

renal tubule *REE-nel TU-bule* The tubule portion of a nephron, along which toxins are added and nutrients recycled to the blood, forming urine. 505

renin *REN-in* A hormone that elevates the level of aldosterone, an adrenal hormone that enhances reabsorption of Na$^+$ in the kidney, salivary glands, sweat glands, and large intestine. 510

residual air *reh-ZID-u-el AIR* The air in the bottom third of the lungs, which is not exchanged with each breath. 455

respiratory chain *RES-pir-ah-TOR-ee CHANE* A series of electron-accepting enzymes embedded in the inner mitochondrial membrane. 123

resting potential *REST-ing po-TEN-shel* The electrical potential (-65 millivolts) on the inside of a neuron not conducting a nerve impulse. 317

restriction enzyme *re-STRIK-shun EN-zime* A bacterial enzyme that cuts DNA at a specific sequence. 270

restriction fragment length polymorphism *re-STRIK-shun FRAG-ment LENGTH POL-e-MORF-iz-um* Differences in restriction enzyme cutting sites between individuals. 303

reticular activating system (RAS) *rah-TIK-u-lar AK-tah-vay-ting SIS-tem* A diffuse network of cell bodies and nerve tracts extending through the brain stem and into the thalamus; screens sensory input approaching the cerebrum. 335

retina *RET-nah* A sheet of photoreceptors at the back of the human eye. 353, 355

retinal *RET-in-al* The pigment portion of rhodopsin, a molecule involved in black-and-white vision. 357

rhinoviruses *RI-no-vi-rus-ez* Viruses that cause the common cold. 459

rhodopsin *ro-DOP-sin* A pigment molecule stored in the rod cells of the retina in the eye. Light splits rhodopsin, which depolarizes the rod cell, provoking a nerve impulse. 357

rib cage *RIB KAGE* The part of the axial skeleton that protects the heart and lungs, consisting in the human of 10 paris of ribs attached to the sternum, plus two floating ribs. 399

ribonucleic acid (RNA) *RI-bo-nu-KLAY-ik AS-id* A single-stranded nucleic acid built of nucleotides containing a phosphate, ribose, and nitrogenous bases adenine, guanine, cytosine, and uracil. 253

ribosomal RNA (rRNA) *RI-bo-SOAM-el* RNA that, along with proteins, comprises the ribosome. 258

ribosome *RI-bo-soam* A structure built of RNA and protein upon which a gene's message (mRNA) anchors during protein synthesis. 72, 258

rods *RODZ* Specialized neurons clustered around the edges of the retina that provide black-and-white vision and night vision. 357

root apical meristem *ROOT AP-eh-kel MER-eh-stem* Dividing tissue at root tips in a plantlet. 578

root cap *ROOT KAP* A thimble-shaped protective structure covering the tip of a root. 563

root hairs *ROOT HAIRZ* Trichomes that appear near root tips and absorb water and minerals from soil. 554

rosettes *ro-ZETTZ* Nonelongated stems, such as in banana. 557

round dance *ROUND DANC* A dance in which bees communicate to members of the colony that food is nearby and is of a certain sweetness. 692

rugae *RU-guy* Folds in the mucosa of the stomach. 470

S

S phase *FAZE* The synthesis phase of interphase, when DNA is replicated and microtubules are produced from tubulin. 133

saccule *SAK-yul* A pouch in the vestibule of the inner ear filled with a jellylike fluid and lined with hair cells, containing calcium carbonate otolith granules that move in response to changes in velocity, firing action potentials. 363

sacrum *SAY-krum* The five fused pelvic vertebrae. 398

saliva *sah-LI-va* A secretion in the mouth that is produced when food is smelled or tasted. 468

salivary amylase *SAL-eh-var-ee AM-eh-lase* An enzyme produced in the mouth that begins the chemical digestion of starch into sugar. 468

salivary glands *SAL-eh-vare-ee GLANDZ* Three pairs of glands near the mouth that secrete saliva, a fluid containing water, mucus, and salivary amylase. 468

saltatory conduction *SAL-teh-tore-ee kon-DUK-shun* The jumping of an action potential between nodes of Ranvier in myelinated nerve axons. 321

sapwood *SAP-wood* Wood located nearest the vascular cambium, which transports water and dissolved nutrients within a plant. 568

sarcolemma *SAR-ko-LEM-ah* The cell membrane of a skeletal muscle cell. 407

sarcoplasmic reticulum *SAR-ko-PLASZ-mik rah-TIK-u-lum* The endoplasmic reticulum of a skeletal muscle cell. 407

saturated (fat) *SAT-yur-ray-tid* A triglyceride with single bonds between the carbons of its fatty acid tails. 52

savanna *s ah-VAN-ah* A grassland. 729

scales *SKALZ* A subunit of a pinecone bearing two ovules. 583

scavengers *SKAHV-en-gerz* Animals that eat the leftovers of another animal's meal. 718

school *SKUL* A formation of fishes swimming at particular distances and angles from each other. 687

Schwann cells *SCHWAN SELZ* Fatty cells that wrap around neurons in the peripheral nervous system, forming myelin sheaths. 320

scientific method *SI-en-TIF-ik METH-id* A systematic approach to interpreting observations, involving reasoning, predicting, testing, and drawing conclusions, which are put into perspective with existing knowledge. 3

sclera *SKLER-ah* The outermost, white layer of the human eye. 353

sclereids *SKLER-ridz* Plant cells with a gritty texture found in pears and in the hulls of peanuts. 553

sclerenchyma *sklah-REN-kah-mah* Elongated supportive plant cells with

thick, nonstretchable secondary cell walls. 553

scoliosis *SKOL-ee-O-sis* An abnormal spinal curvature in which the vertebrae shift sideways. 399

scotopsin *sco-TOP-sin* The protein portion of rhodopsin, a pigment molecule important in black-and-white vision. 357

scramble competition *SKRAM-bel KOM-pah-TISH-un* Direct competition of individuals in a population for a limited resource. 705

seasonal affective disorder (SAD) *SEE-son-al AF-fek-tiv DIS-or-der* A form of depression that occurs mostly in the winter and seems to respond to therapy of exposure to light. 677

seasonal ovulator *SEE-son-al OV-u-LAY-ter* A female mammal that has a period of sexual receptivity and fertility. 382

secondary consumers *SEK-on-DAIR-ee kon-SU-merz* Animals that eat herbivores, forming a third trophic level in a food chain. 718

secondary growth *SEK-on-DER-ee GROWTH* Thickening of a plant due to cell division in lateral meristems. 552

secondary immune response *SEK-on-DAIR-ee IM-mune ree-SPONZ* The immune system's response to subsequent encounters with a foreign antigen. 518

secondary nutrient deficiencies *SEK-on-dare-ee NU-tri-ent dah-FISH-en-seez* Too little of a particular nutrient due to an inborn metabolic condition. 488

secondary production *SEK-on-DAIR-ee pro-DUK-shun* The energy stored in the tissues of herbivores and carnivores. 718

secondary structure *SEK-en-DAIR-ee STRUCK-sure* The shape assumed by a protein caused by chemical attractions between amino acids that are close together in the primary structure. 53

secondary succession *SEK-on-DAIR-ee suk-SESH-un* The arrival of new species in an area that already has life. 723

second messengers *SEK-ond MESS-en-gerz* Biochemicals that modulate neurotransmitter action. 325

secretin *sah-KREE-tin* A hormone produced in the small intestine that triggers the release of bicarbonate from the pancreas, which neutralizes stomach acid. 473

seed *SEED* A temporarily dormant sporophyte individual surrounded by a tough protective coat. 578

seed coat *SEED COAT* A tough outer layer protecting a dormant plant embryo and its food supply in a seed. 579

segmentation *SEG-men-TA-shun* Localized muscle contractions in the small intestine that provide mechanical digestion. 472

segregation *SEG-rah-GAY-shun* The distribution of alleles of a gene into separate gametes during meiosis. 219

seismonasty *SIZ-mo-NAS-tee* A nastic (nondirectional) movement resulting from contact or mechanical disturbance. 594

selectively permeable *sah-LEK-tiv-lee PERM-ee-ah-bul* A biological membrane that admits only some substances. 317

semicircular canals *SEM-ee-SIR-ku-ler kah-NALZ* Fluid-filled structures in the inner ear that provide information on the position of the head. 362

semidwarf rices *SEM-i DWARF RI-ses* Highly productive varieties of rice. 545

semilunar valves *SEM-i-LOON-er VALVZ* A ring of tissue flaps in the arteries just outside each ventricle that maintains unidirectional blood flow. 434

seminal vesicles *SEM-en-el VES-eh-kels* In the human male, the paired structures that add fructose and prostaglandins to the sperm. 155

sense strand *SENSE STRAND* The side of the DNA double helix for a particular gene that is transcribed. 257

sensory adaptation *SEN-sore-ee ah-DAP-TAY-shun* The phenomenon of a sensation becoming less noticeable once it has been recognized. 349

sensory (afferent) neuron *SEN-sore-ee (AF-fer-ent) NEUR-on* A neuron that brings information toward the central nervous system, with long dendrites that transmit the message from the stimulated body part to the cell body near the spinal cord, and a short axon. 315

sensory areas *SEN-sore-ee AIR-ee-ahs* Parts of the cerebral cortex that receive and interpret messages from sense organs concerning temperature, body movement, pain, touch, taste, smell, sight, and sound. 337

sensory (neural) deafness *SEN-sore-ee (NEUR-al) DEF-nes* Hearing loss resulting from an inability of the cochlea to generate action potentials in response to detecting sound. 360

sensory pathways *SEN-sore-ee PATH-wayz* Nerve tracts in the peripheral nervous system that transmit impulses from a stimulus to the central nervous system. 342

sensory receptor *SEN-sore-ee re-CEP-ter* A specialized dendrite of a neuron that is specific to detecting a particular sensation and firing an action potential in response, which is transmitted to the spinal cord. 333

sepals *SEE-pelz* Leaflike structures that enclose and protect inner floral parts. 574

severe combined immune deficiency *sah-VEER kom-BIND im-MUNE dah-FISH-en-see* An inborn deficiency of T and B cells. 525

sex chromosome *SEX KRO-mo-soam* A chromosome that determines sex. 225

sex hormones *SEX HOR-moanz* Hormones that provide secondary

sexual characteristics and prepare an animal for sexual reproduction, such as estrogen, progesterone, and testosterone. 378

sex-influenced inheritance *SEX IN-flu-enced in-HAIR-eh-tence* An allele that is dominant in one sex but recessive in the other. 225

sex-limited trait *SEX LIM-eh-tid TRAIT* A trait affecting a structure or function of the body that is present in only one sex. 225

sex-linked *SEX LINKED* A gene located on the X chromosome or a trait that results from the activity of such a gene. 238

sex ratio *SEX RAY-she-o* The ratio of males to females at conception (primary), birth (secondary), and 10-year intervals thereafter (tertiary). 246

sexual dimorphism *SEX-u-al di-MOR-fiz-um* The difference in appearance between males and females of the same species. 696

sexual reproduction *SEX-u-el RE-pro-DUK-shun* The combination of genetic material from two individuals to create a third individual. 42, 158

sexual selection *SEX-u-el sah-LEK-shun* Natural selection of traits that increase an individual's reproductive success. 627

shoot apical meristem *SHOOT AP-eh-kel MER-eh-stem* Dividing tissue at the tip of a shoot in a seedling. 578

short-day plants *SHORT-day PLANTZ* Plants that require light periods shorter than some critical length to flower. 596

sieve cells *SIV SELZ* Less specialized conducting cells in phloem. 555

sieve plate *SIV PLATE* End walls of aligned sieve tubes in a plant's phloem. 555

sieve pores *SIV PORZ* Perforations in phloem, through which solutes move from cell to cell. 555

sieve tube members *SIV TUUB MEM-berz* More complex and specialized conducting cells in phloem that form long sieve tubes. 555

Silurian period *sah-LUR-ee-an PER-ee-od* The period following the Ordovician period, 435 to 395 million years ago, when organisms first ventured onto the land. 657

simple carbohydrates *SIM-pel KAR-bo-HIGH-drates* Monosaccharides and disaccharides. 50

sinoatrial node (SA node) *SI-no-A-tree-al NOOD* Specialized cells in the wall of the right atrium that set the pace of the heartbeat. Also called the pacemaker. 438

skeletal muscle *SKEL-eh-tel MUS-sel* Voluntary, striated muscle consisting of single, multinucleated cells that are contractile due to sliding filaments of actin and myosin. 87, 405

skull *SKULL* A hard, bony structure protecting the brain. 397

sleep apnea *SLEEP AP-nee-ah* A sleep disorder in which breathing stops several hundred times a night, for 20 to 60 seconds each time.

sliding filament model *SLY-ding FILL-eh-ment MOD-el* The movement of protein myofilaments past each other to shorten skeletal muscle cells, leading to muscle contraction. 409

slow twitch-fatigue resistant fibers *SLO TWITCH fah-TEEG re-ZIS-tent FI-berz* Skeletal muscle fibers that contract slowly but are resistant to fatigue because of a plentiful supply of oxygen. 413

smooth muscle *SMOOTH MUS-sel* Involuntary, nonstriated contractile tissue found lining the digestive tract and other organs. 87, 405

sodium-potassium pump *SO-dee-um po-TAS-ee-um PUMP* A mechanism that uses energy released from splitting ATP to transport Na^+ out of cells and K^+ into cells. 317

softwoods *SOFT-woodz* Woods of gymnosperms, such as pine, spruce, and fir. 566

solution *so-LU-shun* A homogenous mixture of a substance (the solute) dissolved in water (the solvent). 98

somaclonal variation *SOAM-ah-KLON-al VAR-ee-AY-shun* Genetically variant embryos or plantlets grown from callus initiated by somatic cells. 608

somatic cell *so-MAT-ik SEL* A body cell; a cell other than the sperm or ovum. 131, 157

somatic embryo *so-MAT-ik EM-bree-o* A plant embryo grown from callus. 605

somatic hybrid *so-MAT-ik HI-brid* A plant regenerated from a protoplast fusion of cells from two types of plants. 605

somatic nervous system *so-MAT-ik NER-ves SIS-tum* Part of the motor pathways of the peripheral nervous system that leads to skeletal muscles. 342

somatostatin *so-MAH-toe-STAH-tin* A pancreatic hormone that controls the rate of nutrient absorption into the bloodstream. 378

Southern blotting *SOU-thern BLOT-ting* Use of DNA probes to identify specific fragments of DNA. 302

speciation *SPE-she-AY-shun* The appearance of a new type of organism. 621

species *SPE-shez* A group of similar individuals that interbreed in nature and are reproductively isolated from all other such groups. 19, 621

sperm *SPERM* The male sex cell. 155

spermatogenesis *sper-MAT-o-JEN-eh-sis* The differentiation of a sperm cell, from a diploid spermatogonium, to primary spermatocyte, to two haploid secondary spermatocytes, to spermatids, and finally to mature spermatozoa. 163

sphincters *SFINK-terz* Muscular rings that control the passage of a substance from one area to another. 470

sphygmomanometer *SFIG-mo-mah-NOM-eh-ter* A gauge that measures blood pressure by the displacement of a column of mercury. 432

spinal cord *SPI-nal KORD* A tube of neural tissue extending from the base of the brain to just below the lowest rib that carries impulses to and from the brain. 331

spinal nerves *SPI-nal NERVZ* Thirty-one pairs of somatic nerves that exit the spinal cord and emerge from between the vertebrae. 344

spinal reflex *SPI-nel RE-flex* A neural connection made entirely within the spinal cord. 333

spindle apparatus *SPIN-del AP-ah-RAH-tis* A structure built of microtubules that aligns and separates chromosomes in cell division. 133

spines *SPINZ* Leaves modified to protect plants from predators and excessive sunlight. 561

spleen *SPLEEN* An organ located in the abdomen that produces and stores lymphocytes and contains reserve supplies of red blood cells. 442

spongy bone *SPON-gee BONE* Flat bones and tips of long bones that have many large spaces between a web of bony struts. 393

spongy mesophyll *SPON-gee MEZ-o-fil* Irregularly shaped chlorenchyma cells separated by large spaces that are found below the palisade layer in leaves. 561

spontaneous generation *spon-TAY-nee-us JEN-er-RAY-shun* The idea, proven untrue, that living things can arise from nonliving matter. 59

sporophyte *SPOR-o-fight* The part of a plant's life cycle when spores are produced. 28, 573

spring turnover *SPRING TURN-o-ver* The rising of nutrient-rich lower layers of a lake and sinking of oxygen-rich layers from the top, often causing algal blooms. 734

stabilizing selection *STA-bil-I-zing sah-LEK-shun* When extreme phenotypes are less adaptive than an intermediate phenotype. 637

stable isotope tracing *STA-bel I-so-toap TRAC-ing* A technique that analyzes the proportions of certain isotopes in tissue samples, providing clues to which types of organisms consume others. 719

stamens *STA-menz* Male reproductive structures in flowers built of stalklike filaments bearing pollen-producing anthers at their tips. 574

stegosaurs *STEG-ah-SORZ* Herbivorous dinosaurs with panels down their backs. 659

stem cell *STEM SEL* A cell that divides often. 139

steroid hormone *STAIR-oid HOR-moan* A hormone composed of lipid that can pass through the target cell's membrane and enter the cell's nucleus. 369

stigma *STIG-mah* A pollen receptacle at the tip of a style in a flower. 574

stirrup *STIR-up* One of the bones in the middle ear. 359

stolons *STOL-onz* Stems that grow along the soil surface; also called runners. 558

stomata *sto-MAH-tah* Pores in a plant's cuticle through which water and gases are exchanged between the plant and the atmosphere. 558

storage leaves *STOR-age LEEVZ* Fleshy leaves that store nutrients. 562

stress test *STRESS TEST* An electrocardiogram taken while the subject is exercising. 440

stroma *STRO-ma* The nonmembranous inner region of the chloroplast. 116

stroma lamellae *STRO-ma la-MEL-i* Loosely packed inner membranes of the chloroplast, containing pigment molecules. 116

style *STILE* A stalk forming from an ovary in a flower. 574

subapical region *sub-APE-eh-kel REE-jen* The region behind the root cap, which is divided into zones of cellular division, cellular elongation, and cellular maturation. 563

subclinical *sub-KLIN-eh-kel* The stage of a nutrient deficiency when abnormalities can be detected with biochemical tests, but symptoms are not yet experienced. 488

suberin *SU-ber-in* A waxy, waterproof biochemical in the interior of a root's cortex. 564

succulent *SUK-ku-lent* Fleshy plant tissue that can store large amounts of water. 558

summation *sum-A-shun* An increase in the strength of contraction of a muscle that is stimulated a second time very soon after an initial stimulation. 413

superior vena cava *su-PER-ee-er VEE-nah KAH-vah* The upper branch of the largest vein that leads to the heart. 434

supernormal releaser *su-per-NOR-mal ree-LEAS-er* In animal behavior, a model that exaggerates a releaser and elicits a stronger response than the natural object. 670

suppressor T cells *su-PRES-ser T SELZ* T cells that inhibit the response of all lymphocytes to foreign antigens, shutting off the immune response when an infection is under control. 521

suprachiasmatic nuclei (SCN) *SU-pra-KI-as-MAT-ik NU-klee-i* Two clusters of 10,000 neurons each in the hypothalamus that control certain biological clocks in some species. 677

survival of the fittest *ser-VI-val of the FIT-tist* The idea that those individuals best able to reproduce healthy offspring contribute the most genes to the next generation. 627

symbiosis *SYM-bee-o-sis* An intimate relationship between two types of organisms. 14

sympathetic nervous system *SIM-pah-THE-tik NER-ves SIS-tum* Part of the autonomic nervous system that mobilizes the body to respond to environmental stimuli. 344, 439

sympatric species *SIM-pat-rik SPE-shez* Two closely related groups of organisms that occupy the same geographic region but cannot reproduce successfully with each other. 638

synapse *SIN-apse* A space between two adjacent neurons. 321

synapsis *SIN-ap-sis* The gene-by-gene alignment of homologous chromosomes during prophase of meiosis I. 159

synaptic knobs *sin-AP-tik NOBZ* The enlarged tips of branches at the ends of axons. 321

synaptic vesicles *sin-AP-tik VES-eh-kelz* Small sacs within synaptic knobs at the ends of axons that contain neurotransmitters. 321

synovial joint *sin-OV-ee-el JOINT* A capsule of fluid-filled fibrous connective tissue between freely movable bones. 401

synovial membrane *sin-OV-ee-el MEM-brane* The lining of the interior of a joint capsule, which secretes lubricating synovial fluid. 401

systole *SIS-toll-ee* The heart's contraction. 438

systolic pressure *SIS-tol-ik PRESH-yur* The blood pressure at its peak, when the ventricles contract. 432

T

taiga *TI-gah* The northern coniferous forest, north of the temperate zone. 729

taproot system *TAP-root SIS-tum* A plant in which the first root (the radicle) enlarges to form a major root that persists through the life of the plant. 563

target cell *TAR-get SEL* A cell that is affected directly by a particular hormone. 368

tarsals *TAR-salz* The ankle bones. 400

taste receptors *TASTE ree-CEP-terz* Specialized neurons that detect taste. 351

taxonomy *tax-ON-o-mee* The branch of biology concerned with classifying organisms on the basis of evolutionary relationships. Taxonomic levels include, in order, kingdom, phylum (or division), class, order, family, genus, and species. 19

tectorial membrane *TEK-TORE-ee-al MEM-brane* The membrane above the hair cells in the cochlea of the inner ear that is pressed by the hair cells responding to the basilar membrane's vibration in the presence of sound waves. 360

telophase *TELL-o-faze* The final stage of cell division, when two cells form from one and the spindle is disassembled. 135

temporal isolation *TEM-por-al I-so-LAY-shun* When members of two populations do not crossbreed because they have different mating seasons. 368

tendon *TEN-din* A heavy band of fibrous connective tissue that attaches a muscle to a bone. 406

tendrils *TEN-drilz* Shoots or modified leaves that support plants by coiling around objects. 558, 561

teosinte *TE-o-SIN-tee* A grass that may have been ancestral to corn. 544

teratogen *teh-RAT-eh-jen* A chemical or other environmental agent that causes a birth defect. 202

territory *TEAR-eh-TOR-ee* A portion of land defended by an individual. 694

tertiary consumers *TER-she-AIR-ee kon-SU-merz* Carnivores that eat other carnivores, forming a fourth trophic level. 718

tertiary structure *TER-she-air-ee STRUK-sure* The shape assumed by a protein caused by chemical attractions between amino acids that are far apart in the primary structure. 53

test cross *TEST CROSS.* Crossing an individual of unknown genotype to a homozygous recessive individual. 221

testes *TES-teez* The paired, male gonads, containing the seminiferous tubules, in which sperm are manufactured. 155, 374

tetanus *TET-nes* A smooth and continuous muscle contraction resulting from repeated strong stimulations that occur before the muscle has time to relax. Also, an infectious disease called "lockjaw."

tetraploid *TET-rah-ploid* An individual with four sets of chromosomes, usually resulting from self-fertilization in a diploid plant. 639

thalamus *THAL-eh-mus* A gray, tight package of nerve cell bodies and glia beneath the cerebrum that relays sensory input to the appropriate part of the cerebrum. 335

thecodonts *THEK-o-dontz* Descendants of the Permian cotylosaurs that were ancestors of the great dinosaurs. 659

therapsids *ther-AP-sidz* Reptiles living in the Mesozoic era, which had some characteristics of mammals. 659

thermal stratification *THER-mal STRAH-tah-fah-KAY-shun* Layers within lakes that have different temperatures. 734

thermocline *THER-mo-kline* A middle layer of a lake where water temperature changes rapidly and drastically. 734

thermoluminescence *THER-mo-LU-mah-NES-ence* A technique that measures the formation of tiny holes in crystals over time, caused by exposure to ionizing radiation. This measurement is used in absolute dating of fossils up to 1 million years old. 650

thigmomorphogenesis *THIG-mo-MOR-pho-GEN-ah-sis* A plant's responses to mechanical disturbances, including inhibition of cellular elongation and production of thick-walled supportive tissue. 596

thigmotropism *THIG-mo-TRO-piz-um* A plant's response toward touch. 592

thoracic vertebrae *thor-AS-ik VER-tah-bray* The 12 vertebrae in the upper back. 398

thorns *THORNZ* Stems modified for protection. 558

threat posture *THRET POS-tur* A visual display marking a territory. 694

thrombophlebitis *THROM-bo-flah-BI-tis* Inflammation of a vein wall complicated by the formation of blood clots. 438

thromboplastin *THROM-bo-plas-tin* A protein released from blood vessel walls following injury that, in the presence of calcium, converts the blood protein prothrombin into thrombin. 428

thrombus *THROM-bus* A blood clot that blocks a blood vessel or the heart. 428

thylakoids *THI-lah-koidz* Membranous discs comprising the inner membrane of a chloroplast. 81, 116

thymine *THI-meen* One of the two pyrimidine bases in DNA. 57, 253

thymus *THY-mis* A lymphatic organ in the upper chest where lymphocytes called T cells learn to distinguish foreign from self antigens. 442

thyroid gland *THI-roid Gland* A gland in the neck that manufactures thyroxine, a hormone that increases energy expenditure. 112

thyroid stimulating hormone (TSH) *THY-roid STIM-u-lat-ing HOR-moan* A hormone made in the anterior pituitary that stimulates the thyroid gland to release its two hormones. 375

thyroxine *thy-ROX-in* A thyroid hormone that increases the rate of cellular metabolism. 375

tibia *TIB-ee-ah* The larger of the two bones of the lower leg. 400

tidal volume *TI-del VOL-yum* The amount of air inhaled or exhaled during a normal breath. 455

tinnitus *tin-I-tus* A condition in which a persistent ringing sound is heard. 361

Ti plasmid *TI PLAZ-mid* A ring of DNA in the microorganism *Agrobacterium tumefaciens* that is used to introduce foreign plant genes in recombinant DNA technology. 611

tissue *TISH-u* In multicellular organisms, groups of cells with related functions. 40

tonsils *TAWN-silz* Collections of lymphatic tissue in the throat. 442

trachae *TRAY-ki* A branching system of tubules that brings the outside environment in close contact with an organism's cells so that gas exchange can occur. 446

trachea *TRAY-kee-ah* The respiratory tube just beneath the larynx, held open by rings of cartilage. Also called the windpipe. 449

tracheids *TRA-kee-idz* Less specialized conducting cells in plants that are elongate, are dead at maturity, and have thick walls. 555

tracheophytes *TRAY-key-o-fights* Plants that have specialized tubes to conduct water and nutrients. 29, 571

transcription *tranz-SKRIP-shun* Manufacturing RNA from DNA. 257

transfer RNA (tRNA) *TRANZ-fer* A small RNA molecule that binds an amino acid at one site and an mRNA codon at another site. 258

transgenic organism *TRANZ-jen-ik OR-gan-niz-um* Genetic engineering of a gamete or fertilized ovum, leading to development of an individual with the alteration in every cell. 146, 610

translation *tranz-LAY-shun* Assembly of an amino acid chain according to the sequence of base triplets in a molecule of mRNA. 257

translocation *TRANZ-lo-KAY-shun* Exchange of genetic material between nonhomologous chromosomes. 280

transverse (T) tubules *TRANZ-verse TU-bules* Portions of the sarcolemma that jut into the sarcoplasmic reticulum of a skeletal muscle cell. 407

Triassic period *tri-AS-ik PER-ee-od* The period from 225 to 185 million years ago, when small ancestors of the great dinosaurs flourished. 659

trichomes *TRI-koamz* Outgrowths of a plant's epidermis that provide protection. 554

triiodothyronine *TRI-i-ode-o-THY-ro-neen* A thyroid hormone that increases the rate of cellular metabolism. 375

trilobites *TRI-lo-bitz* Insectlike organisms that appeared in the seas of the Cambrian period. 657

trisomy *TRI-som-mee* A cell with one extra chromosome. 280

trophic level *TRO-fik LEV-el* A feeding level in a food chain or web. 717

trophoblast *TRO-fo-blast* A layer of cells in the preembryo that develops into the chorion and then the placenta. 173

tropical rain forest *TROP-e-kel RAIN FOR-est* A warm, moist terrestrial region where rainfall is 79 to 157 inches (200 to 400 centimeters) per year; life is diverse and plentiful, and nutrient cycling is rapid. 728

tropic hormone *TRO-pik HOR-moan* A hormone produced by one gland that influences the secretion of a hormone by another gland. 371

tropism *TRO-piz-um* Plant growth toward or away from an environmental stimulus. 591

tropomyosin *TRO-po-MI-o-sin* A type of protein in the thin myofilaments of skeletal muscle cells. 407

troponin *tro-PO-nin* A type of protein in the thin myofilaments of skeletal muscle cells. 407

trypsin *TRIP-sin* A pancreatic enzyme that participates in protein digestion in the small intestine. 472

tube nucleus *TUUB NU-klee-us* A haploid cell resulting from the mitotic division of a microspore, in male plant reproduction. 574

tubercle *to-BER-kel* A section of lung walled off by a fibrous connective tissue capsule as a result of tuberculosis. 461

tuberculosis *to-BER-ku-LO-sis* A bacterial infection of the lungs. 460

tubers *TU-berz* Swollen regions of stems that store nutrients. 558

tundra *TUN-drah* A band of land running across the northern parts of Asia, Europe, and North America, where the climate is harsh and few organisms live. 729, 733

turgor pressure *TER-ger PRESH-yur* Rigidity of a plant cell caused by water pressing against the cell wall. 100

twitch *TWITCH* A rapid contraction and relaxation of a muscle cell following a single stimulation. 413

twitch types *TWITCH TYPEZ* Varieties of skeletal muscle fibers distinguished by how quickly they contract and tire. 413

tympanal organ *TIM-PAN-al OR-gan* A thin part of an insect's cuticle that detects vibrations and therefore sound. 359

tympanic membrane *TIM-PAN-ik MEM-brane* The eardrum, a structure upon which sound waves impinge. 359

U

ulcer *UL-sir* A raw, craterlike sore. 470

ulcerative colitis *UL-sir-AH-tiv koal-I-tis* Inflammation of the inner lining of the colon and rectum, producing pain, bloody diarrhea, and weight loss. 477

ulna *UL-nah* One of the two lower arm bones. 400

umbilical cord *um-BIL-ik-kel KORD* A ropelike structure containing one artery and two veins that connects mother to unborn child. 168

unconditioned stimulus *un-kon-DISH-ond STIM-u-lus* A stimulus that normally triggers a particular response. 673

uniformitarianism *U-nah-FOR-mah-TER-ee-ah-niz-um* The view that the earth's surface is continually remolded. 621

unsaturated (fat) *un-SAT-yur-RAY tid* A triglyceride with double bonds between some of its carbons. 52

upwelling *up-WELL-ing* The movement upward of cooler,

nutrient-rich bottom layers of the ocean, causing nutrients to bloom. 737

uracil *YUR-eh-sil* One of the two pyrimidine bases in RNA. 257

urea *u-REE-ah* A nitrogenous waste derived from ammonia. 502

ureter *u-REE-ter* A muscular tube that transports urine from the kidney to the bladder. 504

urethra *u-RETH-rah* The tube leading from the bladder through which urine exits the body. 505

uric acid *YUR-ik AS-id* A nitrogenous waste derived from ammonia. 502

urinary bladder *YUR-eh-NAIR-ee BLAD-er* A muscular sac in which urine collects. 505

urinary tract infection *YUR-eh-NAIR-ee TRACT in-FEK-shun* A bacterial infection of the urethra, with symptoms of frequent, painful urination and sometimes fever and lower abdominal pain. 511

uterus *U-ter-us* The muscular, saclike organ in the human female in which the embryo and fetus develop. 157

utricle *U-trah-kel* A pouch in the vestibule of the inner ear filled with a jellylike fluid and lined with hair cells, containing calcium carbonate otolith granules that move in response to changes in velocity, firing action potentials. 362

V

vaccine *VAK-seen* A killed or weakened form of, or part of, an infectious agent that initiates an immune response so that when the real agent is encountered, antibodies are already available to deactivate it. 529

vagus nerve *VA-ges NERVE* The one cranial nerve that innervates internal organs, rather than the head or neck. 344

variable regions *VAIR-ee-ah-bul REE-genz* The sequence of amino acids comprising the upper portions of heavy and light antibody chains, which varies greatly in different antibody types. 518

varicose veins *VAR-eh-kos VANEZ* Distension of the superficial veins in the legs. 438

vascular bundles *VAS-ku-ler BUN-delz* Organized groups of vascular tissues in stems. 557

vascular cambium *VAS-ku-ler KAM-bee-um* A thin cylinder of meristematic tissue found in roots and stems that produces most of the secondary plant body. 566

vas deferens *VAS DEF-er-enz* In the human male, a tube from the epididymis that continues to become the vas deferens, which joins the urethra in the penis. 155

vasoconstriction *VAZ-o-kon-strik-shun* The narrowing of blood vessels, which raises blood pressure. 433

vasoconstriction area *VAZ-o-kon-STRIK-shun AIR-ee-ah* Part of the brain's vasomotor center that stimulates circulation by constricting blood flow. 439

vasodilation *VAZ-o-di-LAY-shun* The widening of blood vessels, which lowers blood pressure. 433

vasodilation area *VAZ-o-di-LAY-shun AIR-ee-ah* Part of the brain's vasomotor center that dilates blood vessels. 439

vasomotor center *va-ZOM-eh-ter CEN-ter* A part of the brain that controls blood flow to the heart and heart rate by sending nerve impulses through the spinal cord to the sympathetic nervous system. 439

veins *VANEZ* Large blood vessels arising from venules that return blood to the heart. 428

veins *VANEZ* Strands of vascular tissue in leaves. 561

venous valves *VEEN-is VALVES* Flaplike structures in veins that keep blood flow in one direction. 432

ventricles *VEN-tree-kelz* Spaces in the brain into which cerebrospinal fluid is secreted. Also, the two muscular chambers of the heart located beneath the atria. 342

venules *VANE-yules* Vessels that arise from capillaries and drain into veins. 428

vertebral column *VER-teh-bral KOL-um* Bones along the back and neck that protect the spinal cord.

vertical stratification *VER-tah-kel STRAH-tah-fah-KAY-shun* The formation of layers of different types of organisms beneath the canopy of a tropical rain forest, caused by competition of organisms for sunlight. 728

vessel elements *VES-el EL-eh-mentz* More specialized conducting cells in plants that are elongate, are dead at maturity, and have thick walls. 555

vestibule *VES-teh-bule* A structure in the inner ear that provides information on the position of the head with respect to gravity and changes in velocity. 362

vestigial *ves-TEEG-el* A structure that seems not to have a function in an organism but resembles a functional organ in another type of organism. 651

villi *VIL-i* Tiny projections on the inner lining of the small intestine, which greatly increase surface area. 473

viroid *VEAR-oid* Infectious genetic material. 43

virus *VI-rus* An infectious particle consisting of a nucleic acid (DNA or RNA) wrapped in protein. 42

vital capacity *VI-tel kah-PASS-eh-tee* The maximal amount of air that can be moved in and out of the lungs during forceful breathing. 455

vitamin *VI-tah-min* An organic molecule essential in small amounts for the normal growth and function of an organism. 58

vitreous humor *VIT-ree-es U-mer* A jellylike substance behind the lens, comprising most of the volume of the eye. 356

vocal cords *VO-kel KORDZ* Two elastic bands of tissue stretched over the glottis, which vibrate as air passes, producing sounds. 449

W

waggle dance *WAG-gel DANC* A bee's dance signifying that food is farther from the hive than a round dance would indicate. The speed of the dance, the number of waggles during the straight part, and the duration of buzzing signal the distance to the food source. 692

white blood cell (leukocyte) *WHITE BLOOD SEL* A cell that helps fight infection. 83, 424

white matter *WHITE MAT-ter* Myelinated nerve fibers, found in pathways that transmit impulses over long distances. 321

wild type *WILD TYPE* A phenotype or allele that is the most common for a certain gene in a population. 220

X

X inactivation *X IN-ak-tah-VA-shun* The turning off of one X chromosome in each cell of a female mammal at a certain point in prenatal development. 239

xylem *ZI-lum* Tubules in a plant that transport water and minerals from the roots to the leaves. 29, 555

Z

zona pellucida *ZO-nah pel-LU-seh-dah* A thin, clear layer of proteins and sugars surrounding a secondary oocyte. 171

zone of cellular division *ZONE of SEL-yu-ler dah-VISH-on* The meristematic part of the subapical region in a plant's root. 563

zone of cellular elongation *ZONE of SEL-yu-ler e-long-GAY-shun* The middle part of the subapical region of a plant's root, where rapid cellular elongation lengthens the root. 563

zone of cellular maturation *ZONE of SEL-yu-ler MAT-ur-AY-shun* The hindmost region of the subapical region of a plant's root, where tiny root hairs protrude from epidermal cells. 563

zygomycete *ZI-go-my-SEAT* A fungus with sexual spores, such as bread mold. 27

zygote *ZI-goat* In prenatal humans, the organism during the first 2 weeks of development. Also called a preembryo. 172, 573, 578

Credits

Chapter 32

32.1: © Wilfred G. Oltis/ William E. Ferguson Photography; 32.2: © Elliot Meyerowitz; 32.3: © Dr. Jeremy Burgess/ Science Photo Library/ Photo Researchers, Inc.; 32.5a (all): © Christian T. Harms; 32.7: Courtesy, Calgene/ SCIENCE AND THE FUTURE YEARBOOK, 1986, p. 105 Encyclopedia Britannica; 32.8a, b, c, d: © Runk/ Schoenberger/ Grant Heilman; 32.9a: © Ted Spiegel/ Black Star; 32.9b: DNA Plant Technology; 32.10 (both): © Dan McCoy/ Rainbow; 32.11: © Curt Maas/ Pioneer Hi-Bred International; 32.15: Courtesy, Calgene; 32.16 (all): © Dr. Paul Christou; 32.17: Courtesy, Monsanto; 32.17b: Courtesy, Calgene/ SCIENCE AND THE FUTURE YEARBOOK, 1986, p. 114 Encyclopedia Britannica; page 615 (top): Courtesy, DNA Plant Technology, (bottom): © Mike Greenlar/ The Image Works

Chapter 33

33.2: © William E. Ferguson; 33.3: © Trans Lanting/ Photo Researchers, Inc.; 33.4: © William E. Ferguson; 33.6a1: © Lynn Rogers; 33.6a2: © Michael Viard/ Peter Arnold, Inc.; 33.6b1: © Ralph Eagle/ Science Source/ Photo Researchers, Inc.; 33.6b2: © Jeff Rotman/ Peter Arnold, Inc.; 33.8: © S. J. Krasemann/ Peter Arnold, Inc.; 33.9a: © Tom McHugh/ Photo Researchers, Inc.; 33.9b: © Tom McHugh/ Rapho/ Photo Researchers, Inc.; 33.9c: © Robert and Linda Mitchell; 33.9d: Field Museum of Natural History, Chicago, IL, Negative Number CKIT

Chapter 34

34.1: © Sandy Macys/ Gamma Liaison; 34.7: © William E. Ferguson; 34.8: © Porterfield/ Chickering/ Photo Researchers, Inc.; page 639: © Ray Pfortner/ Peter Arnold, Inc.; 34.9b: Courtesy, W. Atlee Burpee and Company; 34.9d: © Michael Viard/ Peter Arnold, Inc.; 34.10a: © Jonathan Blair/ Woodfin Camp and Associates; 34.10b: © Glenn Izett/ United States Dept. of Interior, Geological Survey; 34.12: © Jonathan Blair/ Woodfin Camp & Associates; page 644 (top right): © Leonard Lee Rue III/ Animals Animals, (bottom right): © Barb Zurawski; 34.13: © William E. Ferguson

Chapter 35

35.1a: © Jonathan Blair/ Woodfin Camp and Associates; 35.1b: © Albert Copley/ Visuals Unlimited; 35.2a: Courtesy Department Library Services/ American Museum of Natural History, Neg. No. 320496; 35.2b: © George O. Poinar, Jr.; 35.6: Zoological Society of London; 35.7a1: © Ellan Young/ Photo Researchers, Inc.; 35.7a2: © Lynn Rogers; 35.7a3: © Steve Kaufman/ Peter Arnold, Inc.; 35.7a4: © Tom McHugh/ Photo Researchers, Inc.; 35.11, 35.12a: © William E. Ferguson; 35.15a: Field Museum of Natural History; 35.15b: © Martin Land/ Science Photo Library/ Photo Researchers, Inc.; 35.19a: © Cabisco/ Visuals Unlimited; 35.19b: © John Reader/ Science Photo Library/ Photo Researchers, Inc.

Chapter 36

36.1: J. A. L. Cooke; page 668: © Laura Riley; 36.3a: © Doug Vargas/ The Image Works; 36.4: © Roger Wilmshurst/ Bruce Coleman; 36.7: © Marty Snyderman/ Visuals Unlimited; 36.9: Nina Leen/ LIFE Magazine; 36.10: Courtesy, Dr. Martin Ralph/ "CLOCKWORK IN THE BRAIN," Dr. Martin Ralph, BIO-SCIENCE," Vol. 39, No. 2, p. 76; 36.11: © Gary Meszaros; 36.13a: © Charles Walcott; 36.14: © Lynn Rogers; page 675a: © Laura Dwight/ Peter Arnold, Inc.; page 675b: © Bill Bachman/ Photo Researchers, Inc.; page 675c: © Laura Dwight/ Peter Arnold, Inc.; page 675d: © Bob Busby/ Photo Researchers, Inc.

Chapter 37

37.1: © Runk/ Schoenberger/ Grant Heilman; 37.2: © Stephan Dalton/ Photo Researchers, Inc.; page 685 (bottom): © Raymond A. Mendez; 37.3: © Louis Quitt/ M.A.S./ Photo Researchers, Inc.; 37.4: © Horst Schafer/ Peter Arnold, Inc.; 37.5: © Laura Riley/ Bruce Coleman, Inc.; 37.6: © Oxford Scientific 2 films/ Animals Animals; 37.7: © J. P. Thomas/ Jacana/ Photo Researchers, Inc.; 37.8: © 1990 Scott Canazine; page 691 37.9a, b: © Charles H. Janson; page 691 (top): © M. Marchaterre/ Cornell University; 37.11: © Jonathan Scott/ Planet Earth Pictures; 37.12: © Charles H. Jason/ NATURAL HISTORY, February, 1986, p. 444; 37.14: © Professor Axel Michelsan; 37.15: © G. Ziesler/ Peter Arnold, Inc.; 37.16: © John Alcock; 37.17: © V. Arthus-Bertrand/ Peter Arnold, Inc.; 37.18: © Bildorchiv Okapia/ Photo Researchers, Inc.

Chapter 38

38.1: © Bob Thomas/ Gamma Liaison; page 702 (left): © C. Gable Ray; page 702 (right): Montana Department of Fish, Wildlife and Parks; 38.8a: © Stephen J. Krasemann/ Peter Arnold, Inc.; 38.8b: © Jonathan Scott/ Planet Earth Pictures; 38.10: © Gregory G. Dimijian, M.D./ Photo Researchers, Inc.; page 711: © Alan Reininger/ Contact Press Images

Chapter 39

39.2a-f: Courtesy, Dr. Stuart Fisher, Department of Zoology, Arizona State University; 39.3a: © Fritz Polking/ Peter Arnold, Inc.; 39.4: © Charlie Ott/ Photo Researchers, Inc.; 39.6b: © Steven C. Amstrup/ U.S. Fish and Wildlife; page 727: © Ken Spencer; 39.14a: © Gordon Wiltsie/ Peter Arnold, Inc.; 39.14b: © Jim Zippo/ Peter Arnold, Inc.; 39.14c: © Luiz C. Marigo/ Peter Arnold, Inc.; 39.14d: © L. West/ Photo Researchers, Inc.; 39.14e: © Gregory G. Dimijian, M.D./ Photo Researchers, Inc.; 39.14f: © Toni Michaels; 39.14g: © John Bova/ Photo Researchers, Inc.; 39.14h: © Stephen J. Krasemann/ Peter Arnold, Inc.; page 732 (both): © Space Biospheres Ventures; 39.16: © G. Ziesler/ Peter Arnold, Inc.; 39.17a: © David Hall/ Photo Researchers, Inc.; 39.17b: © Peter Parks/ Oxford Scientific Films/ Animals Animals

Chapter 40

40.1a, b: © Al Grillo/ Picture Group; 40.2: © TASS/ Sovofoto; 40.3: © Ray Pfortner/ Peter Arnold, Inc.; page 746: © C. C. Lockwood/ Animals, Animals; 40.4: © Joel Simon/ Society Expeditions; 40.5a: © Ray Pfortner/ Peter Arnold, Inc.; 40.7: © Michael Nichols/ Magnum Photos; 40.9a: © George H. Harrison/ Grant Heilman; 40.9b: © Imre De Pozsgay/ Alpine Color Lab; 40.11: © George Antonelis, National Marine Fisheries Service

Appendix

Page A.2 (top): © Leonard Lessin/Peter Arnold, Inc.; page A.6 (left): USDA/ Science Source/Photo Researchers, Inc., (right): © William E. Ferguson; page A.7 (left): © Michel Viard/Peter Arnold, Inc., (middle): © Martin Land/Science Library/ Photo Researchers, Inc., (right): © Tom Branch/Photo Researchers, Inc., page A.8 (left): © Fred Bavendam/Peter Arnold, Inc., (middle): © Andrew Martinez/Photo Researchers, Inc., (right): © Carl Purcell/ Photo Researchers, Inc.

Text/Line Art

Chapter 2

2.10c: From Eldon D. Enger, et al., *Concepts in Biology*, 5th ed. Copyright © 1988 Wm. C. Brown Publishers, Dubuque, Iowa. All Rights Reserved. Reprinted by permission.

Chapter 3

3.26: From E. Peter Volpe, *Understanding Evolution*, 5th ed. Copyright © 1985 Wm. C. Brown Publishers, Dubuque, Iowa. All Rights Reserved. Reprinted by permission.

Chapter 4

4.5: From Boston Medical Library in The Francis A. Countway Library of Medicine. Used with permission. 4.7: Frederick C. Ross, *Introductory Microbiology*, 2nd ed. Reprinted by permission of the author.

Chapter 5

5.13, 5.14: From Bruce Alberts, et al., *Molecular Biology of the Cell.* Copyright © 1983 Garland Publishing, Inc., New York, NY. Reprinted with permission.

Chapter 7

7.2: From Stuart Ira Fox, *Human Physiology*, 3d ed. Copyright © 1990 Wm. C. Brown Publishers, Dubuque, Iowa. All Rights Reserved. Reprinted by permission. 7.7: From Bruce Alberts, et al., *Molecular Biology of the Cell.* Copyright © 1983 Garland Publishing, Inc., New York, NY. Reprinted with permission. 7.12a-e: Reprinted with permission from *Chem. Eng. News,* February 25, 1985, 63(8), p. 16. Copyright © 1985 American Chemical Society.

Chapter 8

8.8: From Linda R. Maxson and Charles H. Daugherty, *Genetics: A Human Perspective*, 2d ed. Copyright © 1989 Wm. C. Brown Publishers, Dubuque, Iowa. All Rights Reserved. Reprinted by permission.

Chapter 9

Page 178, fig. 3: Gilbert, *Developmental Biology,* Second Edition, 1988. Reprinted by permission of Sinauer Associates, Inc., Sunderland, MA. 9.4, 9.9 (text): From Kent M. Van De Graaff, *Human Anatomy,* 2d ed. Copyright © 1988 Wm. C. Brown Publishers, Dubuque, Iowa. All Rights Reserved. Reprinted by permission. 9.9 (line art): From Kent M. Van De Graaff and Stuart Ira Fox, *Concepts in Human Anatomy and Physiology,* 2d ed. Copyright © 1989 Wm. C. Brown Publishers, Dubuque, Iowa. All Rights Reserved. Reprinted by permission. 9.16: From K. L. Moore, *Before We Are Born: Basic Embryology and Birth Defects,* 3d ed. Copyright © 1989 W.B. Saunders Company, Philadelphia, PA. Reprinted by permission of the publisher and author.

Chapter 10

10.8: Reprinted with permission of Macmillan Publishing Company from *July 20, 2019; Life in the 21st Century* by Arthur C. Clarke. Copyright © 1986 by Serendib, B. V. and OMNI Publications International, Ltd; and From *July 20, 2019: A Day in the Life of the Future,* edited by Arthur C. Clarke. Reprinted by permission of the author and the author's agents, Scott Meredith Literary Agency, Inc., 845 Third Avenue, New York, New York 10022.

Chapter 11

11.2: From E. Peter Volpe, *Biology and Human Concerns,* 3d ed. Copyright © 1983 Wm. C. Brown Publishers, Dubuque, Iowa. All Rights Reserved. Reprinted by permission. 11.4, 11.9: Reproduced by permission from Nagle, James J.: *Heredity and human affairs,* ed. 3, St. Louis, 1984, Times Mirror/Mosby College Publishing.

Chapter 12

12.5b: From Linda R. Maxson and Charles H. Daugherty, *Genetics: A Human Perspective,* 2d ed. Copyright © 1989 Wm. C. Brown Publishers, Dubuque, Iowa. All Rights Reserved. Reprinted by permission.

Chapter 13

13.7, 13.8a: From *Genetics,* 2/e by Peter J. Russell. Copyright © 1990 by Peter J. Russell. Reprinted by permission of HarperCollins Publishers. 13.8b: David Hogness, Department of Biochemistry, Stanford University School of Medicine, Stanford, California as in *Proceedings of the National Academy of Sciences,* U.S., Vol. 71 (1974), p. 135. 13.12: From A. L. Lehninger, *Principles of Biochemistry,* Worth Publishers, New York, 1982. Reprinted by permission.

Chapter 14

14.4b: From *Human Genetics: An Introduction to the Principles of Heredity* 2/E. By Sam Singer. Copyright © 1978, 1985 by W.H. Freeman and Company. Reprinted by permission. 14.5: From *Human Genetics* by Elof Carlson. Copyright © 1984 by D.C. Heath and Company. Reprinted by permission of the publisher. 14.9: From Stuart Ira Fox, *Human Physiology,* 3d ed. Copyright © 1990 Wm. C. Brown Publishers, Dubuque, Iowa. All Rights Reserved. Reprinted by permission. 14.10: Reprinted by permission of Macmillan Publishing Company from *Genetics* by Monroe W. Strickberger. Copyright © 1985, Monroe W. Strickberger. 14.13b: Source: Terman and Merrill, *Measuring Intelligence.* Copyright © 1937 Houghton Mifflin Company, Boston, MA. Table 14.2: From Heredity, Evolution, and Society 2/E. By I. Michael Lerner and William J. Libby. Copyright © 1968, 1976 by W.H. Freeman and Company. Reprinted with permission.

Index

Hybrid vigor. *See* Over-
dominance
Hydra, 30, 34, 333, 446, 734
Hydrocarbon, 47
Hydrocephaly, 205, 291, 301
Hydrochloric acid, 470-71, 473,
477, 479
Hydrogen, 44-45, 48
Hydrogen bond, 46-49, 53, 253,
258-59
Hydrogen ion, 46
Hydrogen sulfide, 114
Hydroid, 31
Hydrolysis, 50
Hydrolytic enzyme, 464-65
Hydronasty, 594
Hydrophilic compound, 95-96
Hydrophobic compound, 95-96
Hydrostatic skeleton, 390-91,
402
Hydrotropism, 594
Hydroxide ion, 46
Hydroxyapatite, 86
Hydroxyl group, 52
Hyena, 706, 729
Hyla chrysoscelis, 640
Hyla versicolor, 640
Hypercholesterolemia, familial,
286-87
Hyperparathyroidism, 377
Hyperpolarized membrane, 324
Hypersomnia, 326
Hypertension, 293, 383, 385,
434, 437-38, 487, 511
Hyperthermia, 149
Hyperthyroidism, 377
Hypertonic solution, 100
Hypertrophy, muscle, 417-18
Hyperventilation, 47, 458
Hypha, 27
Hypocotyl, 578, 580
Hypodermis, 564
Hypoglycemia, 379
Hypophyseal artery, 372
Hypophyseal vein, 372
Hypotension, 434
Hypothalamus, 335, 345-46,
371-72, 381, 386-87, 500,
676
Hypothesis, 3, 7, 10-11
Hypothyroidism, 376
Hypotonic solution, 100
Hysterosalpingogram, 198

I

IAA. *See* Indoleacetic acid
I band, 407-8
Ibuprofen, 534
Ice, 49
Ice age, 641-42
Ice-minus bacteria, 613-14
Ichthyosaur, 625, 659
Ichthyosis hystrix, 239, 241
ICSH. *See* Interstitial cell
stimulating hormone
Identical twins, 176
Idiotype, 519
Ig. *See* Immunoglobulin
Ileocecal valve, 475
Ileum, 467, 472, 475
Iliac artery, 430, 433
Iliac vein, 430, 433
Ilium, 398
Imaginal disc, 178
Imbibition, 49, 580-81
Imitation, 688
Immigration, 701
Immortality, cellular, 142
Immovable joint, 397-98
Immune infertility, 196

Immune response, 517
primary, 518
secondary, 518, 529
Immune system, 92, 94, 514-35
altering function, 529-35
cells and chemicals, 517-21
development, 522
in pregnancy, 194
problems, 95, 523-28
Immunity
active, 522
cellular, 518, 521, 535
humoral, 518, 520, 535
passive, 522, 535
Immunoglobulin (Ig). *See*
Antibody
Immunoglobulin A (IgA), 520
Immunoglobulin D (IgD), 520
Immunoglobulin E (IgE), 520,
525-26
Immunoglobulin G (IgG), 520,
526
Immunoglobulin M (IgM), 520
Immunosuppression, 529-31
Impact theory, mass extinction,
640-42
Impala, 729
Implantation, 157, 173-74, 199-
200
Imprinting, 673-75
Inborn error of metabolism, 252,
254, 287-88, 306
Inbreeding, 195, 285, 633-35,
644
Inclusive fitness, 692, 697
Incomplete dominance, 225-27,
234
Incomplete penetrance, 227, 234
Independent assortment, 160-61,
163, 166, 222-24, 234
Indigo bunting, 679
Individual, 40
Indoleacetic acid (IAA), 589
Induced mutation, 635
Induced ovulator, 382
Industrial carcinogen, 147-48
Industrial melanism, 635-37
Infant
herpes infection, 69
immune system, 522
jaundice, 479
skull, 397-98
Infant formula, 495
Infanticide, 710
Infantile respiratory distress
syndrome, 201, 453, 461
Infant mortality, 701
Infection, 84
Infectious disease, diagnosis, 303
Inferior mesenteric artery, 430
Inferior vena cava, 430, 432-35,
442, 505, 508
Infertility, 211-12
female, 197-200
male, 196-97, 199, 383, 525
Inflammation, 384, 424, 427,
515-16, 534-35
Influenza, 188, 459, 462
Influenza virus, 621
Ingen-Housz, Jan, 119
Inhalation. *See* Inspiration
Inheritance
acquired characteristics, 622,
627
mendelian, 217-24
organisms studies, 244-45
Inhibitory synapse, 324
Initiator tRNA, 262-63
Innate behavior, 667-71, 681
Inner cell mass, 173-75, 191
Inner ear, 359

Inner membrane, chloroplast,
116
Insect, 30, 32, 34
eye, 352-53, 357
hearing, 359
nitrogenous waste, 502-3
pheromone, 385-86
pollination by, 571, 576-77
social, 684-85, 688
temperature regulation, 499
vision, 349
Insect bite, 528
Insecticide, 148, 324
genetically-engineered, 273
plant-based, 29
Insight learning, 338, 674-75
Insomnia, 325, 676-77
Inspiration, 453-55, 461
Inspiratory center, 457-58, 462
Insulation, 52, 499-500, 512
Insulin, 53, 111, 263, 370-71,
378-80, 386-87
genetically-engineered, 73,
251, 272-73
Insulin-dependent diabetes, 95,
203, 379, 525
Insulin-independent diabetes,
379
Insulin receptor, 380
Intelligence, 291-92, 337
Intercalary meristem, 552
Intercalated disk, 405, 417, 434,
438
Interferon, 149, 273, 515, 518,
534
Interleukin-1, 518
Interleukin-2, 518, 534-35
Intermediate-day plant, 596
Internal gill, 446
Interneuron, 317, 328, 332-33
Internode, 557, 568
Interphase, 131-33, 150, 159
Interstellar dust, 59
Interstitial cell stimulating
hormone (ICSH), 373-75,
382, 386-87
Intertidal zone, 735-36, 739-40
Intestinal gas, 475-76
Intestinal secretions, 49, 472
Intestine. *See also* Colon; Small
intestine
cancer, 146
flora, 475
hormone-secreting cells, 383
Intracellular digestion, 465, 479
Intrauterine device (IUD), 208-
11
Intron, 265-66
Intuitive ability, 338
Inversion, 279-80, 298
Invertebrate
digestive system, 465
eye, 352-53, 357
skeleton, 390
In vitro fertilization, 205-7, 212
Involuntary muscle, 405
Iodine, 58, 375-76, 484-85
Ion, 46
Ion channel, 317-20, 324, 460
gatekeeper protein, 318
Ionic bond, 46
Iridium, 641-42
Iris (eye), 353-55, 365
Iris (flower), 596
Iron, 58, 484-85
deficiency, 426, 488, 490
Irritability, 40-42, 62
Ischium, 398
Island, evolution on, 619-21,
626, 629
Islets of Langerhans, 378-79

Isolette, 201
Isoleucine, 485
Isotonic solution, 100
Isotope, 45, 650, 718-19
Isotretinoin, 202, 204
IUD. *See* Intrauterine device

J

Jackdaw bird, 696
Jack pine, 723, 749
Janssen, Johann, 69
Janssen, Zacharius, 69
Jarvik, Robert, 423
Jaundice, 478-79
Jaw, 416
Jawless fish, 33, 657
Jawworm, 31
Jejunum, 467, 472
Jellyfish, 30-31
Jenner, Edward, 9, 530
Jet lag, 674, 677
Jewish population, 636
Johanson, Donald, 663
Johnson, Ben, 383
Joint, 391, 400-402
aging, 401
freely movable, 401
immovable, 397-98
in lever system, 414
movable, 400
synovial, 401-2
Joint capsule, 401
Jojoba, 540
J-shaped curve, 700-701, 710
Jugular vein, 430
Jumping Frenchmen of Maine
syndrome, 229
Jumping genes, 9, 267
Jurassic period, 641, 659, 664
Juvenile-onset diabetes. *See*
Insulin-dependent diabetes

K

Kangaroo, 33, 35
Kangaroo rat, 733
Kaposi's sarcoma, 523
Karyokinesis, 131, 133, 135, 150
Karyotype, 279, 298-99, 310
Katydid, 21
Kellogg brothers, 544
Kelp, 719
Kennedy, John F., 378
Keratin, 140
Kernel, corn, 544
Keystone herbivore hypothesis,
643
Kidney, 49, 84, 377, 504-12
artificial, 511
blood flow, 433, 505-8
cancer, 147, 298, 534
failure, 511-12
fetal, 181
hormonal control, 510
problems, 511-12
transplant, 512, 529
water resorption, 100-101
Kidney bean, 541
Kidney stone, 511-12
Killed vaccine, 529
Killer T cells, 521-22, 524, 534-
35
Kilocalorie, 484-85, 494
Kinetic energy, 109
Kingdom, 21-22, 36
King George III, 231
Kin selection, 692-93, 697
Klinefelter syndrome, 245, 282,
294
Knee, 401
Knuckle walking, 662

Köhler, Georges, 531
Komoda dragon, 195
Krebs cycle, 122-28
Krill, 713-14, 716-17
Kuru, 233-34
Kwashiorkor, 490-91, 494

L

Labellum, 577
Labia majora, 156-57
Labia minora, 156-57
Labor, 168, 184-86, 191, 375
La Brea tar pits, 649
Lacks, Henrietta, 141-42
Lactase, 473
Lactate dehydrogenase, 208
Lacteal, 441, 473-74, 479
Lactic acid, 122
muscle, 410
Lactic acid fermentation, 121-
22, 127-28
Lactobacillus bulgaricus, 73
Lactoferrin, 495
Lactose, 50
Lactose intolerance, 472-73
Lacunae, 85-86, 391, 393
Lag phase, growth curve, 139,
150
Lake, 716, 733-35, 740
pollution, 753-54
Lake Maracaibo residents, 304-5
Lake Tahoe, 753-54
Lamarck, Jean-Baptiste, 622, 627
Lancelet, 33
Landfill, 745
Land pollution, 751-53, 759
Landscaping, 746
Langston, J. William, 327
Language skills, 335, 338-40, 675
Lanugo, 183, 191, 490
Laparoscope, 198, 205
Laparotomy, 198
Large intestine. *See* Colon
Large-scale cell culture, 268
Larynx, 449, 451, 461
cancer, 148
Latent learning, 674
Lateral meristem, 552, 558, 566,
568
Latitude, 713, 728
Law of use and disuse, 622
Laxative, 191
LDL. *See* Low-density
lipoprotein
L-dopa, 327
Lead, 58, 204
Leader sequence, 260, 262-63
Leaf, 552-53, 555, 559-62, 568
abscission. *See* Abscission
alternate, 559-60, 568
autumn colors, 599-600
compound, 559-60, 568
opposite, 559-60, 568
palmate, 559-60, 568
pinnate, 559-60, 568
simple, 559-60, 568
whorled, 559-60, 568
Leaf-cutting ant, 729
Lean tissue, 493
Learning, 335, 337, 341-43, 346,
667-68, 672-74
enhancement by group living,
688
human child, 675
insight, 338, 674-75
latent, 674
Learning disability, 202-4
Leconora esculenta. *See* Manna
lichen
Leeuwenhoek, Anton van, 69